A CENTURY
OF GOLF

WESTERN GOLF ASSOCIATION
1899-1999

BY TIM CRONIN

Western Golf Association (Golf, Ill.)
A century of golf : the history of the Western Golf Association /sponsored by the Western Golf Association.
p. cm.
ISBN 1-886947-36-8
1. Western Golf Association (Golf, Ill.)-History.
2. Western Golf Association (Golf, Ill.)-Centennial celebration, etc.
I. Title.
GV969.W5W47 1998 98-9688
796.352'06'877311-dc21 CIP

Sleeping Bear Press
121 South Main
P.O. Box 20
Chelsea, MI 48118
www.sleepingbearpress.com

Printed and bound in the United States of America.

10 9 8 7 6 5 4 3 2 1

Arnold Palmer looks just a little amazed after winning the 1961 Western Open.

BY ARNOLD PALMER

The Western Golf Association is one of the oldest, and certainly one of the most prestigious, associations in golf in the United States. I remember with pride my victories in the 1961 Western Open at Blythefield Country Club in Michigan and the 1963 Western Open at Beverly Country Club in Chicago.

My first Western Open win, in 1961, actually carried a nostalgic note, as I defeated one of the game's living legends, Sam Snead, by just two strokes. Snead had won the 1949 and 1950 Western Opens, and to win my first Western Open over such a great name in golf made the victory that much more satisfying.

When the Western Golf Association is mentioned in golf circles, though, it's not just the names of Sam Snead, Ben Hogan, Gene Sarazen, Walter Hagen, and the many other Western Open champions that come to mind. I also think of the name of Chick Evans, the man who came up with the idea of giving college scholarships to caddies. His dream changed the focus of the Western Golf Association forever. I personally have been a long-time supporter of the Western Golf Association's Evans Scholarship Program, contributing annually to the WGA Par Club to help fund these scholarships for deserving caddies.

I think all of us who have found success in golf owe it to the game to give something back, and one of the best ways I've found to do that is through the Evans Scholarships. Not everyone is blessed with the God-given talent and opportunity to pursue a career as a professional golfer, but almost everyone has the ability to earn a college education if given the chance. The Western Golf Association gives many young men and women that hope. It is a mission and a tradition unique in all of golf.

In my many years of competitive golf, I have met many people and made many friends, including the hard-working volunteers of the Western Golf Association. These are dedicated people, who give of their time and money to enhance the game of golf and to help the communities they live in by building better citizens through education.

I recall with fondness the many Western Golf Association championships in which I have competed and congratulate the association and its volunteers on this celebration of 100 years of service to golf. Your contributions to the game and to the lives of thousands of caddies is unparalleled. Best wishes for another 100 years of championships and scholarships.

Arnold Palmer

BY JACK NICKLAUS

As a professional golfer who has enjoyed a successful competitive career, I have always respected and admired the many men and women who volunteer unselfishly to support the game of golf.

The Western Golf Association, now celebrating its 100th anniversary, epitomizes the volunteer ideal through its long-standing sponsorship of both golf championships and college scholarships for caddies.

One of my first victories in a national championship came in 1961 when I won the Western Amateur championship at New Orleans Country Club. I still remember the devotion to amateur golf shown by the Western Golf Association officials at the tournament. Six years later, in 1967, I won the first of my back-to-back titles in the Western Open. Those victories, at Chicago's Beverly Country Club and Olympia Fields Country Club, remain among my most cherished championships. I am hon-

Jack Nicklaus drives to victory at the 1968 Western Open.

ored to know that my name is engraved on the J.K. Wadley Cup along with the names of golf legends such as Walter Hagen, Gene Sarazen and, of course, Chick Evans, founder of the Evans Scholarships for caddies.

The Western Golf Association and its Evans Scholarship Program are held in high esteem by those of us who play the game of golf professionally. I am especially proud to be a life member of the WGA Par Club, which funds Evans Scholarships for more than 800 caddies annually.

I join with the entire golf community in congratulating the Western Golf Association on a century of service to golf and in wishing the WGA continued success in the next 100 years.

F O R E W O R D

BY BOB HOPE

I t has been an honor to be a part of the Western Golf Association for the past 50 years. I can't believe it's been 50 years. It seems like just yesterday we decided to train our own set of caddies. (It's the only way to go if you want to make sure they know how to add up your scorecard!)

My thanks go out to all the wonderful people who work to keep the memory of Chick Evans alive in such an inspiring way.

Happy Birthday, Western Golf.

Bob Hope getting the lowdown on the Evans Scholars Foundation from WGA officials Jerome Bowes, Cameron Eddy, and Scotty Fessenden in the late 1940s.

Bob Hope hams it up to the delight of Bing Crosby, Chick Evans, and Ben Hogan during the filming of "Honor Caddie," the star-studded caddie training film.

F O R E W O R D

BY TIGER WOODS

I 've spent a lifetime in competitive golf and throughout my career I have always held the Western Golf Association and its people in highest regard. They conduct first-class championships, and they do it for a first-class cause, the Evans Scholarships for caddies.

The Western Golf Association played a major role in my development as a tournament golfer. I played in the Western Junior in 1992, and the Western Amateur for four years, from 1993 to 1996, winning in 1994. I played in the Motorola Western Open as an amateur in 1994 and 1995 and then won the championship in my first full year on the PGA Tour in 1997. I'll always remember walking down the 18th fairway on the final day of the 1997 Motorola Western Open, with thousands of fans spilling onto the fairway to join me in my victory walk to the 18th green. It was one of the most exciting moments I've ever experienced. I also remember how thrilled I was when I won the Western Amateur in 1994. It was my first win in a major amateur championship, an event I consider to be the Masters of amateur golf.

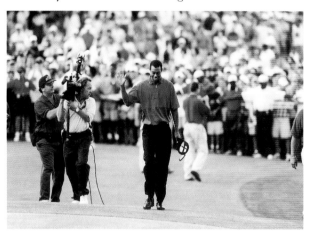

With his fans in the background, Tiger Woods salutes the gallery at Cog Hill on the final green of the 1997 Western Open.

It means a lot to have my name on the WGA trophies along with the names of the legends of golf, such as Walter Hagen, Sam Snead, Ben Hogan, Jack Nicklaus, and Arnold Palmer. I expect to play in many more Western Opens, and I hope to be fortunate enough to have my name engraved on the championship's Wadley Cup more than once.

I'm thankful for the opportunities and support the Western Golf Association staff and volunteers have provided me in my development as a championship golfer. Congratulations on your celebration of 100 years of service to golf, and best wishes for another 100 years of success.

TABLE *of* CONTENTS

T A B L E *of* C O N T E N T S

A CENTURY OF CHAMPIONSHIPS AND SCHOLARSHIPS

BY H. GRANT CLARK, JR., WGA PRESIDENT, AND DONALD D. JOHNSON, WGA EXECUTIVE DIRECTOR

As we celebrate the Western Golf Association's centennial year in 1999, we salute the thousands of golfers, past and present, who have served golf through their support of our championships and scholarships.

The Western Golf Association has been a national leader in golf since our founding in 1899, when representatives of 11 Chicago-area clubs signed the original charter incorporating the WGA to conduct golf championships and coordinate tournament events at member clubs.

In that same year, our organization sponsored the inaugural Western Open and Western Amateur championships at the Glen View Club in Golf, Illinois, a village nestled in Chicago's near north suburbs where we now maintain our headquarters. In 1914 the WGA held the first national junior championship, the Western Junior, at the Chicago Golf Club in Wheaton, Illinois.

Much has changed in the past 100 years, yet our goal at the Western Golf Association remains constant: to serve golf and those who play the game. Although our original mission focused on conducting national championships, we expanded that mission in 1930 when we joined with amateur golf great Charles "Chick" Evans, Jr. in founding the Evans Scholarships for caddies. Since then, nearly 7,000 young men and women have realized the dream of earning a college degree as Evans Scholars. Today, the WGA is devoted to the development and growth of caddie programs and the continuation of golf's favorite charity, the Evans Scholarships.

Each year, more than 800 Evans Scholars are enrolled in college through the generosity of 28,000 WGA Par Club members who annually donate $150 or more to the program. The Par Club contributions and further donations for WGA Bag Tags have

H. GRANT CLARK, JR.
President
Western Golf Association President H. Grant Clark, Jr. is a member of the Glen View Club in Golf, Illinois, site of the first Western Open and Western Amateur championships held in 1899. He is the WGA's 57th president.

earned the Evans Scholarships a reputation as the nation's largest individually-funded college scholarship program.

We are grateful to our many contributors for their support of the Evans Scholarships. In addition, we are proud to have sponsored more than 270 national championships for professional, amateur and junior golfers. All proceeds from our three annual national championships benefit the Evans Scholars Program.

Those of us associated with the WGA have always recognized and appreciated the merits of the Western Golf Association's unique standing in golf. Every golf association sponsors championships. Only the Western Golf Association also sponsors a national scholarship program with nearly 7,000 Alumni and more than 200 new Scholars every year. We are supported in this effort through our affiliation with 23 regional golf associations. All of us involved in this undertaking are proud of our Evans Scholars and of our combined roles in making their dreams possible. By helping these young Scholars obtain a college education, we are changing lives and society for the better.

More than 500 member clubs in states throughout the nation also support the Western Golf Association and our Evans Scholars Foundation. We are governed by volunteer officers and directors, who share a love of golf and a willingness to give of themselves to serve the best interests of the game. Our directors, who serve without pay, assist in many ways, including fund-raising, caddie development, tournament operations, scholarship recruitment, legal matters, and administrative affairs. Our championships and the Evans Scholars Program have weathered many challenges through the years thanks to the guidance of capable leaders who, through a combination of vision and talent, have adapted our programs to the ever-changing landscape of golf.

The most pressing challenge we have met successfully in the past decade has been to improve our financial standing to ensure the Evans Scholarships will continue well into our second 100 years. In the mid-1980s, we were living hand to mouth, with no reserve fund to draw upon in case of a financial emergency. We now have sufficient assets to begin to guarantee the perpetuity of the program. Our endowment fund has grown from a few hundred thousand dollars to more than $16 million, well on the way to our first-stage goal of $20 million.

Recognizing that healthy caddie programs are vital to our mission of sending caddies to college, we have added a part-time caddie services director to assist clubs in caddie recruitment and training.

We also have upgraded our Evans chapter houses on almost every one of the 14 college campuses—including building a new $1.6 million chapter house at Indiana University to replace one destroyed by a 1997 fire.

Most impressively, the Evans Scholars Alumni have shown their appreciation for our efforts by contributing more than $1 million to the program annually during the 1990s. Their cumulative contributions now total more than $13 million. This is a tribute to the character of the men and women who receive the scholarships and to the pride they take in being Evans Scholars.

Their support, in addition to the efforts of our volunteer directors and of our WGA Par Club and Bag Tag contributors, gives us confidence that our first 100 years will prove to be the foundation for an even more successful second century of serving golf.

This centennial book recognizes our unique history and our promising future by reviewing our past in three parts. In the first part, we describe our founding years and the development of our tournaments up to the start of World War II, when the championships were suspended. In the second part, we take an in-depth look at the origins of the Evans Scholarships and the remarkable growth of the program under the sponsorship of the Western Golf Association. In the last part, we follow our championships' continued development in the booming postwar years as golf's popularity benefited from the advent of television and the nation's overall prosperity.

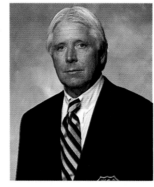

Our history is rich in tradition. The roster of Western Open champions includes our own Chick Evans, Walter Hagen, Gene Sarazen, Sam Snead, Ben Hogan, Arnold Palmer, Jack Nicklaus, and Tiger Woods, to name a few. The Western Amateur and Western Junior have enjoyed equally illustrious pasts, with many of golf's greatest names also inscribed on their trophies.

The roster we are most proud of, however, is the long list of names of caddies who have earned the Evans Scholarships and have graduated from college as Evans Scholars. That list of nearly 7,000 names is the true legacy of our first 100 years.

In our next 100 years, we look forward to adding many more names to our cherished rosters of golf champions and Evans Scholars.

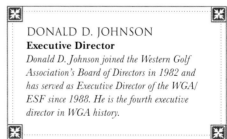

DONALD D. JOHNSON
Executive Director
Donald D. Johnson joined the Western Golf Association's Board of Directors in 1982 and has served as Executive Director of the WGA/ESF since 1988. He is the fourth executive director in WGA history.

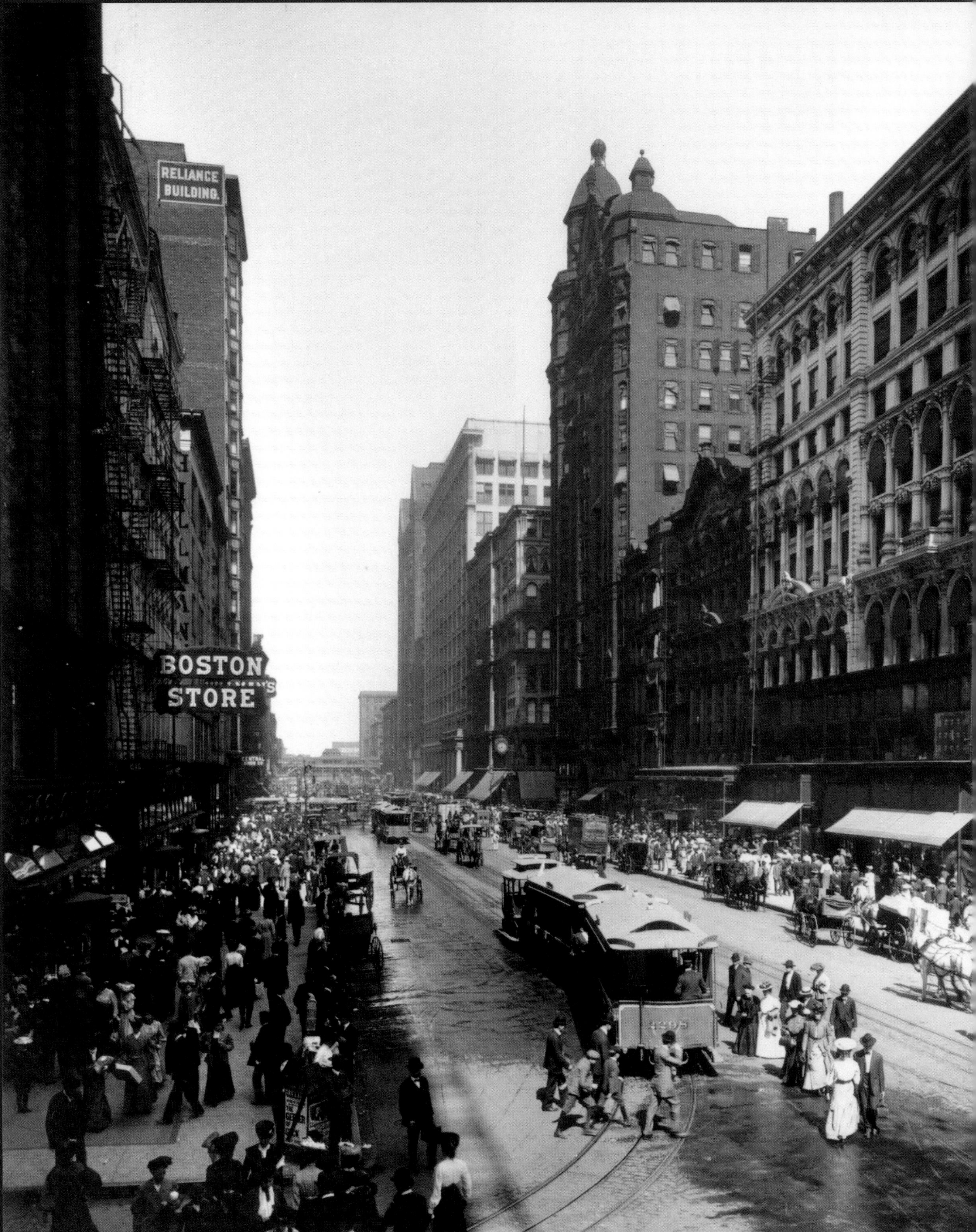
RELIANCE
BUILDING.
BOSTON
STORE

1

GOLF IN THE WEST TAKES FORM

*C*hicago in late April of 1899 was unseasonably hot. A wet, late winter and early spring turned into a balmy imitation of summer with little warning. Flowers bloomed ahead of schedule. The outdoors beckoned.

The world of 1899 was far different from ours. Chicago, the giant of the Midwest, was 28 years removed from the great fire, but closer in spirit to 1799 than 1999. The city had looked to the future with the Columbian Exposition of 1892, but for the average citizen, life was a grind. Automobiles were few, horses many. Most people traveled by train, and they didn't go very far unless it was absolutely necessary. The six-day work week was standard.

Chicago was a toddlin' town at the turn of the century, and State Street was its mercantile core.

On Thursday, April 27, the papers were full of the battles in the Philippines and preparations for the unveiling of a statue of General Ulysses S. Grant—the nation's 18th president—in Philadelphia.

It was 83 degrees and steamy in downtown Chicago under overcast skies when 19 golfers gathered in the German Room of the Grand Pacific Hotel in the Loop. A few miles away, at West Side Park, Chicago's entry in the National League, the Orphans, were celebrating Opening Day with a 4-3 win over Cincinnati before a crowd estimated at 10,000.

Unlike the multitude at the ballpark, the gentlemen gathering downtown didn't have the host Orphans and visiting Redlegs on their minds. Rather, the purpose of the meeting, the second at the posh hotel in a fortnight, was to formalize arrangements for the Associated Golf Clubs of Chicago. In the same back

1

A formally attired gallery eyes the action in the 1915 Western Amateur at Mayfield Country Club in Cleveland.

room on April 13, these gentlemen had agreed that the AGCC was needed. Their proposed association would encompass any club desiring to join, as long as it was within a 35-mile radius of Chicago's City Hall.

Golf wasn't played in Chicago until 1892, but the game found a brisk and enthusiastic acceptance. When the *Chicago Times-Herald* previewed the season in March of 1899, it was able to list plans for tournaments, course improvements, and the arrival of Scottish-born and bred professionals at 17 clubs. Fourteen of those clubs were near enough to qualify as AGCC members.

In 1898, many of the same clubs had held tourna-

ments simultaneously. Players complained that they wanted to play in all of them and could not. A golf clearing house, one that could approve dates of tournaments and interclub matches, as well as issue handicaps, was needed.

Arthur P. Bowen, the new captain of Riverside Golf Club, decided to take action. On March 2, 1899, Bowen wrote the captain of every other area club, proposing a group similar to New York's Metropolitan Golf Association. He also saw to it that the letter landed on the desk of the *Chicago Daily Inter Ocean's* golf writer. It ran in the *Inter Ocean* the next morning.

Most of the letter pertained to inter-club matches.

The last paragraph was the critical one:

"I would also like an expression from you as to the desirability of holding a meeting at an early date of the committees of different clubs having these matters in charge, for the purpose of exchange of ideas on this and other subjects pertaining to the game," Bowen penned.

He already knew what the response would be. Bowen told the *Inter Ocean*, "I have spoken to several prominent

Arthur P. Bowen, seeing a need for cooperation among Chicago-area clubs, started the movement that led to the WGA's formation.

players, and they favor the formation of a local association, and a local championship, and my letter is really to get the proper people together and decide what to do. Occasional meetings or dinners would give us an opportunity of determining the needs of the game, as well as the proper laying out of courses, and I have no doubt that local golf would benefit much from such gatherings."

In 1899, golf in Chicago was more royal than ancient. The factory worker, even if he wanted to play golf, had little leisure time and, until May of that year, nowhere to play. When a nine-hole layout at Jackson Park on Chicago's south side opened for the general public, it quickly was overwhelmed with players.

Charles Blair Macdonald, founder of the Chicago Golf Club, was responsible for the introduction of the game to Chicagoans. Having been schooled in St. Andrews, Scotland, in the early 1870s, he developed a love for golf that was quickly communicated to friends upon his return to Chicago.

Macdonald laid out a seven-hole course on the grounds of an estate in Lake Forest in 1892. Finding his original concoction wanting, Macdonald moved on to an area called Belmont, a rolling prairie west of Chicago. There, on the grounds of a cattle farm, he designed the nine-hole Chicago Golf Club. By the following spring, nine more holes were added. And by 1894, Macdonald and his group had raised the princely sum of $28,000 to buy a 200-acre farm in Wheaton for the Chicago Golf Club's new layout, also designed by Macdonald.

The Chicago Golf Club's Wheaton links, a midwest-

ern approximation of a Scottish links in every detail that Macdonald could conjure up, was a far cry from the seven-hole Lake Forest layout he had quickly abandoned.

That original estate course, however, was the cradle of the game in Chicago. The estate belonged to Senator John B. Farwell, whose son-in-law, Hobart C. Chatfield-Taylor, was a friend of Macdonald's. Chatfield-Taylor, an early convert to the game and a charter member of Chicago Golf, convinced his friends to band together to form their own Lake Forest club, Onwentsia. And he would be the first president of the Western Golf Association.

Chatfield-Taylor was not at the April 13 meeting at the Grand Pacific when 30 representatives of 13 clubs agreed in principle that the time for the Associated Golf Clubs of Chicago had come. Bowen took the floor

The hidden hand of Charles Blair Macdonald ensured that the new organization would be regional rather than local in scope.

and argued that a local group was both necessary and desirable to organize the tournament schedule and to handicap players. The assembly was in favor of the idea, and immediately tried to saddle Bowen with the job of handicapping each player. He wisely declined, and that task was shelved to be dealt with at a later time.

It was agreed that only clubs already members of the United States Golf Association could join. A seven-man committee, including Bowen, Onwentsia's David Forgan, Chicago Golf's R.S. Emmett, and C.L. Williams of Glen View Golf and Polo Club, was formed to write a constitution and bylaws. Four days later, huddling at an office in the Rookery, they adopted most of the New York-based Metropolitan Golf Association's guidelines as their own and agreed to hold an annual members-only handicap tournament.

There was a notion among some in the first meeting that a local group wouldn't meet the needs of golf in the area; that something on a wider scale, along the lines of the Western Lawn Tennis Association, would be better suited. The *Inter Ocean* had already noted that a few delegates were interested in forming a sectional group, which the paper thought could be called the Western Golf Association. They were believed to be in the minority, however, and the idea of an association that stretched beyond the local boundaries was considered as likely to be adopted as the curious notion that the association hold a tournament limited only to American-born players.

The April 27 meeting in the Grand Pacific's German Room featured a Chicago-style delegation of responsibility. Those not in the room were given jobs by those in the room. Chatfield-Taylor, in New York arranging matches between Onwentsia and eastern clubs, was elected president. Bowen, who spearheaded the movement but missed the meeting because of business, was elected vice-president. Somehow, Phelps B. Hoyt of Glen View was elected secretary and George R. Thorne treasurer even though they were in the hall.

Macdonald, who had kept abreast of the AGCC's first steps, also missed the meeting. A force in the formation of the USGA, Macdonald believed a regional association was preferable to a local group. So did

The Grand Pacific Hotel at Jackson and Clark in downtown Chicago was where the WGA was formed in 1899.

Hobart Chatfield-Taylor, golf enthusiast and member of Chicago's upper crust, was the WGA's first president.

Forgan and Emmett. They designed the constitution for local purposes, but knew what they really wanted.

A reading of the constitution proposed by the committee commenced. Forgan, a Macdonald ally from the Lake Forest estate days, moved that the name of the group should be changed from Associated Golf Clubs of Chicago to the Western Golf Association. The motion was carried without dissent or discussion. A few moments later, fellow Onwentsia delegate Sydney Williams moved that the 35-mile limit be expanded to 500 miles.

In two quick steps, a local group had become a regional association, as Macdonald wished. The Western Golf Association, which would become a

leader in golf nationally, sometimes challenging the USGA, at other times supporting it, was born.

Members of 11 clubs were at the meeting. By September, 21 clubs were in the association, the majority of them in Chicago. Member clubs also came from as far east as the Pittsburgh suburb of Sharpsburg, site of the Allegheny Country Club, and as far west as Kansas City.

Clearly, an association encompassing the greater portion of the United States couldn't do with just a handicap tournament. In short order, it was decided that two tournaments, one a stroke-play open championship, the other a match-play championship in which only amateurs would be eligible, would be held. By late spring, Glen View was awarded the first WGA championships, to be played in early September, just before the USGA's Open and Amateur were to be conducted in the East.

Curiously, the influential Macdonald, at this point the sole Westerner on the USGA's Executive Committee, and the winner of the first official U.S. Amateur, never played in a WGA event.

He was not the only absentee when the first Western Amateur and Western Open championships commenced at Glen View in early September. Also missing were several of the day's best professionals, who decided to skip the 36-hole Western Open on Wednesday, September 6, because they thought the WGA wasn't offering enough prize money.

The WGA put up $150 for the Western Open purse, with $50 and a gold medal designated for the winner. Second through fifth place would earn $40, $30, $20, and $10, respectively. To the outsider, this looked like good money for playing a game. To many of the professionals, it looked like chicken feed. They were used to playing for much more.

A tournament at Chicago's Belmont Golf Club in June awarded $80 to winner Willie Smith, the head professional at Midlothian. Glen View head professional Laurie Auchterlonie collected $35 for second and Alex Smith of Washington Park earned $25 for placing third.

In August, a tournament at the Country Club of Oconomowoc, Wisconsin, featured 10 professionals playing for a $200 purse, with $100 pocketed by winner Harry Turpie, the head professional at Edgewater. Walter Dupee of Chicago, a club member, was so delighted by the play, he threw $50 into the pot to be

5

divided by the six players who failed to cash.

In that era, when a men's suit could be had at Carson Pirie Scott for $15, when Marshall Field and Co. sold fancy "Windermere" ladies hats for $3, and when a billing clerk in an office might earn $12 a week, the

Alex Smith led a boycott of the inaugural Western Open, protesting the purse of "only" $150.

$8.33 each of the six received for a day playing golf could pay for a caddie, dinner at a local restaurant, and train fare home, with something left over.

It was in the lucrative atmosphere of Oconomowoc that Alex Smith, who earned $50 for finishing second, said of the upcoming Western Open, "The prizes are too trifling. We won't play. The prizes ought to amount to about $1,000."

That was easy for Smith to say, but even the USGA, whose Open Championship would be played for the fifth time about 10 days after the Western, was offering "only" a $750 purse, with $150 to the champion.

The WGA, trying to satisfy the players, had already boosted its purse from $125 to $150. Chatfield-Taylor was said by the *Chicago Tribune* to be "keenly disappointed" at the stance of the professionals, but found, after taking a survey, that most professionals would play. An unnamed WGA official told the *Tribune*, "They want too much. Because the Belmont club gave purses of $75, some of the professionals seem to expect correspondingly large purses from the other organizations. This cannot happen, and they will realize it sooner or later."

Not all were satisfied. Alex Smith, runner-up in the 1898 U.S. Open, would not be at Glen View when the first Western Open began. Nor would U.S. Open champion Fred Herd, who had beaten Smith the year before at Myopia Hunt Club in Massachusetts, nor the famous Foulis brothers. Neither James, the 1896 U.S. Open champion, nor David filed an entry for the Western Open. When September 6 dawned, they were conspicuous by their absence.

What they missed was a thrilling inaugural that went into overtime. Under ideal conditions, Willie Smith and Auchterlonie, the favorite, tied at 2-under-bogey 158 after 36 holes, outdistancing Turpie by four strokes and the rest of the 16-man field by nine and more.

Smith and Auchterlonie came back the next morning and played 18 holes, under an unceasing sun and in stifling 94 degree temperatures, for the championship. Auchterlonie, as the host professional, was still the favorite. Since arriving from Scotland in the spring, he had established the course record of 72 in a noncompetitive round. But Smith ran away with the title, going out in 37, nine strokes better than Auchterlonie, and coming home in like fashion. Smith's 74-84 rout in the playoff earned him the $50 first prize and the WGA's gold medal. Two weeks later, he added the 1899 U.S. Open to his victory list.

The Western Amateur Championship, which began while Smith and Auchterlonie were preparing for their playoff, opened with an 18-hole stroke-play qualifying tournament in the morning, the low 16 advancing to the first match-play rounds in the afternoon.

With 82 entries from member clubs, the Amateur was wide open. If anyone rated an edge, it was fifteen-year-old William Holabird, Jr., the son of the famous architect (and Glen View member) who had recently annexed his third straight club championship and was rated a scratch player against bogey. But Forgan, as skillful a player as he was a persuader in meetings, carded the low score in qualifying with an 84. He would earn a berth in the 36-hole final, as would fellow Onwentsia member Walter Egan, whose qualifying round 86 earned him the WGA's medal for the low score by a player who learned his golf in the United States. Egan beat host club hopeful Holabird in their semifinal match.

Apparently, the skills picked up on foreign shores were more complete, for Forgan trumped Egan in the final, winning 6 and 5. Forgan won five straight holes to assume a 3-up lead during the morning's front nine, and Egan could never catch him.

George R. Thorne, the WGA's treasurer, was so delighted by the fledgling organization's success, he donated $500 to buy the trophy for the Western Amateur.

Three-time U.S. Amateur champion Walter J. Travis and 1901 Western Open winner Laurie Auchterlonie eye the path of a tee shot at Glen View Club at the first Western Open in 1899.

While the final was the feature at Glen View on Saturday, September 10, it wasn't the only competition. Phelps B. Hoyt's net 74, taking into account his 6 handicap, earned first place in a handicap tournament. The Glen View Club conducted a long-driving championship, with Forgan winning the prize for carry and Skokie's A.G. Bennett top honors for overall distance.

With that, and the knowledge that Midlothian president George Thorne, the WGA's treasurer, was going to donate a $500 trophy for the Western Amateur winner, the Western Golf Association's first year of activity was complete. The concept for a local golf association had grown into a flesh-and-blood organization with a 21-club membership that, excepting the absence of clubs from the East, was as far-flung as the USGA itself. The squabble with the professionals over prize money aside, the first year of the WGA had been a success. What the future and the new century would bring to the newly formed Western Golf Association and the game itself could only be hypothesized.

THE CHARTER CLUBS

Founding WGA member club Midlothian's clubhouse was one of the grandest of its time.

Eleven clubs were represented at the April 27, 1899, meeting at which the Western Golf Association came into existence, emerging full-born from the larval stage that was the Associated Golf Clubs of Chicago. By year's end, 21 clubs, all of them private clubs, were members of the WGA, ten more having joined along the way. All 21, having joined before the first championships were played, are considered charter members of the Western Golf Association.

The Original Eleven, all of them located in Illinois, were:

Belmont Golf Club, Belmont

Chicago Golf Club, Wheaton

Edgewater Golf Club, Edgewater

Evanston Golf Club, Evanston

Glen View Golf and Polo Club, Golf

Midlothian Country Club, Blue Island

Onwentsia Country Club, Lake Forest

Riverside Golf Club, Riverside

Skokie Country Club, Glencoe

Washington Park Club, Chicago

Westward Ho! Golf Club, Oak Park

Of those 11, all but Evanston and Skokie were represented at the April 13 meeting at which the AGCC was brought into being. Delegates from Exmoor Country Club and River Forest Golf Club were also at that meeting.

8

The ranks of the Original Eleven have been depleted over the years. Only seven of the 11 remain, though golf is still being played at the site of two former clubs, Belmont and Edgewater.

Although Belmont Golf Club disbanded, the game is still being played on the site, which today is the municipally-owned Downers Grove Golf Course in Downers Grove.

Edgewater, where Chick Evans broke into the game as a caddie and later spent years honing his game, nearly was lost to developers in the late 1960s. However, action was taken, and today a nine-hole course, the Chicago Park District-controlled Robert Black layout, sits on portions of the former Edgewater property, encompassing many of the original holes. Listed in 1899 as being located in Edgewater, by that time the neighborhood was actually part of Chicago.

Westward Ho!, which like the British club of the same name used an exclamation point in its sobriquet, fell to development in the first half of the century. Washington Park was in fact located inside the racetrack of the same name but eventually was abandoned.

On May 9, five more clubs were admitted to membership:

Exmoor Country Club, Highland Park, Illinois
Kenosha Country Club, Kenosha, Wisconsin
Milwaukee Country Club, Milwaukee, Wisconsin
Rock Island Arsenal Golf Club, Rock Island, Illinois
The Town and Country Club, St. Paul, Minnesota

Three more clubs joined the burgeoning WGA roster on May 29:

Allegheny Country Club, Sharpsburg, Pennsylvania
Cincinnati Golf Club, Cincinnati, Ohio
The Country Club of Kansas City, Missouri

Before the summer was out, two more clubs had joined the movement:

The Country Club of Detroit, Michigan
St. Louis Field Club, St. Louis, Missouri ◻

With a horse-drawn contraption in the background, a golfer putts out on the second green of Edgewater's original course.

WILLIE SMITH

Things could have been worse for Willie Smith in 1899. He could have stayed at Shinnecock Hills on Long Island rather than move to the Chicago area and become the head professional at the year-old Midlothian Country Club near Blue Island.

He could have followed the lead of his older brother, Alex, and decided not to play in the first Western Open.

He could have been intimidated by the older Laurie Auchterlonie, the head professional at Glen View Golf and Polo Club, when the two men met on Auchterlonie's home turf in an 18-hole playoff for the championship.

Yes, things could have been worse. But he moved West, as did many professionals, and set up shop at Midlothian. He ignored Alex's stance and played. And he beat Auchterlonie by 10 shots to win the new championship.

Things were very good for the twenty-four-year-old Smith in 1899. Less than two weeks later, he'd win the fifth playing of the U.S. Open. Indeed, if a money list had been kept, Willie Smith would have been near, if not at, the top. Here's what he won and where he won it in 1899:

Date	Tournament	Place	Money
June 10	Belmont Open	First	$80
Aug. 3	Oconomowoc Open	Third	30
Sept. 6-7	Western Open	First	50
Sept. 14-15	U.S. Open	First	150

▶ Total $310

Smith knew how to finish. He won the Belmont Open by 12, coasted to the aforementioned 10-stroke win over Auchterlonie in the Western Open playoff, and captured the U.S. Open by 11 strokes, a record then and now.

He was one of five brothers who hailed from Carnoustie, Scotland, with Alex and Macdonald making an impact on the game as well. Both also won the Western Open. Alex abandoned his boycott to capture the title in 1903 and 1906; Macdonald, the youngest, won in 1912, 1925, and 1933. Alex also won the U.S. Open in 1906 and 1910.

Willie Smith, winner of the inaugural Western Open, in formal attire with his dog.

Willie Smith never won another major. His best subsequent Western Open finish was a tie for second in 1902, five strokes behind Willie Anderson. Smith had a chance to win two other U.S. Opens, in 1906 and 1908. He was tied for the lead after one round in 1906, but eventually finished second to Anderson by seven strokes. In 1908, he led after each of the first three rounds, but was caught by Fred McLeod in the afternoon of the final day and fell to McLeod in a playoff.

While most professionals rarely stayed at one club for more than a year or two, Smith was an exception. He left Midlothian after five years, an eternity then, to become the head professional at the Mexico City Country Club, as exotic a position as there was in the game. He stayed there for the rest of his life, dying of a reported case of pneumonia on December 26, 1916, at age forty-one. ◻

Willie Smith's 1899 Western Open win received plenty of coverage in newspapers, including the Chicago Tribune...

...and fledgling golf magazines, including Western Golfer.

CHAPTER

2

THE SMITHS, THE EGANS, AND WILLIE ANDERSON

After the successful formation of the Western Golf Association in the spring of 1899 and the championships held in the fall, there seemed little doubt that the WGA had only one place to go: forward.

The steps would not be measured, or constant, or all in the right direction. Like any organization or family, there would be missteps along the way. But the WGA would go forward, moving to a leadership position in golf, and quickly.

The first decade of the 1900s—"the oughts," they were christened by some—saw the WGA expand into women's and team championships. They saw the cessation and resumption of the Western Open. They saw

Macdonald Smith followed in the footsteps of brothers Willie and Alex to win the Western Open, and did so three times, boosting the family total to six championships.

the first brush with the United States Golf Association over the rules of the game. And they saw a revolution in equipment threaten to change golf.

In the latter regard, little has changed in the last century. In 1900, remember, the featherie had gone out of style just 50 years before, and the gutta-percha ball, which had replaced the featherie, was just about to be supplanted by the rubber-cored ball as the WGA was formed. Technology was seen as the ruination of the game, threatening to make courses and the records set on them obsolete. Golf would never be the same.

That was also said, but in a positive sense, when the WGA came on the scene. An aggressive tournament program helped put the fledgling organization on the map. By 1901, it was conducting three individual championships and a team competition, outpacing the USGA. That was in contrast to 1900, when, as in 1899,

13

Laurie Auchterlonie compiled an astonishing record in the early days of the Western Open, with nine top-10 finishes in the first 10 championships, including a victory in 1901.

With those circumstances in place, the board accepted Field's offer. Without any announcement, the Western Open was canceled.

Golf went on regardless of the absence of the professionals. The host team from Onwentsia would win the first Marshall Field Trophy competition, while William Waller, an Onwentsia member, fought off the gritty challenge of William Holabird, Jr., by this time sixteen-years-old, in the championship final of the Western Amateur. Holabird was 4 down with eight holes to play but mounted a stirring rally to tie the match with a 4 on the 17th. Waller, stirred rather than shaken, captured his 1-up victory over the prodigy with a six-foot putt for a 3 on the home hole.

The following year saw the return of the Open, played, along with the Amateur, at Midlothian Country Club in Blue Island, Illinois. In the 1899 Open at Glen View Club, it was Midlothian's Willie Smith beating Glen View's Laurie Auchterlonie. Now the visiting professional was Auchterlonie, and he beat David Bell, the Midlothian professional who had joined Smith at the club, by two strokes with a 36-hole total of 160. Auchterlonie earned a $125 slice of the $310 purse. The larger purse had attracted most of the professionals who had boycotted two years earlier, though Alex Smith, the most vociferous of the critics, still stayed home.

To this point, despite the presence of clubs from Detroit, Pittsburgh, and Kansas City, the WGA was primarily a Chicago-based organization. Its headquarters was a suite in the Grand Pacific Hotel, and all of its first championships were played in the area. That began to change in 1902, when the Open was awarded to the Euclid Club in Cleveland.

In the next 10 years, the Open would be played out of the Chicago District six times, and while Cincinnati and St. Louis were the most distant outposts, the trend was obvious. The WGA would be a leader in taking its championships to areas of the country which had never before seen championship golf played.

On the links, two other trends were playing themselves out. First, it was a virtual lock that a Scottish-born professional would win the Western Open, and second, that a member of the Egan family would be odds-on to capture the Western Amateur.

the WGA ran two tournaments, but one of them wasn't the Western Open.

There was no Western Open in 1900. It was scheduled for the Onwentsia Club in Lake Forest, Illinois, for September 26, the day before the Western Amateur would start. That was the same format as employed in 1899, but between May 21, when the date and site was fixed, and the day of the tournament, the WGA board members had second thoughts.

They remembered how several professionals, led by Alex Smith, stayed away from the first Western, disappointed by the $150 purse and $50 first prize. They knew that the U.S. Open was slated to be played at the Chicago Golf Club in Wheaton on October 5-6. They also had an offer of a new trophy for a team competition from department store magnate Marshall Field.

The professional side was also monopolized, in a way, by one family. Willie Smith was the first winner of the Western Open, but his triumph in the inaugural Western Open was hardly the last for his family. Four years later, in 1903, Alex Smith, who had arrived in the United States in 1898 and who finally played in the Western Open in 1902, joined his younger brother as a WGA champion, defeating Auchterlonie and David Brown by two strokes in Milwaukee. Alex Smith would win again three years later, scoring a three-stroke victory over John Hobens at Homewood Country Club, which is known as Flossmoor Country Club today.

Alex wasn't the last of his clan to win. In 1912, six years after Alex's second success, Macdonald Smith, the youngest of the family, won at Idlewild Country Club, just down the street from Homewood. It was the first of his three well-spaced Western Open titles. The second came in 1925, and the last in 1933, a wire-to-wire six-stroke win over Tommy Armour at Olympia Fields Country Club. By winning the Open so many years apart, the smooth-swinging Smith established records for the time between triumphs and, in the latter case, became the oldest Western Open champion at the time. He was forty-three.

A scan of the records indicates that Arthur Smith won the 1905 Western Open. He was from Scotland, all right, but he wasn't from the Carnoustie-based Smiths. Alex, Willie, and Mac Smith were joined as professionals by brothers George and Jimmy. George Smith's best Western Open finish was a tie for 19th in 1907, but no record of Jimmy playing can be found.

The Smiths didn't have the "oughts" to themselves.

The Egan cousins, Chandler and Walter, book-end this group of caddies at Onwentsia in 1900.

Another Scot, North Berwick native Willie Anderson, dominated the game in the first decade of the century as nobody would until Bobby Jones came along. From 1901 to 1909, Anderson won eight major championships, four U.S. Opens, and four Western Opens. Anderson, the son of a professional whose schooling came mostly on the links and in the pro shop, was the favorite in every event he entered and rarely failed to place out of the top 10.

Sadly, his life was cut short, some say because he drank heavily. Whatever the reason, his death in 1910, attributed to "hardening of the arteries" at the tender age of 30, stole from the game its first star attraction.

In seven Western Open appearances, he was always in the top five. That, incredibly, was his poorest showing, a tie for fifth in 1903 at the Milwaukee Country Club. It came a year after his record-setting achievement in the Western Open at the Euclid Club in Cleveland.

Euclid was the setting for the first 72-hole Western Open, a two-day affair that brought it equal in length with the Open Championship, as the British Open was universally known, and the U.S. Open. At that pace, 36

Between them, cousins Walter Egan (left) and H. Chandler Egan captured five of the six Western Amateurs from 1902 through 1907.

A pair of 30s on the back nine keyed little-known Arthur Smith's win in the 1905 Western Open. It must have been the hat.

holes followed by 36 more, not only would the golfer's game be challenged, so would his psyche. How would it hold up under the increasing pressure?

Fine, if your name was Willie Anderson. Euclid Club's course, at 6,000 yards with a bogey of 86, was one of the finest of its day, and Anderson proceeded, after an opening-round 80, to take it apart. He posted second- and fourth-round scores of 75, with an astonishing 69 in the third round. That second morning score was, by five strokes, the best in the history of the Western Open.

If that weren't enough, his total of 299 set a record for a major championship. Break 300 strokes in a golf championship? It was unheard of, but it happened, and it put the Western Open on the map nationally.

The noted golf expert Herbert Tweedie was moved to call Anderson's performance, achieved with a ball that, if struck perfectly, would travel barely 250 yards, "a splendid exposition of two days' golf. . . to be remembered—to be thought of—to be conjured over, and finally to be put on the record shelf."

For his performance, Anderson won $150. In his seven Western Open appearances, Anderson would collect $912.50, a good sum for the day. More than that, however, he would make history. His scoring records would last only three years, but by winning three more Western Opens—his third and fourth coming in succession at St. Louis' Normandie Country Club in 1908 and Skokie Country Club in Glencoe, Illinois, in 1909—he would stamp an indelible imprint on the championship.

So, for one year, would the aforementioned Arthur Smith.

A native of Yarmouth, England, Smith headquartered at Columbus, Ohio, after stops in Montreal and the Pittsburgh area. He entered the Western Open of 1905 because it was being played down the tracks, at the Cincinnati Golf Club, and found himself very much on his game.

Because the CGC links were hardly long—when stretched to their limit, they measured 4,620 yards—Smith soon found himself setting scoring records. Laurie Auchterlonie fired a Western Open record 66 in the afternoon of the first day, but Smith earned notice by going around the back nine in 30 strokes in the morning.

Clearly, Cincinnati's course was one to be trifled with, and on the second day, Smith slapped it around again. A second incoming 30 in the third round keyed his 66, and by coasting home with a final round 74, he managed, with a total of 278 strokes, to set a Western Open scoring record that would stand for 24 years.

It was Arthur Smith's career highlight. He played in the 1906 Western Open at Hinsdale Golf Club in Clarendon Hills, Illinois, placing sixth, but was never a factor in that or subsequent Westerns.

The Smiths, and, to a degree, Anderson displayed longevity on the professional side, but for true staying power, it's hard to rival the Egan family. Cousins Walter and H. Chandler Egan made the Western Amateur their personal battleground for much of the century's first decade.

Three times, they faced each other in the championship match, and twice, took matters to the 37th hole. What's more, Chandler Egan, who was being schooled at Harvard, proved that while amateur golf in the West might be a family affair, it wasn't a second-class affair. He took time out from playing his cousin to win the

H. Chandler Egan's form earned him a quartet of Western Amateur titles.

U.S. Amateur in 1904 and 1905, then generally composed of a field dominated by Easterners.

Walter Egan was the first fine golfer in the family, dropping the decision to David Forgan in the inaugural Western Amateur and matching Fred Hamlin to share medalist's honors in 1901. But Chandler was the first Egan to win the championship, and he had to beat Walter to do so. Chandler won in 1902 at the Chicago Golf Club in Wheaton, Illinois, at the ripe age of 19 and in so doing, set off on a personal run of four victories.In defeating Walter for his first Western Amateur title, Chandler took a 2-up lead into the afternoon round and into the final nine holes, but not before getting a scare.

On that final nine, Walter authored a rally that climaxed with a sensational shot out of Chicago Golf's long rough to within inches of the cup. It won the 36th hole and forced a return to the first tee for the first time in Western Amateur history. When Chandler outscrambled Walter, 5-6, on the first hole, he had won family and WGA honor.

A year later at the Euclid Club, Walter again faced Chandler in the final. And once again, the championship match would go to the 36th hole and beyond. This time, it was Walter who held together on the extra hole, winning it 4-5 and squaring the family rivalry.

Chandler would win again in 1904, regaining the title by defeating Ned Sawyer of Wheaton 6 and 5 at Exmoor Country Club in Highland Park, Illinois, where he was a member. He did so a day before turning twenty-one. He then beat cousin Walter in 1905 for his third championship in four years, this time scoring a 3 and 2 victory at Glen View Club.

For H. Chandler Egan, this was the pinnacle. He was champion of both the Western Amateur and U.S. Amateur for two years running. And two years after that, in 1907, he captured his fourth Western Amateur in a half-dozen years. The twenty-three-year-old administered a 5 and 4 whipping to Herbert Jones of Wheaton at the Chicago Golf Club, a favorite Egan haunt.

Four championships in six years, and two U.S. Amateurs thrown in for good measure. Surely nobody could come along and top that performance, went the common wisdom.

In fact, in that very year of 1907, a new face on the golf scene—Charles "Chick" Evans, Jr.—was in the process of arriving. He would proceed to not only rewrite the WGA's record books, but add a unique chapter to the story of golf in America.

Smiling Chick Evans (second from left) with fellow competitors at Kent Country Club during the 1914 Western Amateur.

THE MARSHALL FIELD TROPHY

The Marshall Field Trophy was awarded to the winner of the WGA's team competition from 1900 through 1909.

Chicago merchant and philanthropist Marshall Field was not only a premier marketer but an avid golfer, and in 1900, when WGA officials decided not to hold the Western Open, he offered a trophy for a team competition.

His offer was accepted enthusiastically, and the Marshall Field Trophy competition was soon underway. Any WGA member club could enter a five-man team. It was a simple stroke-play event, though in the years before par, holes in a course were rated against "bogey," the score a good golfer such as the mythical Colonel Bogey would be expected to make. In the Field competition, scoring was summarized as against bogey, much as TV coverage of golf today concentrates on under-par or over-par scores to simplify things. In the case of bogey, the concept was reversed. Players (and teams) scoring higher than bogey for a round were considered "down" to the bogey. Players under bogey were called "up."

Thus, when the host Onwentsia Club team won the inaugural competition on September 26, 1900, its total of "30 down to bogey" in the 36-hole competition was prominently displayed. Bogey at Onwentsia Club in Lake Forest, Illinois, was 85, high for the era. Walter Smith and Walter Egan broke bogey, with first round scores of 81 and 82, respectively, in leading Onwentsia to a 40-stroke win over Glen View, the closest of the seven other teams in the field.

The competition, held the day before the Western Amateur, was enough of a hit that WGA officials decided to make it an annual feature.

However, there were only nine more Marshall Field Trophy tournaments, with the last held in 1909, won by Exmoor Country Club, Highland Park, Illinois. The WGA decided that with a new nationwide club competition, the Tom Morris Cup, underway, having a similar event that evolved into a local contest was superfluous. The WGA wanted the 1908 Field showdown to be the last, but was prevailed upon to put it in play for one more year.

The four previous winners—Exmoor, Glen View, Midlothian, and Onwentsia—were invited to play for the Field trophy in 1909 at Homewood Country Club, in south suburban Chicago. Onwentsia boycotted, and Exmoor's team, which included Walter Egan (who played on Onwentsia's original winning team) and Chick Evans, beat Midlothian by four strokes to secure the Marshall Field Trophy for good. ◘

THE OLYMPIC CUP

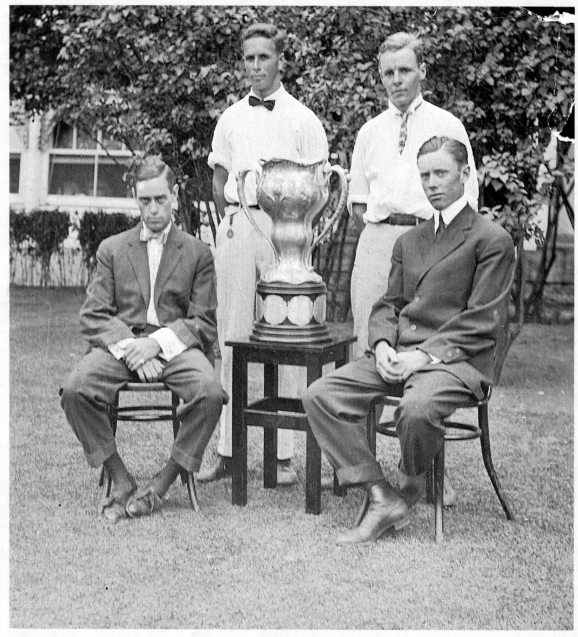

A pensive Chick Evans (seated right) with the Olympic Cup and WGA teammates Albert Seckel (seated left), Robert A. Gardner, and Paul Hunter after winning the 1910 competition by 31 strokes at Minikahda.

There is little question that the Games of the III Olympiad, held in St. Louis in 1904, were the most disorganized of modern times and perhaps of ancient times as well.

Held as an adjunct of the St. Louis World's Fair after having been originally awarded to Chicago, they barely resembled the fast-paced Olympics of today. They took some six months to complete, for one thing. There were as many sideshows as competitions. An Olympic gold medal for the tug of war? One was awarded.

And, under the rules of the day, countries could enter more than one team in any particular competition. So it was in the golf competition, held in the Olympics for the first, and, as it turns out, last time.

The WGA's 10-man team romped in the 36-hole team competition at Glen Echo in St. Louis. Headed by H. Chandler Egan, the WGA won by 21 strokes, scoring 1,749 strokes to the 1,770 registered by the Trans-Mississippi Golf Association. The team from the United States Golf Association finished third and last, taking 1,839 strokes.

In celebration, the WGA inaugurated the Olympic Cup competition, designed to commemorate its win. The first OC was played under WGA direction at the Chicago Golf Club in 1905, the day before the U.S. Amateur commenced at the same club. The four-man team of the Western Pennsylvania Golf Association, one headed by Oakmont notable W.C. Fownes, Jr., captured the Cup in the 12-team competition. Their five-stroke victory over the WGA's team was keyed by four sub-80 rounds of the eight played.

In an effort to broaden the competition, the WGA tried to play the Olympic Cup at the site of the U.S. Amateur whenever possible.

That paid off again in 1907, when it was held at the Euclid Club in Cleveland. Not only did the Metropolitan Golf Association's team, led by Jerome Travers, win by eight strokes, but billionaire John Rockefeller, celebrating his sixty-eighth birthday by getting away from the business of Standard Oil for a day, strolled around the course, watching Travers and Fownes.

Rockefeller, who took up the game late in life, was asked why he wasn't playing in the tournament.

"I am getting too old, my boy," he told a reporter. "It's too much of a nervous strain."

The following year in Rock Island, Illinois, the Olympic Cup was played in advance of the Western Amateur. Travers, Fownes, and his teammates weren't there. Rockefeller wasn't dispensing bon mots along with his trademark dimes. The Olympic Cup was never as big again and eventually was caught up in controversy.

In 1909, no Eastern teams entered, even though it was again played before the U.S. Amateur, apparently because WGA rules, rather than USGA rules, would be in effect. In 1912, two teams representing the WGA played—one, the official entry, and one, essentially official but finally playing under the name of the USGA. They finished 1-2. The WGA regulars, with Chick Evans aboard, won by seven strokes. The MGA, a team including Travers and Walter Travis, was third, 16 strokes behind the winners.

The MGA and other regional associations were upset, and rightfully so. Protests ensued, and enough heat was generated that the WGA, at its 1913 annual meeting, passed an amendment to its constitution limiting the competition to one team per association. At the same time, the WGA reaffirmed its notion to pick players for its team who resided in the Chicago area, so as not to cherry-pick the best players available to other associations. And it upgraded the individual awards, handing out gold rather than bronze medals to the winning team.

With that tempest quelled, the Olympic Cup went on. The WGA won the 1913 title, its sixth straight, but in 1914, the spanking new Chicago District Golf Association captured the crown and won it again a year later.

In 1919, the Olympic Cup came full circle. It was played at Sunset Hill Country Club in St. Louis, where the Olympics had been played, and was won by the St. Louis District Golf Association, its team including George Herbert Walker, who conceived the Walker Cup and who was the grandfather of President George Bush.

That was also the last year the Olympic Cup was played as a separate competition. Beginning in 1920, the OC was held in conjunction with qualifying rounds for the Western Amateur. The Southern Golf Association was the last winner of the Olympic Cup, capturing it at the Hinsdale (Illinois) Country Club in 1924.

The 1925 Olympic Cup competition was never held. In the spring of 1924, a raging fire destroyed the Roebuck Country Club, where the trophy was on display. Uninterested in getting a replacement, the WGA's executive committee abandoned the competition. ◘

3

THE KID FROM EDGEWATER

The story is too good to be true, but it is. A young boy moves from Indianapolis to Chicago with his family late in the nineteenth century, lives near a golf course, and is attracted at the tender age of eight years to the game and the money a youngster can earn as a caddie.

He becomes a fine caddie and a finer player. He begins to enter tournaments. He begins to win them.

He becomes the first amateur to win a major American championship open to professionals. He becomes the first player to win the U.S. Open and U.S. Amateur in the same year.

He wins at least one significant event each year for well over a decade. Often, he carries just seven clubs in his bag.

Chick Evans: unique in golf and philanthropy.

He plays in national tournaments for six decades and scores important victories 50 years apart. He's eventually in the vanguard when it comes to organizing senior tournaments, just as, decades before, he pushed for the formation of the PGA.

Despite doing that, he spurns temptations to turn professional. Money earned from a series of golf lessons on phonograph records—the forerunner of today's video golf lessons—is instead placed in a fund to help caddies go to college.

He remains an amateur even after a bankruptcy caused by errant investments in the stock and commodities markets.

A traditionalist, he nonetheless embraces the new technology of steel shafts.

An armchair architect, he helps design some courses.

A patriot, he raises hundreds of thousands of dollars

for the Red Cross by playing exhibitions during World War I.

And in real life, away from the limelight of the links, after spending the 1920s at a brokerage firm, he is, finally, for decades, a milk salesman.

Chick Evans lived that life, and more.

A part of the game for 81 of his 89 years, Charles Evans, Jr. saw golf revolutionized by changes in every aspect of the game, including who participated in it. What was a sport for the privileged few when he entered the scene, turned into a sport for the working class, in part because of his successes.

It was happenstance that Evans and golf connected in the early fall of 1898. His parents, Charles, Sr. and Lena, could just as easily have moved to a different house than the one down the block from Edgewater Golf Club on Chicago's north side, one that might have taken young Chick down a different path. To that house, though, they moved—Charles and Lena and Chick's older brother Eliot, who would become a lawyer, and sister Gertrude. Once Chick stepped on the fairways of Edgewater, he fell in love with the game and its people.

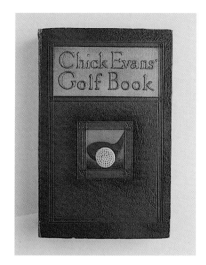

Thousands read Chick Evans' first-person story of his upbringing and his early championships when Chick Evans' Golf Book *was published in 1921.*

Besides, he confided in *Chick Evans' Golf Book*, his 1921 autobiography, he earned 35 cents for carrying—or, more accurately, alternately carrying and dragging—the bag of Miss Amy Jones, the daughter of one of Edgewater's five founding members and the women's club champion at the time.

Far younger than most caddies at the club, he scrapped for what links work he could get. As he grew, so did his reputation as a good caddie and one who, unlike many, abhorred cheating and got into at least one fistfight over his player's honor. By the time he was fourteen, he was Edgewater's best caddie, adept at finding golf balls in the rough. He would roll on the ground until he felt the ball under him. That unorthodox style helped earn him the No. 1 caddie badge.

That badge of honor, however, would soon become only a reminder of his caddie days. In that child-labor era, the stern rules of the game were reflective of the time. The combination of turning sixteen and working as a caddie meant said bag-toter was a professional. Evans had no interest in becoming a child professional, even though he'd become a reasonably proficient player, making it to the second round of the Chicago City Championship at Jackson Park in 1905, not long after his fifteenth birthday. Now, a year later, by ending his caddie career he'd stay an amateur, but also would lose his privileges to play at Edgewater.

He would have, that is, had he not been such an agreeable lad. The members had taken to Evans, and besides, head professional Tom O'Neil frequently needed help in the pro shop. So Evans, at sixteen, was allowed to hang around Edgewater, a private club, and work on his game. Had he been barred, the only public

The Evans family, including young Chick, first took up residence in Chicago at 1413 Pratt Avenue in the Rogers Park neighborhood.

USGA President George Herbert Walker presented the original Havemeyer Trophy to Chick Evans after his 1920 U.S. Amateur triumph.

course in Chicago, in Jackson Park, was 15 miles and over an hour away by the streetcar and elevated lines. It was an unlikely place to further develop a game that already was advanced.

His play had received considerable notice, including his inaugural appearance in a Western Golf Association championship, the 1906 Western Amateur in St. Louis, where he lost to Homewood's George Klingman 3 and 2 in the first round.

In 1907, winning would become Evans' trademark. He would win the Interscholastic title, emblematic of Chicago area high school supremacy. He would win the Edgewater Open on his home course. He would grab the city championship, the Westward Ho! golf club's Western Junior, and he would finish 14th in the Western Open at Hinsdale Golf Club. At age seventeen, Chick Evans was on his way to greatness.

In the next 10 years, before the Great War halted tournament play and spurred Evans to a fund-raising frenzy, Chick would win the Western Open, the U.S. Open, the first of two U.S. Amateur titles, and the first four of the eight Western Amateur crowns he would eventually wear. He won in the United States and he won overseas, capturing the 1911 French Amateur. He won on sand greens at Pinehurst's North and South Amateur.

And Chick Evans did all this even though putting, the heart of scoring, was the weakest part of his game.

The quality of Evans' considerable talents from tee to green carried him far, but, for all the brilliant long-iron shots his sweet and deceptively powerful swing produced, it couldn't do everything. In match-play competition, he had a habit of advancing to the semifinals, but no further. He even penned a poem about it, and *The American Golfer*, the eminent links publication of the day, carried it:

> *I've a semi-final hoodoo, I'm afraid.*
> *I can never do as you do, Jimmy Braid.*
> *I've a genius not to do it,*
> *I excel at almost to it,*
> *But I can never go through it, I'm afraid.*

Some Eastern-based observers believed Evans would never win anything big. By January 1912, when the poem was published, Evans had already captured his first Western Amateur title and the 1910 Western Open, the first of two to be played at match play. While the Western Amateur then was restricted to U.S. citizens living west of the Alleghenies and Canadians, the Western Open was open to anyone in the world.

It was in the U.S. Amateur that his semifinal jinx was most evident. In 1909, the second of his record 49 U.S. Amateur appearances—the last 48 consecutively—he had been beaten in the semifinals by H. Chandler Egan. In 1910, W.C. Fownes, Jr. did him in, and in 1911 it was Fred Herreshoff playing the eliminator's role in the penultimate round.

Chick Evans (center) and Walter Hagen (second from right) pose before teeing off in a 1917 Red Cross fund-raising exhibition at Scioto Country Club.

In 1912, when the U.S. Amateur was played at the Chicago Golf Club for the third time in eight years, Evans finally broke through into the final. He was clobbered in the title match by Jerome D. Travers.

The East's eminent amateur since Walter J. Travis and until Francis Ouimet came along, Travers administered a 7 and 6 whipping to Evans in the 36-hole final, coming from three holes down. Jerry Travers' comeback was made in a blistering heat wave, one which Evans later admitted he allowed to get to him by believing the burned-out conditions favored Travers. As a result, the match became as one-sided as the fire which had destroyed the main building of Chicago Golf's clubhouse just a few days before.

Evans was just as hot, explaining in his autobiography, "After the usual exchange of congratulations I went back to the clubhouse and took the silver medal that I had won and threw it as hard as I could up against the wall."

It wasn't his putter betraying him on that occasion, but his mind. The following year, Evans carried four putters in his bag in the U.S. Amateur. No matter. He lost in the semifinals again.

He would, finally, break through in USGA competition and did so spectacularly. He beat his hoodoo, his semifinal jinx, call it what you will, in 1916. Using just seven clubs, Evans raced to a two-stroke victory in the U.S. Open at the Minikahda Club in Minneapolis, setting a scoring record that would stand for 20 years. Three months after that, at Merion Cricket Club on Philadelphia's Main Line, Evans finally captured the U.S. Amateur.

Nobody, not Travers or Ouimet or Travis, had accomplished the feat of winning both championships in the same summer. "The Double Crown," it was called. Astounding was a better word for it.

Two years earlier, in 1914, Evans had entered the U.S. Open for the first time, principally because it was played at Midlothian Country Club in Chicago's then sparsely-settled southwest suburbs. He had finished a stroke behind Walter Hagen. Evans, while he didn't use it as an excuse, was playing the championship with an injured ankle. He was staying with a family adjacent to the course and sprained the ankle during an impromptu race with Dorothy Ellis, the daughter of his hosts, to the first tee and back.

Bad ankle or not, Evans—playing three holes behind Hagen—closed the gap to two strokes coming to the 18th tee, and nearly drove the green of the 277-yard home hole. A chip-in eagle would tie Hagen, and the hometown crowd was beside itself.

Presently, they quieted. Hagen, who had birdied the hole in each round, strolled out of the clubhouse to view the scene, and Evans lined up his chip. It scooted across the green, but just to the left of the cup, stopping nine inches away. Evans would make the tap-in birdie to fall a stroke short, the gallery groaned, and almost immediately, the critics noted that his missing a three-footer back on the ninth hole cost him the tie.

"I can't describe to you how I felt," Hagen told Evans on the green.

Chick smiled and said, "I can describe to you how I felt when I looked from the 15th tee over to you finishing on the 18th and you had a 20-footer with about a four or five-foot borrow and it went in." Evans was being typically modest.

He remembered his 1910 Western Open triumph as modestly, noting he had entered only because Beverly Country Club head professional George O'Neil was the brother of Edgewater professional Tom. Upon his arrival at the South Side bastion of the game, good things started to happen.

"I don't know how it happened, but when the qualifying scores were posted, there was my name right up at the top with 71," Evans recalled. "Then they had the match-play rounds, and somehow I happened to win them all."

Evans, then a twenty-year-old student at Northwestern University, squeaked through the first round, was taken to the 17th hole in the next two matches, and crushed LaGrange Country Club head professional George Simpson 6 and 5 in the final match. The youngest winner in the Western Open's history, then and now, Chick was in complete command.

It would be six years before Evans would find the same success in the 1916 U.S. Open at Minikahda. His score of 2-under-par 286—breaking George Sargent's seven-year-old record by four strokes—established a standard that would not be surpassed until 1936, when Tony Manero came home in 282 strokes at Baltusrol. By then, golf's equipment revolution had come to see steel shafts employed, and improving agronomy made fairways truly fair. Yet, Evans' mark stood for 20 years, an indication of what he accomplished.

His U.S. Open win at Minikahda quickly placed Evans in the national limelight.

"As early as the 15th tee of the final round," Evans recalled in a 1975 letter, "a man put $1,500 in cash in my hand and said I could have it if I won while playing with the Pneumatic Golf Ball. What a mistake I would have made then, for I doubt if anyone in the world of golf now knows there ever was a Pneumatic Golf Ball."

Chick Evans and his mother, Lena Young Evans, pose with the U.S. Open and U.S. Amateur trophies after Chick's Double Crown in 1916.

The gallery at Mayfield Country Club in Cleveland watches from near and far as Chick Evans beats Jess W. Sweetser in the 1923 Western Amateur semifinals, avenging his loss to Sweetser in the previous year's U.S. Amateur championship match.

There were more temptations, all of them turned down at the behest of Lena Young Evans, Chick's mother and his biggest fan. She saw sport as sport, not as a jumping-off point to business. While she is not believed to have played the game, she saw golf as even more than that, going so far as to compose a prose poem, "The Religion of Golf."

Even as Evans and his mother walked to the award presentation, an official of the A.G. Spalding Company took her aside. She told Chick, "He handed me a $10,000 check." It was payable to her, to keep Evans' amateur status technically correct. It was for Evans' endorsement for a line of clubs, with a substantial percentage royalty.

"Let's look at the check," Evans told his mother.

"I gave it back to him," she answered.

The offers kept coming. One for $300 to endorse a cigar. One for $3,000, from vaudeville impresario Martin Beck, to go on tour demonstrating golf shots. One for no less than $25,000 from Studebaker to endorse their cars. (Notre Dame football coach Knute Rockne, also offered the Studebaker deal, accepted it, and endorsed the car until he died in a 1931 plane crash.)

Wrote Evans in 1970, "This mother's advice came as quick as a flash as more money than I had ever heard of was ringing in my ears before, during and after the gold medal was in my pocket. It was a lot of money to turn down."

It was clear. Chick Evans was going to remain an amateur, no matter that a fortune was being offered him. Years later, he said, "I knew I was still an amateur when Jock Hutchison said, ' You are the champion and have only a gold medal, but I got money.' "

Later in the year, Evans would become twice a national champion.

The U.S. Amateur was played on Merion's classic East Course and, for a change, there was no sign of Evans' trademark poor putting. On this go-around, Chick was in control. He qualified for match play easily and had his closest call in the first round, Nelson Whitney of the Audubon Club taking him all the way to the 35th hole before Evans could finish him off, 3 and 1.

After that, it was the proverbial walk in the park. Evans lashed W.P. Smith of Pine Valley 10 and 9 in the second round, coasted past John Anderson of Siwanoy 9 and 8 in the quarterfinals—thus avenging a semifinal loss three years earlier—and took Baltimore Country Club's D. Clarke Corkran 3 and 2 in the semifinals.

He would meet a near-neighbor, Robert A. Gardner of the Hinsdale Golf Club, in the final. Gardner had won the Amateur the year before. That presented the large Philadelphia gallery, nearly 10,000 by one estimate by day's end, with a dream matchup for the title: the defending U.S. Amateur champion against the current U.S. Open champion.

Chick Evans in 1910, the year he burst upon the national scene by winning the Western Open.

Robert A. Gardner fell to Chick Evans in the final of the 1916 U.S. Amateur thanks to a run of uncharacteristically fine putting by Evans.

Evans won the first hole and never trailed in the match. Four times, Gardner came back to square the match, once from a three-hole deficit, but could never take the lead, and Evans took a 4 and 3 victory, finally earning the elusive Havemeyer Trophy.

It wasn't really great golf—Evans' morning-round score on the par 72 course was 77, Gardner's 82—but that didn't matter in match play. The kid from Edgewater had beaten his hoodoo forever. He was now a nationally-known star, just 26 and the first winner of the U.S. Open and U.S. Amateur in the same year. He was also the first to win the Western Open and Western Amateur as well, which is to say, every major title of his day on this side of the Atlantic.

Harry Vardon, who had lost to Ouimet three years earlier, called Chick Evans America's best golfer.

Evans, who spurned money for himself, would soon become America's best golf fund-raiser. With the entry of the U.S. into the Great War, the United States Golf Association canceled its 1917 championships, playing only a fund-raising tournament in Philadelphia. Evans, as the reigning national champion, was much in demand to play fund-raising exhibitions.

By now working in a brokerage firm and waiting for assignment to the Army's aviation service—for which he was ultimately rejected—Evans was eager to help in a big way. He saw, correctly, that an organized series of events would do far more for the cause than a scattershot collection of exhibitions.

As the national champion, Evans also saw the USGA as the natural organization to put such a series together. They turned down his request and the WGA stepped in. With Evans leading the way, the WGA-sponsored events helped raise over $300,000 for the American Red Cross.

After the war, his impact on the American golf scene continued. Evans won the 1920 U.S. Amateur, the interruption meaning he had captured two titles in three playings of the event. He would win four more Western Amateur crowns, giving him eight in all, the last six in consecutive appearances, and—with his 1910 Western Open win—he owned a record nine WGA championships.

His many victories kept Evans in the public eye, so much so that, while keeping his amateur status (the rules being different in that era), he was able to pen a golf column for the *Chicago Examiner* and record a series of golf lessons with the Brunswick Company.

Reading about how to play was one thing. Evans' record album deal was another. Buy a set of 78s, wind up the Victrola, and Chick Evans himself would tell you how to draw the ball like a champion.

But what to do with the money? Evans' mother, seeing how his association with golf had brought him first attention, then titles, then fame, and finally the spoils in the form of fancy finances, suggested that he put his money into a scholarship fund, thus continuing his amateur career and benefiting boys who started as he did.

It was a splendid idea, one that should have gained support. It wouldn't be that easy.

Chick Evans was rejected for the Army's aviation service during World War I, but that didn't stop him from getting into the air as a wing-bound passenger.

EVANS' U.S. OPEN WIN

A bunker on the seventh hole of Minikahda Country Club's course proves no problem for Chick Evans en route to the 1916 U.S. Open title.

By 1916, the occasion of its 22nd playing, the U.S. Open was recognized for three challenges: having generally difficult course
conditions, featuring the most impressive field of the season, and generating the most pressure on the competitors.

Despite Francis Ouimet's stunning 1913 playoff victory over Harry
Vardon and Ted Ray at The Country Club, in Brookline, Massachusetts,

the U.S. Open still was looked down upon by a segment of golf's intel-
ligentsia simply because it was an Open.

Professionals ought to play better, went the theory, because that's
what they do. It's the amateur who succeeds who is really the player,
for it's just a hobby to him, something done in his leisure hours. And
when an amateur wins, that simply proves the point. It's the U.S.

Not even the fast finish of Jock Hutchison was enough to knock Chick Evans off the lead at Minikahda.

rulemaking bodies decreed that 14 clubs were the limit, might carry two dozen clubs or more.

Evans' real eccentricity was in carrying more than one putter on occasion, to combat his often-poor touch on the greens. He would carry as many as four at one time, but at Minikahda, Evans had only one putter.

While at times in later years his description of the clubs differed, in 1916 Evans carried a brassie, spoon, mid-iron, jigger, lofter, and niblick along with the putter, all of them hickory shafted. Imagine playing today with only a 2-wood, 3-wood, 2-iron, 4-iron, 6-iron and 9-iron or wedge in the arsenal. That, essentially, is what Evans did, but his ability to shape shots, something lost on many players 80 years later, gave him far more flexibility with seven clubs than the overwhelming majority of players have with 14.

Even after the 14-club rule became the norm, Evans believed less was more.

"We'd all learn to play better shots with nine clubs, and I'm sure we'd score about the same," explained Evans, who once used only a mid-iron and a putter to finish second in the city championship. "This would demand the old skills in playing what we used to call 'part strength' shots. And (fewer clubs) would ease the load of the boy who has to caddie double.

"And we would be healthier because we wouldn't be riding in one of those darned carts. We could carry our own clubs in a Sunday bag or have a little boy caddie for us. It takes a high school football player to lug today's big bags."

With seven clubs to lug, caddie Shorty Johnson, whom Chick had befriended at the Chicago Golf Club, had no problem carrying Evans' bag, all 11 pounds of it, at Minikahda. And Evans had little trouble with the course or the field. Often ill in his youth, Evans was hale and hearty for the Open, and showed it from the start.

"The first day of the championship was about the prettiest June day I have ever seen," Evans wrote in his autobiography.

He made it a glorious day, opening with a 32 and finishing his morning round with a 70, a 2-under total that Chick thought could have been better, except that his 32 "surprised me so much that I lost three or four strokes on the next three holes."

By tying the course record, he was tied for the lead, and by breaking the course record in the afternoon with a 3-under 69, he was the leader by three at 5-under 139 and seemed invincible.

Not quite. The 36-hole final day saw Jim Barnes, six strokes back at dawn, mount a mighty charge, but Evans, after a third-round 2-over 74, still led by three strokes going into the afternoon's final round.

Amateur that's the real championship. The Open? That's just a sideshow for the professionals to showcase their skills.

In the last 80 years, such class distinctions have blessedly fallen by the wayside, but in the mid-teens, the theory lingered. Occasionally, the amateurs would even beat the professionals at their own game. Ouimet did it in 1913, and amateur Jerry Travers won the 1915 U.S. Open at Baltusrol Golf Club in Springfield, New Jersey.

Chick Evans would follow in their footsteps in 1916 at Minikahda, a club in Minneapolis that was the westernmost Open site to that point. Indeed, the USGA didn't take the Open west of Minneapolis until 1938.

Evans would become the third amateur in four years to win the Open and, like Ouimet—another former caddie—he would stun the best professionals of the day. He would do it with just seven clubs in his golf bag, the antithesis of the professionals who, in the years before the

The fourth and 12th holes, each a par 5, were critical. Evans' approach on the fourth buried in a bunker, and after he extricated it, three-putted for a double-bogey 7.

Evans had to wait on the fifth tee, ruminated about what had happened, and said to himself, "Forget it, and keep going." He did, making a birdie 3 on the short fifth, and even a bogey on the eighth hole, and the news that Barnes had tied him didn't get Chick down.

He came to the 12th knowing that Barnes had stumbled at the ninth. Evans also knew he had to at least par the 12th, a par 5 with a creek crossing some 25 yards in front of the green, for Barnes, whose nickname was "Long Jim," was likely to make a birdie. Thus, Evans, after a splendid drive, had a decision to make.

"I decided to risk the creek, and I never played a better shot in my life," Evans wrote. "I listened for the gallery at the green and when the encouraging sounds came echoing thrillingly from the little wood nearby, I was overjoyed."

Evans' brassie shot had found the green, never flirting with the creek. He two-putted for a birdie and parred the next five holes. He three-putted the last for a bogey, but it didn't matter. Barnes faded, and the late rush of Jock Hutchison, whose 3-under 33 gave him a closing 68, wasn't enough. Evans, on a warm Friday in June, was the U.S. Open champion. Hutchison was two strokes behind, Barnes four.

Chick had never been out of the lead. He would set a U.S. Open scoring record, one that would stand for 20 years. He spurned on-the-spot offers to turn professional and later in the year, by winning the U.S. Amateur, he'd make history, becoming the first "double champion," an achievement that so moved his fellow Edgewater members that they bought him a car. It is unlikely that any drive in that roadster was as fulfilling to Chick as the one he launched on the 12th hole at Minikahda on June 30, 1916. ◻

Jim Barnes mounted a charge against Chick Evans on the final day of the 1916 U.S. Open, but faded in the stretch.

THE WESTERN JUNIOR

In 1914, when the first Western Junior was played, teenagers didn't have abundant opportunities to play competitive golf.

Certainly, if they met qualifying standards, they could and did enter tournaments, but few were the players who were that accomplished at such a tender age. In that era, Chick Evans and Chandler Egan were the standout exceptions. Egan won his first Western Amateur at age nineteen. Both had started playing competitively in their teens.

Frederick Wright won the 1917 Western Junior at Exmoor Country Club.

Together, they would go on to win 12 of the first 24 Western Amateurs, and do so in their twenties and early thirties against fields comprised almost exclusively of middle-aged (and older) players.

Most teenagers had to be content with watching from the gallery or caddying.

With that in mind, on January 14, 1914, WGA President John Cady, a fine player who in 1908 had advanced to the semifinals of the Western Amateur in his hometown of Rock Island, Illinois, presented his fellow board members with the concept that the WGA conduct a championship only for junior players.

It would be open to boys at least fifteen, but no older than nineteen, living in the United States and Canada. It would mirror the Western Amateur in that it would be a match-play championship following a qualifying round, if necessary. Along with the 16-player championship flight, it would have two runner-up flights. After all, the idea was to give the boys an opportunity to play golf, and with extra flights, there would be a greater opportunity.

The Western Junior concept was accepted enthusiastically by Cady's audience. In short order, the Chicago Golf Club offered its facilities for the inaugural event, and entries began to trickle in. A field of 77 teed off on July 21, 1914, a steamy Tuesday in Wheaton, and after the three days of competition, University of Chicago student Charles F. Grimes emerged victorious.

Grimes beat medalist John Simpson of Galesburg, Illinois, in the first round, and was never headed after that 5 and 4 rout. He thrashed St. Louis resident Lawson Watts, who was playing out of the Nashville (Tennessee) Golf & Country Club, in the final. The 6 and 5 victory stood until 1931 as the most one-sided in the Western Junior final.

The Western Junior is the oldest national junior tournament. The Metropolitan Golf Association already was sponsoring a junior championship in 1914, but it remains a regional event.

In the Chicago area, Westward Ho!, a club in Oak Park, Illinois, began what was called the Western Junior championship in 1907. As it happened, Chick Evans won that inaugural event as well as the 1908 affair. He referred to it in *Chick Evans' Golf Book,* and from there it was taken that the Westward Ho! event was a WGA championship. It wasn't.

*1921 Western Junior winner
Burton Mudge, Jr. is flanked by
WGA President Albert R. Gates
(left) and Secretary W.W. Harless
at Belle Meade Country Club.*

Through the first half of the century, the designation " Western" referred to anything west of the Alleghenies. What is officially the Big Ten Conference today, for instance, was popularly referred to as the Western Conference early in the century. Indeed, the Western Golf Association itself holds that name for the same reason, though today its membership is national.

The WGA's Western Junior grew quickly, and was soon recognized as the premier junior event in the country. From the original entry of 77 in 1914, it mirrored the growth on the adult side of the ledger. In 1927, 266 players started at the Indian Hill Club. Said WGA Vice-President Robert Cutting at the following winter's annual meeting, "It was only because it was a nice, bright day and it stayed daylight a long time that we were able to finish the situation in daylight."

Eventually, qualifying restrictions were placed on the size of the field, but the Western Junior continued to attract the best and brightest young players in the game. In 1930, the age limit was raised to sixteen and, at least in theory, the name of the tournament was changed to "The Junior Championship of the United States." That didn't catch on, even within the WGA. By December, it was called the Western Junior again. If the name had held, the United States Golf Association, slow to encourage junior golf, might have needed another name for its U.S. Junior Amateur, first played in 1948, 34 years after the Western Junior's inaugural.

From the start, WGA clubs that hosted the Junior embraced it, though at times the Association had to scramble to come up with a course. Invariably, the post-tournament reaction was positive. The kids could play.

Until 1992, the Western Junior championship trophy was named for W.A. Alexander, one of the WGA's early officials.

years Jim Simons, Gary Hallberg, Bob Clampett, Willie Wood, and Jim Furyk have all had their moments.

Nonetheless, a high ranking and the promise of success later in life has little bearing in teenage match-play competition. Thus, when sixteen-year-old Eldrick "Tiger" Woods played in the 75th edition of the Western Junior in 1992, he was knocked out of the quarterfinals at the Chicago Golf Club when Ted Purdy of Scottsdale, Arizona, administered a 3 and 1 defeat.

To date, the only Western Junior champion to also win the Western Open is Jim Benepe, then and now of Sheridan, Wyoming. He captured the Junior in 1982 at Travis Pointe Country Club in Ann Arbor, Michigan, and the Open at Butler National Golf Club in Oak Brook, Illinois, six years later. ◻

In the late 1930s, when the Great Depression still had its grip on the land, the WGA wrestled with the difficulty of finding adequate and economical housing for the junior contestants. It settled on the idea of playing the Junior at university-owned courses, most of them around the Midwest, and using the school dorms for housing.

First attempted at Minnesota in 1938, the idea was well received, and since then, many Western Juniors have been played at university courses, as far east as Duke University's layout in Durham, North Carolina and as far west as Stanford University in Stanford, California.

The Western Junior still travels in an era in which the Western Amateur has remained anchored at Point O'Woods Country Club in Benton Harbor, Michigan, and the Western Open has settled at Cog Hill Golf & Country Club in Lemont, Illinois. The 1997 championship, the 80th renewal, was played at the restored East Lake Golf Club in Atlanta, Bobby Jones' stomping grounds as a junior.

The championship always has attracted a quality field. Future PGA champion Walter Burkemo lost in the Western Junior final. Deane Beman, who would become the PGA Tour's commissioner, lost in the 1956 Western Junior championship match. Andy North, who would win a pair of U.S. Opens, dropped back-to-back final appearances in 1967 and 1968.

More recently, perhaps a reflection of the junior golf tours that have grown up around the country, the winners have enjoyed success down the road as well. While Fred Haas, Jr., the champion in 1934 and 1935, was the first champion to go on to a fine professional career, in recent

1987 Western Junior winner Jim Furyk has gone on to considerable success in the professional ranks.

CHICK VS. BOBBY

Golf's two greatest career amateurs, Bobby Jones and Chick Evans.

Charles Evans, Jr. and Robert Tyre Jones, Jr. were not really contemporaries.

Born 12 years apart, there was a divide between them that had nothing to do with age and everything to do with culture.

Chick Evans could relate to commoners and kings. Bobby Jones, while hailed by commoners, preferred the company of kings, and eventually created his own kingdom in the Augusta National Golf Club.

They never really knew each other. In the first third of the century, before air travel became common, Evans and Jones rarely crossed paths. They saw each other in several Red Cross matches during World War I, but Jones was sixteen then, the kid swinger from the south. Evans, twenty-eight, was the grand attraction, champion of both the United States Open and United States Amateur.

Evans played in USGA and WGA events and a few select tournaments in Chicago and the Midwest. Jones played in the USGA championships and the occasional tourney down south. They were members of the 1922, 1924, and 1928 Walker Cup teams, saw each other at the U.S. Open and U.S. Amateur, and that was virtually it. They met in matches only three times.

It was hardly a rivalry on the level of Arnold Palmer and Jack Nicklaus, born 10 years apart but fierce competitors in a friendly golfing sense, from 1962 on.

Instead, it featured three matches and a relationship that was generally arm's length.

Given their ages, it's understandable that Evans ruled early and Jones late when they met on a golf course.

Their first on-course meeting in something other than a Red Cross benefit was at the Memphis Country Club in the semifinals of the 1920 Western Amateur. Jones played because it was in the neighborhood, and quickly found that his older opponent, while shorter off the tee, was splendid with his approach irons.

This 36-hole affair would go the distance. Chick and Bobby traded the lead back and forth all day.

They were all square starting the second 18, and it was then that Evans took advantage of Jones' miscues. He won the par-3 fourth hole with only his second birdie of the day and led 3-up after 27 when Jones bogeyed three of four holes.

Then the eighteen-year-old rallied. He birdied the 12th, parred the 13th, and birdied the 14th, winning them all to square the match. Jones was charging, and doing so before a partisan crowd who had heard of the Atlanta charmer's bursts of scoring, and now saw it on display. To have set a Western Amateur qualifying record, as Jones did with his

1-over 139, was one thing. To come through in match play was another entirely.

Chick and Bobby halved the next two holes with pars. There were two par 4s to play.

Jones put his second shot on the 17th at the edge of the green. Evans, trying to force the issue, forced his swing instead, pulling his approach into a grass ditch. Faced with an awkward and difficult recovery, he punched out with a niblick, the ball finishing 13 feet above the hole on the canted green.

Jones calmly knocked his mammoth approach putt to within four feet of the cup. The crowd figured that Jones, on Bermuda greens, would make his putt and Evans, a stranger to the surface at the start of the week, would miss his curling downhill 13-footer.

Instead, the opposite occurred. Chick made his 4, Bobby missed his, and they and the crowd went to the 18th with Evans in the catbird seat.

The home hole was anticlimactic in comparison, halved in par to give Evans the win over the medalist and regional favorite.

A month later, they were both in the U.S. Open, the first of eight times each was in the field. Evans finished ahead of Jones in 1920 and 1921, and the reverse was true thereafter.

The pair would share the qualifying medal in the 1923 U.S. Amateur at Flossmoor, but Evans was knocked out in the first round, while Jones was bounced by Max Marston in the second round. A rematch of Memphis would have to wait.

The wait ended in 1926 at Baltusrol. They would meet in the third round, and Jones would come away with a 3 and 2 victory. That, though, was only a preliminary to a meeting in the finals a year later at Minikahda, where Evans had taken the U.S. Open—but left the money—11 years earlier.

Jones would win, and handily, administering an 8 and 7 whipping. *The Chicago Tribune,* usually favoring their hometown hero, called Jones, who had won his second straight British Open earlier in the summer, the "King of Links" in a headline. Harland Rohm wrote that Jones "mercilessly crushed" Evans.

That was true. Jones crushed everyone down the stretch, beating Minikahda member Harrison Johnston 10 and 9 in the quarterfinals, toppling Francis Ouimet 11 and 10 in the semifinals, and then wiping out Evans in yet another 36-hole marathon that had no chance of going the distance. It was a match that drew no less than Walter Hagen as a spectator.

Jones was 6 up at lunch, having no more trouble with the rain than with Evans. Chick won a couple of holes early in the afternoon, threat-

The first Walker Cup team represented the USGA in the 1922 matches at the National Golf Links of America (left to right): Chick Evans, Bobby Jones, Francis Ouimet, Robert Gardner, playing captain William C. Fownes, Jr., Max Marston, Jesse Guilford, Jess W. Sweetser, and alternate Rudy Knepper.

ening to make it a close match, but Jones won the seventh, eighth, and ninth holes of the afternoon side to run away. It was essentially over, but for a strange incident on the 29th and last hole.

In 1963, Evans remembered that he had a two-inch putt to win the hole. At the time, the *Tribune* reported it as a four-footer. Wrote Rohm, "Suddenly he straightened up and walked over to Bobby with his hand extended."

The match was over, and while Jones walked to the clubhouse, the crowd, many of whom saw Evans win the U.S. Open on the same course in 1916, tried to carry Chick off the green. And 36 years later, in an interview with Charles Chamberlain of the Associated Press that was published on Evans' seventy-third birthday, the finish was alive in Evans' memory.

"I thought he might concede the two-inch putt," Evans said. "I

looked at him and he just stood there, about a yard from me, and stared at me. I went up to my ball, and when I put my putter head down, it touched the ball.

"I looked at Jones. 'The ball didn't move,' I said.

"'It sure did,' Jones replied. I just shook his hand and said, 'Congratulations for your fine victory,' and walked away."

Wrote Chamberlain of Evans, "His somewhat bitter feeling toward Jones, regarded by many as the world's greatest golfer, has never been a secret."

If there was a row at the time, it quieted quickly. The following year, Evans and Jones were not only members of the USGA's Walker Cup team, they paired up in the alternate-shot foursomes match, beating Britain's Charles Hezlet and William Hope 5 and 3 at the Chicago Golf Club. ◻

4

CONFLICTS WITH
THE USGA

The question presented during the Western Golf Association's annual meeting in Chicago's Grand Pacific Hotel on January 15, 1910, was simple: What organization should be golf's governing body in the United States?

Should it be the United States Golf Association, which was formed in 1895 after the continual cater-wauling of Chicago's own Charles Blair Macdonald, who complained that the national championships he was losing were not properly conducted?

Or should it be the Western Golf Association, younger by four years and controlled in 1910 by men outwardly conservative but often radical in their ideas?

Francis Ouimet, declared a pro by the USGA, was still an amateur in the WGA's eyes, and won the 1917 Western Amateur. He's proudly displaying his U.S. Amateur trophy here.

This was the issue confronting the delegates, many of whom arrived thinking the biggest issue they would have to vote on would be expanding the match-play portion of the Western Amateur from 16 to 32 players.

Instead, they were being asked to vote on expanding the existing boundaries of the WGA—which then restricted membership to clubs within 500 miles of Chicago—to include all of North and South America.

The motive behind the proposal was simple. Many Western golfers believed the USGA Executive Committee was comprised of a group of elite Easterners who had little concern or interest in the needs of the golfing community in the western United States. They thought the USGA's two-class member-ship system, which allowed active clubs to vote while associate clubs watched from the sidelines, was unfair.

As early as 1904, the WGA had petitioned the USGA

WGA Secretary Albert Gates announced the association's intention to expand in 1910.

to eliminate the separate and unequal categories, which WGA officials believed concentrated power in the East. They wanted a one-club, one-vote policy on important matters. In their minds, it was time for a declaration of golf independence.

WGA Secretary Albert Gates read the resolution. The WGA's name would be changed to the American Golf Association and, he intoned, "Any properly organized club on the continents of North and South America, and islands pertaining thereto, maintaining or controlling a golf course, shall be eligible to membership in this Association."

It was like a thunderbolt. The WGA was not only taking on the USGA, but, in moving outside the borders of the United States, it would be challenging the Royal & Ancient Golf Club of St. Andrews as well.

W.L. Yule, a WGA board member, offered a different option: the WGA should lead a movement to organize the various golf associations of North America, with the overseeing association then becoming the governing body rather than the USGA. A petition from 55 players was submitted at the meeting proposing that the WGA be given authority to conduct the new organization's championships.

All of this was quite a bit to swallow, along with dinner. Yule's concept of the associations banding together found favor, however, and carried. The idea of directly confronting the USGA by becoming the American Golf Association was referred to committee and deferred for a year.

No matter. The battle lines had been drawn. The WGA, in one way, shape, or form, was going to challenge the heretofore undoubted authority of the USGA from boardroom to bunker. Years later, Macdonald, reviewing these events in his autobiography, *Scotland's Gift—Golf,* would call Chicago "the hotbed of recalcitrants."

One year later, in 1911, the name change was voted down, as was the idea of ruling the Western Hemisphere. The delegates settled for accepting memberships from clubs "west of a north and south line made to pass through Buffalo and Pittsburgh" and those in Canada, no matter how far east.

The WGA had backed down because of behind-the-scenes fence-mending by former USGA Executive Committee member Leighton Calkins. He wrote the USGA suggesting they compromise and enact a new, more inclusive constitution.

"There is in the restlessness of the day a danger which threatens the game in some loss of respect for ancient authority," Calkins wrote, "and it is a pernicious theory that different sections of the country are competent to legislate for themselves on the rules of play. There must be joint action and the spirit of compromise."

There was. The USGA had adopted a new constitution on January 20, 1910, just five days after the WGA extended its olive branch. While the two-class membership system was retained, and only a small percentage of clubs still were eligible to vote, peace was expected to reign for generations to come. A potential "war" had been kept to a skirmish settled by a gentlemanly compromise.

However, the two organizations would soon be at odds again, sometimes arguing even though they agreed on matters.

Indeed, six years later came a pair of arguments, one

CONFLICTS WITH THE USGA

of which divided golfers on emotional, rather than regional, lines. Both disagreements involved amateur status.

The first, largely internal, came in the early days of 1916. The owners of the Del Monte Golf and Country Club on the Monterey Peninsula invited the WGA to hold the Western Amateur on its new course, and the California Golf Association offered to throw in a free train trip, from Chicago direct to Del Monte, California, for every distant contestant.

To accept free transportation to a tournament, however, would jeopardize the amateur status of the contestants. So the WGA Board of Directors huddled. The previous two years the Western Amateur had been held in Grand Rapids, Michigan, and in Cleveland. The WGA had ventured as far as Denver, but no further.

Now, a group from the California coast, including Jack Neville, the amateur architect who would design Pebble Beach and happened to be the secretary of the California Golf Association, was offering a free trip to paradise, plus expenses.

The board, mindful that a year earlier it had added a section to the bylaws prohibiting free travel, turned down the transportation offer and sent a wire to the California Golf Association noting that the Western Amateur might still be awarded to Del Monte. The WGA membership would decide that matter at the annual meeting.

As happens in democratic organizations, the board had one idea and the members another. First, the membership awarded the Western Amateur to Del Monte by a 134-71 vote. Next, the issue of the free trip came to the floor. It stayed there until the late hours, the arguments for and against acceptance going back and forth. The day before, USGA President Frank Woodward, a member of the Denver Country Club and an old WGA supporter, had said that to accept free transportation in one instance would open the door toward any number of inducements to attract entrants in amateur tournaments.

Woodward's thoughts, as well as the WGA board's recommendation, went unheeded. By a 100-15 majority, the delegates voted "that it is the sense of this meeting that the invitation of the California Golf Association be accepted and no member of the Western Golf Association attending the tournament in the acceptance of this invitation shall be considered as jeopardizing his amateur status."

There still was no free trip. The USGA quickly announced that any player taking the free ride to the Western Amateur would be barred from playing in the U.S. Amateur and U.S. Open. The WGA's board, by a 6-3 mail ballot vote, then reiterated its original stance: players would have to pay for the trip. The Western Amateur went on with a small contingent of Chicagoans who paid their own way, but Californians dominated, especially Heinrich Schmidt, who paced qualifying and went on to beat fellow San Franciscan Douglas Grant, 7 and 6, in the final match.

That was the first confrontation of 1916, and again the WGA board eventually sided with the USGA. However, another skirmish already was brewing, this time over Francis Ouimet's amateur status. The USGA ruled Ouimet became a professional when he and a friend opened a sporting goods store. That meant he would make money, albeit indirectly, from golf, because golf balls and equipment would be sold at the store.

WGA officials thought otherwise and announced they not only believed Ouimet was an amateur but had revised their

Wildlife and championship golfers coexisted during the controversial 1916 Western Amateur at the Del Monte Golf and Country Club on the Monterey Peninsula.

amateur code and invited him, and other leading Eastern amateurs, to play in the 1917 Western Amateur, previously open only to players living in the WGA's "territory."

Ouimet accepted the invitation and won the championship. Soon after, Ouimet was inducted into the Army, and the USGA reinstated him. But he and other notable Easterners would become semi-regulars at the Western Amateur for years to come.

Curiously, at first the WGA went along with the USGA's tightened code of amateurism. After the annual meeting of January 20, 1917, ended with the swearing in of a new board of directors, however, the new board convened in executive session. Behind closed doors, the board formed a committee that would find no fault with the Ouimets of the world, or with a golf association or club paying expenses to a competition. In other words, if the Del Monte offer came along again, it would be accepted.

Then the arguments began. Former USGA President Silas Strawn, a member of the Glen View Club, a charter WGA member club, stated:

"It has always been a matter of exceeding regret to me that there has been a tendency on the part of some members of the Western Association wholly to misconceive the purpose of its organization and to attempt to put this local association on a parity with the USGA and even to try to take the place of the USGA in the supervision of national golf affairs. . .

"Passing for a moment the merits of the WGA (amateur) definition, can it be presumed that any golfer good enough to win, or even to enter the Western championship, would be eligible to compete for the amateur championship of the United States, under the USGA definition? I cannot imagine such a case.

"Obviously, any man who is good enough to be Western champion is sportsman enough to observe the letter and spirit of the USGA definition."

WGA officials Albert Gates (left) and Crafts Higgins (right), seen here with Chick Evans at the 1920 Western Amateur, were at the forefront of the WGA's argument with the USGA.

Three months later, Ouimet, sportsman and sporting goods shop co-owner, unfit to play in the U.S. Amateur by the USGA's—and Strawn's—standards, won the Western Amateur at Midlothian Country Club in Blue Island, Illinois.

If that argument wasn't enough to cause division, days after Ouimet's acceptance of the Western Amateur invitation was announced, the WGA outlawed the stymie—that vexing rule that prohibited the lifting and marking of balls on the green and forced players to chip over balls close to the hole. Long thought to be an anachronism, especially with the improvement of putting surfaces, the WGA was the first national golf body to outlaw the stymie, setting the stage for 45 years of back-and-forth debate on the issue. Golf's ruling bodies, the USGA and Royal & Ancient Golf Club, finally agreed with the WGA in 1951, abolishing the stymie as the WGA had done decades earlier.

However, the stymie was small fish compared to control of the game overall, and some in the WGA hierarchy were interested in making another bid for control late in 1920.

Once again, WGA leaders broached the idea of changing the name of the WGA to the American Golf Association and allowing clubs from across the country to become members. The WGA, according to its proposal, wanted "to act as the authoritative administrative body for making and enforcing the rules for the playing of golf in the United States."

"DECLARES WAR FOR SUPREMACY IN GOLF," read the headline in *The New York Times.*

Crafts W. Higgins, a WGA official since the 1899 formation, railed against the USGA's dual membership stand, by which associated clubs could vote and allied clubs could not.

"No other sport could exist under such conditions, submitting to the dictation of the few," Higgins said in the WGA's proposal. "It will be contended by many that it is not good for the game in this country to have two associations struggling for national supremacy. But constant efforts for more than 18 years have demonstrated that there is no hope of getting the powers who control the United States Golf Association to change its form of government so as to give all clubs the right to vote."

WGA President Wilbur Brooks said American golfers needed "understandable rules" adapted to American courses and rejected the notion that the WGA was a regional group.

"The WGA is neither a local nor sectional body," Brooks said. "Its membership now extends into 31 states, Canada and Hawaii. The Western Golf Association believes that Americans understand golf and that they play under different conditions from those existing in other countries, and that Americans are entirely capable of formulating the proper rules for playing the game in this country.

"The rules, as published by St. Andrews, should be rewritten in response to the popular demand for a set of understandable rules covering playing conditions in this country."

Even as the USGA responded by stating that its Executive Committee would be expanded by four, all of whom would be representatives of regional golf associations, Brooks revealed that the new WGA constitution had also been submitted to the USGA with the proposal that the USGA adopt it as well.

"The WGA also believes that one golf association in this country is preferable to two or more, and that that one must be representative of American golfers from the Atlantic to the Pacific," Brooks opined. "The idea of one set of rules to govern the game throughout the world is ludicrous, even when climactic conditions alone are considered."

Just before Christmas in 1920, Brooks, Gates (the WGA's secretary in 1910, when the issue last had surfaced, and now the vice- president), former president Charles Thompson, and Trans-Mississippi Golf Association president James Nugent met with USGA brass. A truce was expected.

On January 15, 1921, at the WGA's annual meeting, Gates was optimistic, reporting that the USGA's Executive Committee expansion on a regional basis had met one goal: they had agreed to let the membership decide if it wanted one class of membership or two, and had agreed to work on a revision of the rules.

"These gentlemen have met us more than halfway," Gates said to the gathering in the ballroom of the Blackstone Hotel on Michigan Avenue. "They sent for us. We went there. We were treated splendidly. Everyone sat down with an open mind and we thrashed over the whole matter . . . with but one end in view, and that is, the best interests of golf in the United States."

Gates called the USGA "the parent organization.

While they have not been as liberal as we think they might have been in the past, we believe that they are seeing the light."

Added Nugent, "You must remember that we are not only seeking to avoid a warfare in golf, but are seeking to effect a co-operation between the ruling bodies in golf so that everybody may be benefited."

With that, as in 1910, the entire issue was tabled. It was not forgotten.

Meanwhile, the WGA and USGA huddled in regard to the rules. Here, as in more political matters, the WGA was far more liberal, not only eliminating the stymie, but adopting rules about out-of-bounds and lost balls that differed from those the USGA established. Except for the stymie, the WGA decided to play its rules as local rules, thus avoiding a major confrontation.

In 1922, the USGA also voted to ban the steel shafts that had appeared a few years earlier, on the theory that they would make the game far easier to play. The WGA, which had authorized their use upon their introduction, undertook performance tests featuring Chick Evans and Bob O'Link head pro Bob MacDonald at Edgewater Golf Club in Chicago. It was a windy mid-May day when Evans and MacDonald hit, using both hickory and steel shafts, firing into the wind onto a fairway after a shower, which deadened possible roll.

MacDonald averaged 226 yards with his old hickory shafts and 206 yards with steel. Evans batted 205 yards with wooden sticks and 208 with steel. Using middle-irons, both players averaged about 180 yards with both varieties of instruments.

WGA officials took it all in, slept on the results, and decided no change was necessary. Players could keep using steel shafts in WGA championships. The USGA eventually arrived at the same viewpoint in 1925 and the R&A in 1928.

There was, aside from the stymie and sundry other rules squabbles, one more WGA-USGA battle. It was a third and final attempt by the Western forces to upset the balance of power, this one a palace coup from within the USGA hierarchy itself. It almost succeeded.

Following the expansion of the Executive Committee membership, the so-called "establishment" from the East had less influence. When the 1923 U.S. Amateur was held at Flossmoor Country Club in Flossmoor, Illinois, the Executive Committee considered changing the USGA's name to, what else, the American Golf Association, and adopting a new constitution, similar to the WGA's. Here was the old WGA argument, now being promulgated by Western-based members of the USGA hierarchy.

USGA President J. Frederick Byers of the Allegheny Country Club near Pittsburgh, seeing the tide swing toward the West—seven of the 13 members were expected to vote for a name change at the least—asked for two weeks' time to consult with an advisory committee. The committee was made up of former USGA presidents and most of those Executive Committee members who opposed the changes.

"The Executive Committee could never have delivered the USGA to the WGA without the liveliest fight ever witnessed at an annual meeting," Charles Blair Macdonald wrote five years later. "The original membership of the USGA to a man would have taken umbrage and possibly have disrupted the organization. The Havemeyer Cup and the USGA meant something to the old guard, and they would have resented selling their birthright for a 'mess of pottage.' "

The advisory committee advised as expected. They told the Executive Committee to vote against the changes. It did. There, the matter essentially ended, with the Westerners now having been defeated on the inside as they had been defeated twice before on the outside. The WGA would continue for years to advocate its own rules, but, with a few exceptions—the stymie often being one—there were far more agreements than disagreements between the two organizations.

In fact, Charles O. Pfeil of Memphis, the WGA's president in 1923 and 1924, was highly regarded by both the "Eastern establishment" and WGA regulars for attempting to maintain calm during and after the 1923 Flossmoor uprising.

"It makes everything a great deal easier to have things go on in harmony and everybody play the game under the rules and the sky clear again," said Robert Gardner, a onetime Western Amateur finalist.

Evidently, the USGA thought so as well. Subsequently, Pfeil was nominated to become the USGA's president. He died before the meeting which would feature his election was held.

The war was over.

FRANCIS OUIMET

Francis Ouimet rocketed to fame by winning the 1913 U.S. Open.

Francis Ouimet could do no wrong.

The following year, Ouimet won the U.S. Amateur a fortnight after finishing fifth in his U.S. Open defense. In 1915, Ouimet finished 35th in the U.S. Open, 20 strokes behind fellow amateur Jerry Travers.

In 1916, however, Ouimet played in neither the U.S. Open nor the U.S. Amateur. Because he and fellow Woodland Golf Club member James Sullivan opened a sporting goods store in Boston, they were ruled ineligible to compete in the U.S. Amateur. All but one of the members of the USGA's Executive Committee voted against their continued eligibility on April 13, 1916, basing their decision on more stringent rules against professionalism that had been implemented three months earlier.

Then as now, amateurs ruled national golf organizations, except the Professional Golfers' Association of America. (In 1916, the PGA was just getting organized, with assistance from Chick Evans and WGA President Albert Gates, who helped draw up the papers of incorporation.) Otherwise, the USGA and WGA hierarchies were comprised of amateurs. It wasn't until 1988, when Chicago public golf legend Joe Jemsek was nominated, that a golf professional was a member of the USGA's Executive Committee.

It didn't take much to be tabbed a golf professional in that era. Caddies were professionals if they toted bags after their sixteenth birthday. Golf equipment salesmen were professionals. Architects were even considered professionals for a short time. Just about any-

In winning the 1913 U.S. Open, Francis Ouimet became an overnight national hero. He was the first amateur to win the U.S. Open, prevailing in a playoff against the great British professionals Harry Vardon and Ted Ray

People who didn't care about golf suddenly cared. People who didn't know a mashie from mashed potatoes took up the game. The first great American golf boom embraced by the general public was on, in large part because of Ouimet, the former caddie who won the Open at The Country Club, located across the street from his house in Brookline, Massachusetts.

Francis Ouimet was caught in the middle of a war of semantics not of his own making.

Golfer, publisher, and architect Walter J. Travis railed against USGA "snobbery."

one who could make money from golf was a professional, whether he wanted to be or not.

Yet, amateurs could receive gifts after winning championships, and that was considered acceptable. Thus, Chick Evans' receipt of a roadster from his fellow members at Edgewater Golf Club after winning the U.S. Open and U.S. Amateur in 1916, and another car after his win in the 1920 U.S. Amateur, caused no problems. Evans could even write for the *Chicago Examiner* without raising an eyebrow.

The crazy-quilt code meant that when Ouimet and Sullivan hung their storefront shingle and opened their doors for profit, they lost their amateur status by the USGA's dictates. And Ouimet, the people's champion, was sidelined. (So, for that matter, was Sullivan.)

The people, from the municipal player to the country club elite, were outraged.

George Crump, founder of Pine Valley Golf Club in Pine Valley, New

Jersey, and one of the giants of golf in the East, wrote *The American Golfer* to say, "It has always seemed to me that a professional was one who taught golf or a player who made a business of playing golf in public for money (one or more times). I think a short clear rule is what is wanted, and that the present rule has not filled the want."

Crump, well ahead of his time, was defining the modern professional. What nobody could understand was why the USGA was so worried about professionalism.

"What is the particular cancer eating into the game?" queried eminent amateur Walter J. Travis, editor of *The American Golfer,* in the June 1916 issue. "There is no outward evidence of there being anything 'rotten in the state of Denmark.' And all this needless agitation reflects unfavorably on the game.

"The general tendency of the rule would appear to be to make golf so that only a man with plenty of money can afford to play it. This is snobbery."

Travis, a three-time U.S. Amateur champion, was obviously making money off the game through his publication, but that, like Evans' newspaper column, was all right with the USGA. It ruled him ineligible for amateur events for a short time because he was also a golf architect, then rescinded that decision. Later, in January 1917, the USGA again ruled that architects were professionals.

Seeing this contretemps, and judging the action of the USGA improper, Western Golf Association officials decided to take action. The incoming board ruled on January 20, 1917, that while course architects should be considered professionals, Ouimet was an amateur under their code. They then invited him and other prominent Eastern players to play in the 1917 Western Amateur at Midlothian Country Club in Blue Island, Illinois. The USGA was aghast, and even more aghast when Ouimet accepted the invitation.

It was a fine field, for while Evans was dedicating himself to playing in fund-raising matches exclusively in 1917 and 1918, plenty of other stars were on hand, including Southern Amateur champion Bobby Jones. The fifteen-year-old Atlanta prodigy lost in the first round to Ned Sawyer, who had won the Western Amateur 11 years earlier.

Ouimet was relatively unchallenged, especially in his 36-hole quar-

terfinal match, a 14 and 13 victory over Paul Burnett of Maywood, Illinois. It was the most lopsided win to that point in Western Amateur history. Two days later, Ouimet had a tougher time with Ken Edwards of the host Midlothian Club, taking a 1-up victory by two-putting for a par 4 and a halve on the home hole.

The modest Massachusetts mauler was expected to have a tougher time regaining his USGA amateur status, but fate intervened. In the winter of 1917-18, Ouimet was drafted, and when he went into the service, the USGA saw an opening. Ouimet wasn't at his sporting goods store. He wasn't making money by selling golf equipment. Thus, he wasn't acting like a professional.

The USGA ruled as such on January 25, 1918, and never raised the subject of Ouimet's eligibility again after the war. Ouimet was welcomed back into the USGA fold with open arms and played on the first USGA-sponsored Walker Cup team in 1922. He became a fixture in the event, playing in each Walker Cup through 1934. He won another U.S. Amateur, this one at the Beverly Country Club on Chicago's southwest border, in 1931, and received a signal honor in 1951, when he was the first non-British subject to be elected captain of the Royal & Ancient Golf Club of St. Andrews. ◻

Francis Ouimet (third from left) and Bobby Jones (second from right) were members of a 1921 team of American amateurs which laid a 9-3 defeat on a British squad at Hoylake. The match led to the Walker Cup competition a year later.

THE RED CROSS YEAR

As Chick Evans recalls it, this 1918 Red Cross fund-raiser at Old Elm Club near Lake Forest was the first time the club was opened to the public.

The U.S. Open, PGA Championship and British Open were canceled in 1917 in deference to the Great War. The British Open hadn't been played since the onset of hostilities in 1914.

There was, though, a golf championship played in 1917. The Western Open, alone among golf's major open-to-all events, took place and was won by Jim Barnes. He had first captured the Western title in 1914 and snared top honors in the first playing of the PGA in the summer of 1916. The English-born Barnes, at 6-foot-3 the tallest golfer of note of his time—and one of the most successful tall players of any era—beat defending champion Walter Hagen by two strokes at Westmoreland Country Club in Wilmette, Illinois.

Barnes' victory, for which he earned $300, came in the last major championship until after Armistice Day. By the winter of 1917-18, the increasing scope of the war made the prospect of playing tournament golf impossible, if only because of travel restrictions.

On January 19, 1918, the WGA's annual meeting was held at the Congress Hotel in downtown Chicago. The mood was somber, notwithstanding the association's best-ever financial position, in which $3,000 of the $5,691.97 in the WGA kitty was invested in Liberty Bonds.

Patriotism, not golf, was in the air. Thus, when Westmoreland member S.G. Strickland, a WGA director, offered a motion, it was quickly seconded and carried. The motion:

"That owing to the war, the regular championship tournaments of the Association be abandoned, but if in the opinion of the Board of Directors, the situation in this country is propitious, that they are at liberty to hold such patriotic tournaments as they may judge expedient; the proceeds derived to be dedicated to war charity purposes."

So it would be. The situation was propitious beyond the wildest imagination of Strickland and the rest of the board. By the following May, the American Red Cross had been designated as the body for which funds would be raised. A schedule of one-day exhibitions starring the best players in the United States was being arranged. Other regional golf associations were getting involved.

At the center of it all, star of many of the exhibitions, was Chick Evans.

A Red Cross exhibition was nothing new to Evans. He had played in one in Guelph, Ontario, Canada, in August of 1916, not long after winning the U.S. Open. Canada, as part of the British Empire, was already at war with Germany, and every method of fund-raising was taking place. Why not golf?

It was arranged to have Evans tee it up with George Lyon, the noted Canadian champion, at the Guelph Golf Club. In his autobiography, Evans remembered,

"There was a big crowd out, a good many wounded soldiers among them. No entrance fee was charged, but the money was collected through the sale of pins representing a soldier in khaki. The crowd bought liberally. Individuals, too, gave large sums. It was from this comparatively modest beginning that all the Red Cross golf competitions grew. I believe it was the first of its kind."

The United States entered the war in the spring of 1917, President Woodrow Wilson signing the declaration of war after his golf game was interrupted. Evans decided he would play no tournament golf until the war ended and, as the "duration" U.S. Open and U.S. Amateur champion, he was deluged with invitations to play in charity events.

At his own expense, Evans roamed the Midwest and East, twice playing in Canada. Proceeds went to the Red Cross or the Navy League, as the particular club saw fit. He estimated that $50,000 was raised, but thought that with some planning, a far greater sum could be realized.

The USGA, thought to be in the best position to make an impact nationally, was approached but tabled Evans' request to organize the

matches for 1918. He then went to WGA President Charles F. Thompson, a member of Flossmoor Country Club, and was received far more encouragingly.

Evans proposed that participating professional be paid, that amateurs pay their own way unless the expense was prohibitive, that clubs guarantee a minimum donation, and that the WGA and the clubs handle the organizational details while the players simply played.

WGA President Charles F. Thompson brought the enthusiastic support of the association behind Evans' concept of the Red Cross fund-raisers.

"Our great desire was to put the thing on a high plane to keep the game alive in war time, and to make a wholesome, needed amusement pay a tax for the benefit of the boys at the front," Evans wrote. "The players responded nobly. Not one refused to do his share."

The biggest names of the day joined Evans in the WGA matches. Barnes would play. So would Jock Hutchison, the winner of the Patriotic Tournament in Philadelphia which replaced the U.S. Open in 1917. Walter Hagen stepped up. From the East, Jerry Travers and Fred McLeod took part. So did another regional favorite, a sixteen-year-old fellow from the South with a deceptively powerful swing by name of Robert T. Jones, Jr.

The matches, not all of which involved the tireless Evans, were successful beyond expectation. For a start, an admission fee, new to golf (and which would not be duplicated in tournaments until 1922), was charged. Next, the honor of caddying for the players was often auctioned off. Finally, a ball from each player, suitably adorned with autograph, would go on the block, sometimes twice if the high bidder was in a particularly giving mood.

June 9, 1918, saw one of the biggest fund-raising days. Lake Shore Country Club in Winnetka, Illinois, a picturesque course adjacent to Lake Michigan, raised $35,000 in a day which featured Evans, Barnes, Hutchison and Bob MacDonald, the head professional at nearby Indian Hill Club. The Lake Shore members and their guests added a new wrinkle, auctioning off each player's ball after each hole. Evans guessed that the maneuver brought in about $12,000 by itself.

The WGA Red Cross Matches were not a male-only domain. One of the most heralded matches was played at Westmoreland, where Perry Adair and U.S. Women's Amateur champion Alexa Stirling were paired against Bobby Jones and Women's Western Amateur winner Elaine Rosenthal. When the sun had set, some $2,000 had been raised.

As summer turned to fall, the exhibitions began to wind down. Evans and Rosenthal played against Jones and Stirling in another co-ed match at Scioto Country Club in Columbus, Ohio. It was a match that featured four champions, three already of national renown and

U.S. Women's Amateur champion Alexa Stirling was one of the Red Cross headliners.

one, Jones, the youthful Southern Amateur champion. Eight years later, Jones would return to Scioto and win the U.S. Open.

The WGA organized the matches, with C.M. Smalley and Crafts Higgins doing the detail work, so the clubs could concentrate on the fund-raising. The players could concentrate on the playing.

Evans would end up playing in 48 of the WGA Red Cross Matches, as well as another four arranged independently. His presence was a boon, for when the final tally was made, it was found that more than 80 percent of the money raised came from matches he took part in.

The war ended, as any schoolboy knows, on November 11, 1918, at 11 a.m. in Europe. The world, and the world of golf, would be able to go back to normal. Thus, it was not only with great pride but also a sense that a similar series would not be needed that Thompson, who had taken up Evans on his offer a year earlier, could announce that the WGA Red Cross Matches had raised $303,775, at an expense of only $1,061.50. The net of $302,713.50 went a long way toward relieving the suffering caused by the great conflict. ◘

The foursome of Robert Gardner, Chick Evans, Perry Adair, and sixteen-year-old Bobby Jones entertained a throng at Flossmoor Country Club in 1917.

5

THEY CALLED HIM
SIR WALTER

All eyes were on Walter Hagen when he stepped up to Canterbury Golf Club's 15th tee in the final round of the 1932 Western Open.

How many times since his debut in the 1913 U.S. Open had Hagen been the focus of attention? Hundreds? Thousands? The easy answer is the right one. Hagen was the cynosure of all eyes every time he played.

Now, with four holes to play at Canterbury, Hagen's faithful followers were watching as their star faced imminent defeat. Seeking to win an unprecedented fifth Western Open championship, Hagen trailed Olin Dutra by three strokes.

Hagen and Dutra were playing together, and on this day, none of Hagen's crafty techniques that would unnerve a

lesser opponent bothered the unflappable Dutra.

Dutra had birdied the par-3 11th to pull two ahead and took a three-stroke lead when Hagen bogeyed the par-4 14th. Dutra seemed ready to capture his first major championship.

Hagen, legendary for his astonishing comebacks, refused to fold, even with a stiff wind whipping at his trousers and only four holes left. He blistered his drive on the 372-yard straightaway par 4, keeping it just short of the creek some 100 yards from the green. His pitch to the uphill green stopped some 30 feet above the hole.

Dutra was 20 feet from the cup, in a favorable position. Hagen was faced with a curling downhill putt that would, if it missed, surely run at least 10 feet past the hole.

A gallery estimated at 3,000 was watching. A robin

Power, grace, and a sense of timing for dramatics: Walter Hagen had it all.

One of golf's most stylish threesomes: the Squire, the Silver Scot, and the Haig, a.k.a. Gene Sarazen, Tommy Armour, and Walter Hagen, all of whom captured the Western Open.

as many as Willie Anderson, the turn of the century phenom. Now, chasing an unheard of fifth, he pressed the advantage, hitting the green of the par-5 16th hole in regulation and two-putting for par. Dutra, 100 yards short of the green with his third shot, scrambled for a bogey. They were tied.

It was almost academic now, and Hagen made sure of it with a 230-yard tee shot to within seven feet of the pin on the par-3 17th, an easy birdie that put him in front. Dutra parred, and when they traded pars on the 18th, Hagen was acclaimed as the champion of champions. Once again, he had lived up to his deserved reputation as the most dramatic performer in the game. Dutra would have to wait two months, until the PGA Championship, to win his first major. The Western Open, as always seemed the case, again belonged to Hagen.

When Charles Kimmel, working the first of his more than 50 Western Opens as the scorekeeper, lettered the final summary, it was Walter Hagen's name that received the most lavish flourishes. Dutra's was in smaller, less ornate type. That mirrored reality.

Like most great athletes, Hagen was multifaceted. He was a golfer, first and foremost. He was a showman, unquestionably. He was also a standard-bearer, and demonstrably so, for those in his profession.

Most of all, in combining those three passions, and by pulling off headline-grabbing finishes, he was the absolute leader in making the professional golf tour a reality.

When golf took hold in America, when permanent courses were developed and when country clubs were formed, the concept of a circuit of professional tournaments was not even considered. Professionals were imported from Scotland and England to teach the members how to play and to run the golf shops.

The United States Open? It was, upon its start in 1895, regarded as a once-a-year aberration, a busman's holiday.

flew low across the green. Hagen couldn't help noticing it and said, "I could use a birdie now."

He stepped up, read the line, took aim and sent the ball curling toward, and into, the cup. The gallery whooped it up. Dutra, stunned, sent his matching birdie attempt three feet past the hole, then missed his putt for par. It was a two-stroke swing. Hagen was one behind with three to play.

It was now Hagen, not Dutra, who was in the driver's seat.

Hagen had already won four Western Open crowns,

The Western Open? It became of a piece with the U.S. Open, regarded as a way to let the professionals play the game while playing hooky from their club.

The local professional events splashed on the calendars, especially in the metropolitan areas of New York, Chicago, Boston, Philadelphia, and Detroit, drew little outside interest.

A weekly tour? Dream on. If there was a way for a professional to make real money outside of his shop, it was by giving exhibitions, and the only professionals in demand for exhibitions were the champions. Harry Vardon and Ted Ray were on an American exhibition series in 1913 when they played in the U.S. Open—and

lost to amateur Francis Ouimet—giving a boost to golf on this side of the Atlantic far greater than they could have through any number of stops at country clubs.

Exhibitions were just that. Generally, Vardon and Ray would be teamed against a pair of local players, such as the head professional and leading amateur at a club, or a pair of local professionals. They were paid a guaranteed fee and, if there was money on the line, whatever else they could pick up. Easy money.

In the manner of the vaudeville circuits, these barnstorming tours were invariably popular because not only could residents of the hinterlands see a big-name athlete close-up, they also could pick up a pointer or

Walter Hagen and Tommy Armour draw a large gallery, for the time, at the 1930 Western Open at the Indianwood Club near Detroit.

Harry Vardon preceded Hagen in the touring pro department.

two, either during a clinic or during the round.

Then Walter Hagen showed up and changed the course of the game.

Hagen could play, as evidenced by his fourth-place finish—three strokes out of the famous playoff—in the 1913 U.S. Open. He could do more than play.

Hagen could strut. Hagen could show off. Hagen could get out of trouble with a flourish. Hagen had a tan. Hagen had style. He wore spats and slicked his hair back and looked like either a Hollywood star or American royalty. Maybe both.

"Sir Walter," they called him. "The Haig," more formally.

"Golf has never had a showman like him," Gene Sarazen, who could play a little himself, wrote in his autobiography. "All the professionals who have a chance to go after the big money today should have a silent thanks to Walter each time they stretch a check between their fingers. It was Walter who made professional golf what it is."

Bobby Jones, who kept amateur golf in the forefront, played in the Western Open only at Oakwood Club in Cleveland in 1921, where he held the lead at the halfway point, but faded to fourth thanks to a third-round 83. Hagen, three strokes back after 36 holes, subdued a strong southerly gale on the final day to score a five-stroke victory over Jock Hutchison. Jones skipped the Western Open thereafter, preferring to concentrate on the U.S. Amateur and U.S. Open, as well as a couple of southern events, and as the years went on, the British Open and British Amateur.

While Jones chased, and eventually captured, the Grand Slam, Hagen was winning almost everything else. The Western Open and PGA were his personal playground in the 1920s, keeping those championships in the headlines while Jones dominated the others.

There would be more headlines, and from datelines that previously had no connection with golf.

The so-called "Winter Tour" began with the Texas Open in 1922, played, incidentally, under WGA rules.

Walter Hagen would eventually win five Western Open medals.

Hagen won it the year after, pocketing $1,500. More tournaments were added in outposts such as Corpus Christi and New Orleans. The Los Angeles Junior Chamber of Commerce dug deep and put up $10,000 for the inaugural Los Angeles Open in 1926, when the Western Open's purse was only $1,500. Long Beach and Sacramento weren't far behind in creating tournaments.

Hagen, the drawing card, played in almost all of these events when he wasn't playing in yet another lucrative exhibition. When Bob Harlow, Hagen's manager, began to run the fledgling tour as well, that made for a perfect combination.

More than anything else, Hagen could win. He won more than any professional of his time, more tournaments and more money. He won more than anyone in the 1920s, Jones included.

An argument raged at the time as to who was the greater player, Hagen, who lived to play, or Jones, who played in his spare time. It rages on, with the Hagen camp noting that their man once beat Jones 12 and 11 in a 72-hole match-play showdown. Jones' followers simply point to their man's record vs. Hagen in the U.S. Open and British Open: Jones finished ahead of Hagen nine times in the U.S. Open (and was first or second eight of those times), and Hagen won the British only when Jones was stateside. Their 1921 Western Open showdown, of course, aids Hagen's cause.

Regardless of where he stands against Jones, Walter Hagen was the first great homebred golf professional. He was from Rochester, New York, not St. Andrews, Fife. When he wasn't caddying, he played baseball as a kid, a pitcher who mulled signing a contract with the Philadelphia Phillies but finally decided that golf offered a better future.

What Hagen saw was a day in which professionals would be allowed to walk into the clubhouse via the front door. The members of Inverness Club in Toledo, Ohio, taking Hagen's cue that professional and amateur golfers deserved to mingle under the same roof, invited the professionals inside during the 1920 U.S.

Walter Hagen, here showing off his putting prowess at Winged Foot for Bobby Jones and Jess Sweetser, brought the pro game to the public like no one had before.

Hagen putting on the old sand greens at Pinehurst.

Open. In response, Hagen led a collection to present the club with a grandfather clock, which stands proudly in Inverness' foyer and upon which is inscribed the following:

God measures men by what they are,
Not what in wealth possess.
This vibrant message chimes afar,
The voice of Inverness.

That was typical Hagen style, a grand gesture with meaning behind it. He also foresaw a day in which a regular tour would be organized, a day in which professional golf would thus gain the lion's share of attention of the public, relegating the amateur game,

which dominated the headlines from the start, to the back burner.

He would help that day arrive, along the way becoming the first true professional golfer, one who didn't have to rely on a club job to survive. The Western Open would be one of his major stages.

Those without a sense of history today credit Hagen with 11 major championship titles: two U.S. Opens, five PGA Championships, and four British Opens. Hagen won all those and more. His five Western Open titles should be counted as majors today, as they were considered as much at the time.

Additionally, aside from his considerable presence

on the early Ryder Cup teams, he won the Metropolitan Open—a major title in the first third of the century—four times, and won the North and South Open in Pinehurst, North Carolina, likewise an early-day major, on three occasions.

Today, the Met Open and North and South aren't even lines in record books, so long ago did they vanish from the scene. But his accomplishments in the Western Open endure.

Nobody else has five Western Open titles. Only Anderson had won four Western Opens prior to Hagen, and only Billy Casper has captured four since.

Hagen won the Western Open from behind, as he did in overcoming Jones for the first time in 1921, and won it from the lead. He won it hard and he won it easy. Mostly, it seems, he won it, and in the years he didn't, he almost did.

He won his first Western Open in 1916 and his last in 1932. At the time, the 16-year distance between wins was a record for the championship.

Hagen, when he was on hand, was always in the hunt. He played in 14 Western Opens and was in the top 10 on 13 occasions and placed first or second nine times. The first of his four second-place finishes came in 1917 at Westmoreland Country Club in Wilmette, Illinois.

He tied for fourth in his first Western Open, at hilly Glen Oak in Glen Ellyn, Illinois, in 1915, and would have been closer to the front, if not in the vanguard, but for an opening-round 80. The following year at the Blue Mound Country Club in Milwaukee, he opened with a 70 and hung on to win by a stroke.

Those two tournaments, in essence, sum up Hagen. Occasionally wild, but usually where he should have been. He had a propensity for hitting drives 30 and 40 yards off range, then slamming a recovery shot back to the fairway, or, better yet, the green for a par or a birdie.

Hagen could be forgetful. His image of a late-night carouser was just that, an image. He would party, but not until later in life did he try to live up to his press clippings and drink up to his reputation. In reality, Hagen used the party scene as an image-builder. His last-minute arrivals at the first tee were more a part of the show than anything else.

Hagen was born with a flair for the dramatic. He would sometimes even change into his golf shoes after hitting his tee shot on No. 1; that after pulling up to the tee in a fancy car.

The crowd enjoyed his antics, but sometimes Hagen

was bitten by his poor timing. He was expected to play in the 1920 Western Open at Olympia Fields, but, eschewing a practice round, didn't leave Detroit until the day before. He arrived at the vast club in the south suburbs of Chicago early in the afternoon of the first round. This time, he really was late. He'd missed his tee time by so much,

The program from the 1926 Western Open in Indianapolis is the oldest in the WGA archives.

WGA officials had no choice but to tell him he couldn't tee off.

Hagen was the first golfer to really make a living from playing golf, endorsing products, and the like. He surpassed Vardon, Ray, and J.H. Taylor in working the exhibition circuit. Teaming up with a variety of professionals and then striking out on his own, Hagen was the No. 1 professional attraction in the game. He hired Harlow to book those exhibitions and to keep his calendar straight.

That didn't always work perfectly. Then as now, tournaments built up expectations that the champion of a particular year would return the next year to defend his title. When Hagen won, the anticipation was trebled. It was not always fulfilled.

Hagen won the Western Open at Oakwood in 1921 and didn't play at Oakland Hills in 1922. He was off on an exhibition tour, believing the Western Open was being played on another date. He won his second straight Western (and fourth overall) at Olympia Fields in 1927, winning wire-to-wire, but he didn't show for the 1928 Western Open at North Shore Country Club in Glenview, Illinois. This time, he had decided to play in the Canadian Open, being played the same week.

In 1933, the year after winning Western title No. 5 with his dramatic catch and pass of Dutra on Canterbury's final four holes, he took off on a foreign exhibition tour, rather than defend his title at Olympia Fields.

Officials weren't happy with Hagen's wayward ways, knowing that the gate would be diminished. The other professionals knew with Hagen out, they would move up a place in the field. And when he did appear, Hagen drew the lion's share of the gallery.

Only Hagen could get away with asking for the flagstick to be pulled on the final hole of a British Open, knowing he needed an eagle 2 to tie, and then nearly hole out for that tie from the fairway.

Only Hagen could get away with saying, as he stepped on the first tee, "Who's going to be second?"

Only Hagen, in the Roaring '20s when there were more paper millionaires than real ones, could sound logical when he said, "I don't want to be a millionaire. I just want to live like one." He was a millionaire, eventually, and lived like one.

Hagen was difficult to play with, but not because he was a lout, or severe in his outlook, or all business. On the contrary, he was unfailingly polite. He appeared to approach the game casually. He seemed to have not a care in the world between shots, living up to his dictum, "Take time out to smell the flowers."

His no-grind demeanor put other players at ease, often so much so they would lapse into a Hagenesque nonchalance. But that coolness masked the heart of a hitman. Hagen would, when the time came, study his shot as intently as any player who had come before him, then, often as not, pull himself out of trouble as briskly as he'd entered into it. Ask Dutra, who might still have been watching that robin flying around the 15th green at Canterbury when Hagen lowered the boom.

Hagen's greatest scoring performance in the Western Open came in 1926, at Highland Golf and Country Club in Indianapolis. He opened with a sloppy 5-over-par 75, but closed with a rush while the rest of the field moved in the other direction. He came back with a second round 68, a third round 66 which included an inward 31, and finished with an even-par 70.

The total: 279 strokes, 1 under par for the championship. The margin of victory: nine strokes over Gene Sarazen and "Light Horse" Harry Cooper. Said Sarazen during the lunch break between the third and fourth rounds, when apprised of the 66s Hagen and Cooper scored: "What did those fellows do out there this morning? Go crazy?"

Walter Hagen was crazy, all right. Crazy like a fox.

CHICAGO'S EARLY CLUB PROS

This staged shot spotlighting Chicago-area pros from the 1935 St. Paul Open features (left to right) Henry Picard, longtime Evanston Golf Club pro Johnny Revolta, Glen Oak Country Club stalwart "Light Horse" Harry Cooper, 1935 U.S. Open winner Sam Parks, Jr., and Ky Laffoon, longtime pro at Northmoor Country Club. Revolta and Cooper won the Western Open, Cooper by beating Laffoon in a 36-hole playoff in 1934.

It isn't remarkable how many club professionals won the Western Open in the early days.

Club professionals were the game's only professionals. There was no tour. Professionals played in championships and tournaments on their time off, if they could get time off.

What is remarkable is this: once golf was established throughout the United States, the greatest concentration of club professionals who could play the game—and win championships—was in Chicago.

Through the Roaring '20s and Great Depression, Chicago's roster of professionals reached its peak in national prominence. Following is a short list of what could well be called Chicago's Who's Who of Golf Professionals:

Tommy Armour.

The winner of every major professional title of his era, save the Masters, which commenced just as he was retiring. Armour's instructional classic, "How to Play Your Best Golf All the Time," is still in print, as illuminating today as it was when "The Silver Scot" was on the lesson tee at Medinah Country Club, getting the members to hit the ball straight when he wasn't firing a shotgun at squirrels who dared stray in his direction. Armour, who lost an eye in World War I combat, nonetheless captured the Canadian Open three times, the U.S. Open in a playoff over Harry Cooper in 1927, the Western Open in 1929—and by a record score of 273, which would stand until Ben Hogan surpassed it in 1946—the PGA Championship in 1930 and the British Open at Carnoustie in 1931. Along with his Medinah post, he wintered in Boca Raton, having truly the best of both worlds.

Johnny Revolta.

A splendid teacher who had the pleasure of summering at Evanston Golf Club, Revolta won the Western Open and PGA Championship in 1935—the latter by defeating Armour in an all-Chicago final match—en route to capturing the fledgling tour money title. He earned a princely $9,543 for the year. Revolta, whose first national success came in the 1933 Miami Open, also won the 1939 Crosby and the 1944 Texas Open. Cutting back his tournament play after World War II, Revolta was the professional at Evanston until 1966 and the professional emeritus until his death in 1991.

Harry Cooper.

"Light Horse," so nicknamed by Damon Runyon, enjoyed plenty of success while the head professional at Glen Oak Country Club in Glen Ellyn, one of Chicago's leafy western suburbs. His 1934 Western Open championship came in a marathon playoff, the first extra session in the Western since 1899. Cooper and Ky Laffoon tied at 14-under 274 on the 6,040-yard Country Club of Peoria course, then tied after 67s in an 18-hole playoff. They went out for 18 more—sudden-death for a prestigious title such as the Western's was unheard of at that time—and Cooper scored 66 to Laffoon's 69, pulling away with a rousing frontside 30, to snag the title. Cooper, who won the Los Angeles Open in 1926, when it offered the biggest purse in the world—$10,000 total—also won the Crosby and two Canadian Opens, while finishing second twice in the U.S. Open, including his 1927 playoff loss to Armour. His tour-leading money winnings of $14,138 in 1937 marked the first five-figure total for a professional.

Jock Hutchison.

Already a player of considerable renown when he made his headquarters at Glen View Club, in Golf, Illinois, Hutchison won a Western Open, British Open, PGA Championship, and North and South Open, but never captured a U.S. Open, finishing second twice and third twice. However, Hutchison, like Ben Hogan a generation later, won a wartime substitute for the U.S. Open. He won the Open Patriotic Tournament at Whitemarsh Valley Country Club near Philadelphia in 1917, and did so by seven strokes. Hutchison later played in the PGA Seniors, winning twice, including the inaugural at Augusta National in 1937, and finishing in the top 10 every year through 1951. He and McLeod (who won the second PGA Seniors at Augusta in 1938) were the honorary starters in the Masters for years.

Horton Smith.

One of the game's fastest starters, Smith won eight tournaments in his first year, then settled down to a more leisurely victory pace. The winner of the first and third Masters, Smith ran the pro shop at Oak Park Country Club in Oak Park for years and rose through the ranks to become the PGA of America's president.

Lloyd Mangrum.

The two-time Western Open winner, a World War II hero, played out of George S. May's Tam O'Shanter Country Club in Niles. Unlike the above players and their clubs, Mangrum and May followed one of the fashions of the time. Mangrum was the playing professional at Tam. He didn't have to work behind a counter. He just dropped by now and again to say hello to customers when the tournament trail was closed. ◻

Tommy Armour, about to split the fairway with a big drive.

Ky Laffoon and Harry Cooper just couldn't play enough golf in the 1934 Western Open. Cooper needed 108 holes to eliminate Laffoon and capture the J.K. Wadley Trophy. Laffoon, one of golf's great characters, never won a major championship.

In 1935, Johnny Revolta became the first player since Walter Hagen to win the Western Open and PGA Championship in the same year.

Lloyd Mangrum, who would win the 1952 and 1954 Western Opens, shows off the $10,000 check for winning the 1948 World Championship at Tam O'Shanter Country Club. His playoff win over Sam Snead and Dutch Harrison led to the head pro job at Tam.

When he wasn't tending to his head pro duties at Oak Park Country Club, Horton Smith was making an impact on the course and in the PGA of America's boardroom.

Stylish Jock Hutchison won everything but a U.S. Open while playing out of Glen View Club in the first third of the century, including the 1920 Western Open.

THE STYMIE

Looking back from the end of the twentieth century, when the Rules of Golf have so many loopholes that a full-scale seminar takes four days, it's hard to believe that the stymie hung on for so long.

What was the stymie? A pain in the neck, the one rule that almost all golfers abhorred and, unless they were in tournament competition, ignored.

If another ball was between your ball and the hole, the ball could not be lifted. Tough luck, laddie. You could chip over the stymie ball, brushing the turf with your niblick. It was an acquired skill, but possible to clip the ball squarely and drop it right into the cup that way, or at least get close.

You could putt around the intervening ball, trying to cut the putt. You could try and hit the other ball with your putt, but if the blocking ball fell into the cup, so be it. The player who owned that ball had finished the hole. The knock-in was a bonus. Holes in one had been made that way.

You could curse when stymied. Usually, you cursed.

Everybody talked about the stymie but nobody did anything about it until May 20, 1917, when the WGA ruled the ball nearer the hole would be played first in the Western Amateur.

"If a stymie exists, and the balls lie within a putter's length of each other, the ball furthest from the hole must be lifted on request until the nearer ball has been played, and then replaced in its previous lie. Penalty for violation: loss of hole in match play, two strokes in medal play," read the ruling. "Under no circumstances, except as above, shall a ball on the putting green be lifted."

This reversed the tradition that the more distant player would putt first. It was not a big hit. *The Chicago Tribune's* Joe Davis wrote, "...this gave general dissatisfaction, as the man farthest away knew just what he had to do, while at the same time it robbed the play of much interest to the spectator."

The WGA flip-flopped at the end of 1920. Suddenly, the ball away from the hole would be played first, the nearer ball lifted if within six inches of the cup or another ball. Plus, balls could be cleaned when on the greens regardless of their position. The USGA reacted by ruling a stymied player would be allowed to get a clear line of putt only by conceding his opponent's putt first.

Even before he donated the Western Open's championship trophy, J.K. Wadley was an influential member of the WGA's board.

This was as much a dud as the nearer-first concept. Concede a 15-footer in the way because your ball was 15 feet 3 inches away? The Royal Canadian Golf Association tried the USGA rule and dropped it, going back to the traditional stymie.

Even within the WGA, there was a great division of opinion. On January 21, 1922, during the annual meeting, the question took up most of a 45-minute-plus discussion of the rules, one which had to wear out the stenographers.

"There is nothing more damnable in playing a game than to have a poor player come up, play a poor mashie shot and lay you a stymie," said Bob Jans. "This is one of the bad things about stymie. But if a good player accidentally lays you a stymie, then your knowledge of the game should be such as to permit you to negotiate that shot. It is a consideration in the game."

In response, Bert Hooper of the Kalamazoo Country Club said, "Golf is hard enough, we know. What my friend here says is all true but it just proves the stymie is only for the expert player. Every club has but very, very few expert players."

To that, Guy Gregg of Milwaukee noted, "I will guarantee right now that there is nobody in this room that plays stymie in a social match. If they don't play it in social matches why should they play it in tournaments? The clubs that belong to the USGA in the east do not play stymies except in tournament matches. They don't play it in social matches. They admit it."

J.K. Wadley, a Texas oilman and newly-elected WGA director who within a year would donate the Western Open championship trophy, had the foresight to realize that the USGA, in modifying the stymie rule, was itself in a jam.

"I think, from what I understand of it, the members of the United States Golf Association would not like to see the old stymie rule go back into effect," Wadley intoned. "I think the spirit that dominates them is that they hate to conflict with the Royal & Ancient Golf Club and do not do anything that to their ideas would be contrary to it. "So it went for decades. The stymie was back in force by 1922, then dropped again by the WGA in 1936, five years after a poll found 78.5 percent of responding clubs in favor of abolition.

"The executive committee of the USGA had the question under serious advisement," said WGA president Henry Bartholomay. "I understand the stymie was retained (by the USGA) by a close vote. Our committee felt that the members favored abolishing stymies and we decided to act."

Cracks in the eastern establishment soon became evident. In 1937, the Metropolitan Golf Association, everyone from Shinnecock Hills to Winged Foot to Baltusrol, dropped the stymie.

Early in 1938, the USGA began to allow partial relief. The PGA of America dropped it in 1946, eliminating it from most of the pro tour. The next year, seeing the inevitable, the R&A took a poll on the stymie, and found the world outside the United States divided on the issue.

It didn't stay divided long. The more nonstymie golf was played, the more it was liked. The stymie's death sentence came May 17, 1951, during the USGA/R&A conference that led to worldwide uniformity in the Rules of Golf. The R&A's bluebloods finally buckled, decreeing with the USGA that the stymie would be buried on New Year's Day, 1952.

There was some dissent. Five-time British Open winner J.H. Taylor penned an essay in an Edinburgh golf magazine that expressed his indignation.

"I challenge anyone possessed of a decent mind to dare suggest that the player of any stymie since the game commenced has been actuated by dishonest intention," Taylor railed. "It would be an insult to his intelligence. Something that occurs accidently, without any suspicion of malicious intent, cannot by the stretch of the most elastic conscience be deemed dishonest.

"The ball is the game. Remove it and nothing remains but to beat the air or thump the ground with a stick." ◘

J.H. Taylor believed in keeping your head down at address and keeping the stymie as part of the game.

CHAPTER

6

GULDAHL'S TRIPLE CROWN

There have been many stylish players throughout golf history. The names of Sam Snead, Bobby Jones, and Mickey Wright spring quickly to mind. Each possessed a languid swing that propelled the golf ball at great speed, though seemingly without great force.

Then there is the golf swing of Ralph Guldahl. Stylish and languid it wasn't. Forceful and effective it was.

Guldahl would never win a prize for his swing's form. He would win many for its results. And what results! Guldahl, never a fan favorite, enjoyed what to this day may be the greatest hot streak in golf's major championships.

Never mind his swing, described by contemporary writers as a motion more akin to swinging a sledge-

Ralph Guldahl did what nobody else has managed, winning three straight Western Opens.

hammer than a golf club. Look at the record instead: from 1936 through 1939, Guldahl won three straight Western Opens, two U.S. Opens in succession, and a Masters, and was runner-up at Augusta National twice.

He achieved that unparalleled success after a cold streak so frigid following a near miss in the 1933 U.S. Open that he all but quit the game. After his championship winning streak, his title-controlling game left him again. While he had it, however, nobody had a tighter grip on the major championship trophies than Guldahl. Even Ben Hogan's post-accident run of major titles, impressive in its own right, isn't as concentrated as Guldahl's.

Guldahl's accomplishments, though, have gone nearly unnoticed, in part because the Western Open no longer is considered a major. That is where it ranked, though, in the late 1930s, when Guldahl went

71

on his remarkable run. Recently, a glimmer of light focused on his achievements posthumously when Nick Price won back-to-back Western Opens in 1993 and 1994, giving Price the opportunity to match Guldahl's stretch of three wins in a row.

Guldahl's Western Open run commenced in 1936, when he came from behind with a final-round 64, 7-under-par at Davenport Country Club, to shade Ray Mangrum, the leader for the first three rounds, with a total of 10-under-par 274 or, as writers of the day would have said, "14 under even fours for 72 holes."

It was a sensational finish, not only numerically but in the manner in which Guldahl made his run. His 64 was both a course record and the lowest round in the history of the Western Open to that point. The previous standard of 65 had been set by Emmett French in the first round of the 1921 Western Open at Oakwood Club in Cleveland, Ohio.

Three strokes behind Mangrum after the third round thanks to a 4-over 75, Guldahl gulped down lunch and took the measure of the course in the afternoon. He went out in 3-under 33, closing the gap to a

stroke, then stormed home in 4-under 31. A 40-foot birdie putt fell on the par-4 14th, following birdies on the 12th and 13th, and gave Guldahl the lead as Mangrum, two holes behind, faltered. If that wasn't spectacular enough, Guldahl sank an uphill 50-footer on the par-3 17th.

In a curious finish, the pumped-up Guldahl's approach flew the green of the uphill 18th, but crashed into a motion picture cameraman's film box and stopped two feet from the putting surface for an easy up-and-down. Guldahl earned the J.K. Wadley Trophy, the $500 first prize, and a similar sum from his sponsor, Wilson Sporting Goods.

For the twenty-four-year-old Guldahl, it was a grand comeback from obscurity after a single brush with fame. He had been a good player, one who had come close in some events, but had only one claim to fame: winning the 1932 Phoenix Open.

He was better known for blowing the 1933 U.S. Open at North Shore Country Club in Glenview, Illinois, though that tag wasn't entirely fair. Guldahl had to come from behind in the final round of the Open to

Guldahl's languid follow-through attracts less attention than the flight of the ball off the first tee in an early Masters Tournament. Bobby Jones is among the interested observers.

Through the 1930s, the Western Open featured a galaxy of stars, including this seated gathering from 1937 (left to right): Ralph Guldahl, Sam Snead, Horton Smith, Lawson Little, swimmer-turned-Tarzan Johnny Weissmuller, and big-hitting Jimmy Thomson.

catch amateur Johnny Goodman, already in the clubhouse—and resting on a couch—with a total of 1-under-par 287. Goodman had struggled to a final round 76 despite playing the first three holes in 3-under-par. Presently, there was a ruckus, and Goodman learned that Guldahl, then 21, was overpowering the back nine.

He didn't overpower North Shore's famed 18th. He pushed

The J.K. Wadley Trophy was all Guldahl's for three glorious years in the 1930s.

his 3-iron approach shot into a bunker, wedged out to within four feet of the cup and, needing to sink the putt to tie Goodman and force a playoff, pulled the putt. It slid by an inch to the left.

"I didn't hit it," he said later. "I knew the moment it left the clubhead that it would miss the hole."

If one mistake can tear apart a man's psyche, that missed putt did so to Guldahl. He faded from view, not easy for someone 6-foot-3 and 210 pounds, a giant for the time in golf or any other sport. Fifth in the 1933 Western Open, he was eighth in the 1934 U.S. Open, and tied for 16th in the 1934 Western Open. By 1935, he wasn't close to the leaders. By the end of the year, he was off the tour.

Moe Springer, thirteen when he teed off in the 1937 Western Open at Canterbury Country Club, is believed to be the youngest contestant in the championship's history. He shot 84-90 and missed the cut by 13 strokes.

It was the height of the Great Depression. Most tournaments, the Western Open included, paid only the top 20 pros, no matter how many made the cut. Playing professional golf was a very tenuous lifestyle. Players stayed on the tour because they loved the game, not to get rich. Nobody was getting rich.

Guldahl was married by now, and he and his wife, Maydelle, had a young son, Ralph Jr., nicknamed Buddy. With Buddy aboard, there were three mouths to feed. Guldahl went to work for a living selling cars.

In theory, that might have worked, except that in the Depression no one was buying cars. The only car Guldahl sold was to himself. He then dabbled in golf-course architecture with the same limited success, designing a nine-hole course in Kilgore, Texas, west of his hometown of Dallas. That proved to be his one and only design. Golf courses weren't being built in the 1930s.

Buddy developed a severe cold, so the family moved to the warmer California desert. Guldahl pawned his

golf clubs so Buddy could eat. A near-U.S. Open champion was at the end of the road.

Suddenly, his fortunes turned. Guldahl met a pair of moneyed Hollywood types who remembered Guldahl's near-win in the Open. After playing with him, they saw his game was still sound. They got his clubs out of hock and convinced big Ralph to return to the professional circuit.

Lawrence Icely, the Wilson magnate, bought Guldahl a new suit and the latest weapons. In his first start, Guldahl won $240 at the True Temper Open in Detroit, which buoyed his confidence heading into the Western Open at Davenport. His come-from-behind victory there brought him even more confidence. He roared through the rest of the 1936 season, taking the Harry Radix Trophy for the low scoring average.

The next spring, Guldahl arrived at Augusta National aiming for the pins and led fellow Texan Byron Nelson by three strokes entering the final round. Typically, that 1937 Masters changed dramatically in the final nine holes, starting when Guldahl fired at the flag, cut dangerously on the right side, on the par-3 12th hole. His shot fell short, bouncing off the bank and into Rae's Creek. His double-bogey, followed by a 25-foot birdie by Nelson, playing in the next group, shaved Guldahl's lead to a stroke.

Guldahl kept aiming at the pins, ripping a 3-iron toward the flag on the par-5 13th. It caught the creek for another bogey, after which Nelson came by and chipped in for eagle. Over two holes, Nelson, playing them 2-3 to Guldahl's 5-6, was the beneficiary of a six-shot swing. He beat Guldahl by two.

If that deterred Guldahl, it didn't show at the 1937 U.S. Open. He came from off the pace to beat Ed Dudley and rookie Sam Snead, winning the Open at Oakland Hills with a record score of 7-under 281. The turning point: back-to-back birdies on the 12th and 13th. Guldahl now held two major titles simultaneously.

Guldahl won his second Western Open crown in 1937 at Canterbury Country Club in Cleveland. The leader by a stroke with 18 holes to play, he was caught by Snead at the turn of the fourth round, and, while Snead couldn't keep up, Guldahl ended the day in a tie with Horton Smith. They would meet in an 18-hole playoff.

Guldahl had to be wondering why a fifth round would be needed. He had been cruising along until the 16th hole, when his third shot on the 615-yard par-5 sailed over the green and out-of-bounds. Under WGA

Horton Smith and Ralph Guldahl grip the J.K. Wadley Trophy and grin for photographers before their playoff for the 1937 Western Open title.

Ralph Guldahl sends a chip-and-run toward the hole.

rules, that cost him only distance, not an extra stroke. But his next shot hit a child standing near the green and dropped to the bottom of the hill. Only sinking a 16-footer after chipping onto the green enabled him to save a bogey 6.

The playoff was decidedly less dramatic. Guldahl's easy par 72 beat Smith by four strokes, earning him a second straight title. He was the first Western Open champion to repeat since Walter Hagen in 1926 and 1927, and followed Willie Smith, Willie Anderson, and Alex Smith as winners of both the U.S. and Western Opens in the same year.

In 1938, Guldahl would improve even on those marks. He finished tied for second in the Masters again, this time behind Henry Picard. Then he won the U.S. Open at Cherry Hills in Denver and the Western Open at Westwood Country Club in St. Louis—doing so only five days apart.

Nobody but Guldahl has won two majors in that close a span. Bizarre scheduling had the 1938 Western Open starting on a Tuesday and ending on a Thursday with the traditional 36-hole finish. In that era, the U.S. Open wrapped up on a Saturday. Guldahl defended his U.S. Open title with another come-from-behind finish,

making up four strokes on Dick Metz in the first five holes of the final round, taking the lead with a birdie on the sixth hole and winning by six strokes.

The Western Open featured another Guldahl-Snead showdown, and big Ralph, unruffled, scored 6-under 65 in the final round to win by seven strokes with a total of 5-under 279. Here again, style meant nothing. It didn't matter that Guldahl appeared to be hitting the ball with a bludgeon while Snead struck the ball precisely with his sweet swing. Guldahl was sinking every putt. His 40-footer for eagle on the par-5 13th sealed the victory. His chip-in from 18 feet on the home hole merely added an exclamation point to his unprecedented—and so far unmatched—third consecutive Western Open championship.

In the spring of 1939, Guldahl finally broke through at Augusta National, winning the Masters. By so doing, he captured his sixth major championship in 11 events and had managed a top-two placing in eight of those 11.

In 1939, Ralph Guldahl was twenty-eight years old. His best years should have been ahead of him. Instead, he had already reached his peak. Never having had a formal lesson, having turned professional right out of high school at eighteen, Guldahl had bounced back from the lowest low to the absolute pinnacle of the sport. And for those three Western Open championships, Guldahl earned the handsome sum of $1,750; $500 for each of the first two and $750 for the last.

Then, as quickly as it began, it was over. Guldahl was no longer an automatic in the winner's circle, or even close to the top. His game faded from meteoric to mediocre, and there were several theories: he had tired of the road and preferred a club job; or he had holed all the long putts a man is allotted in a lifetime.

Another theory, which sounded intriguing until the circumstances were investigated, held that, in preparing a golf instruction book, "Groove Your Golf," Guldahl—who had never taken a lesson—had to figure out just why his unorthodox swing was so effective.

Having learned what he was doing, clucked the critics, he could no longer do it. A fascinating angle, but dead wrong. Before his two U.S. Open wins at Cherry Hills and Westwood, he had written a series of lessons that ran in newspapers. No, writing golf lessons didn't hinder Guldahl in the least.

Whatever the reason for his incredibly fast fade,

Guldahl had one more fling with success, advancing to the semifinals of the 1940 PGA Championship. He had never enjoyed much match-play success, and his old pal Nelson beat him 1 up in the 36-hole semifinal.

Guldahl once said, "I never did have a tremendous desire to win." Tell that to Snead, whom he specialized in beating. Or anyone else during his hot streak.

What Guldahl wasn't—and Snead was—was colorful. Big and quiet, and slow, the stoop-shouldered Guldahl's idea of being flashy was combing his hair after a shot.

Guldahl played in a few tournaments in later years and took a club job. He was the head professional at Braemar Country Club in Tarzana, California, for years, and was the professional emeritus when he died in 1987. Four years earlier, he had returned to the Western Open, playing a ceremonial nine holes along with Gene Sarazen, Johnny Palmer, and several other former winners.

Nobody else posing for pictures on the first tee of Butler National that day in 1983 could claim they had done what he did, absolutely ruling the game. Ralph Guldahl knew that on the scoreboard, results beat style every time.

Sam Snead (left, back to camera), Andy Bean, Ralph Guldahl, and Gene Sarazen (far right) were among the participants in the WGA's 1983 salute to past Western Open champions.

MACHINE GUN McGURN AT THE WESTERN OPEN

It has been said that many players have gunned for the Western Open title in the past.

One really had the means to do so.

Ever hear of Vincent Gebhardi?

No? Didn't think so.

Ever hear of Jack McGurn? Machine Gun McGurn?

Or Al Capone? Or the St. Valentine's Day Massacre?

Thought so. Gebhardi by another name was the feared McGurn. When he wasn't mowing down fellow criminals and who knows who else in the pursuit of gangland riches, McGurn played golf.

He was the professional at Evergreen Golf Club, then and now across the street from Chicago's city limits, and adjacent to Beverly Country Club on the city's southwest boundary.

These days, Evergreen is a public course where only birdies and eagles are in danger. Back in the 1930s, it was a prime Capone hangout, featuring golf during the day and sundry other less prim pursuits 24 hours a day. Gebhardi was the front man.

In reality, no matter how dangerous he was with a niblick in hand, he was a killer, through and through, one of the gunmen who cut down the Moran gang on Capone's behalf in the St. Valentine's Day Massacre in 1929.

He also fancied himself a golfer, a good one, and in the summer of 1933, McGurn took it upon himself to enter the Western Open at Olympia Fields Country Club.

There was no qualifying for the Western Open in that era. Players sent in an entry, paid the nominal fee, and received a tee time. Some years, more than 250 teed it up.

The 1933 Western Open field included some 220 hopefuls. Perhaps Gebhardi thought there would be safety in numbers, that his presence in the field would go unnoticed.

If so, the man marked as "Public Enemy No. 5" was wrong. Chicago's chief of detectives, a golf fan scanning the tee times, noticed Gebhardi's name next to the 12:25 p.m second-round tee time. He knew that Gebhardi was McGurn. He knew that under a new "criminal reputation" law, he could pick up the rascal.

Now, he not only knew where McGurn would be but knew he would be in a crowd, on public view, and thus less likely to cause a disturbance or to pull a "15th club" in the form of a tommy-gun out of his bag.

Plans were laid to arrest McGurn during the second round of the Western Open, on Saturday, August 26, 1933. He had fired a 13-over-par 83 in the first round, played over the No. 4 (now North) course. His second round would be on the other side of Olympia Fields' mammoth clubhouse, on the No. 1 course.

Lieutenant Frank McGillen, accompanied by seven Chicago and Cook County police officers, made their way to the club to get their man.

It was a beautiful afternoon for golf, and McGurn started well, scoring 1-under par through six holes. His young wife Louise—famed as the underage "blonde alibi" whose testimony kept him out of jail after the St. Valentine's Day Massacre—was on hand to watch the action.

There also was a small gallery watching him. Or perhaps those spectators were eyeing his wife, for Mrs. Machine Gun was wearing what the newspapers called "a tight white dress, white hat, and anklet stockings," not to mention a tan, a three-carat diamond ring on one hand and a wedding ring on the other. The classic gun moll outfit.

McGillen and two plainclothesmen reached McGurn on the 7th green. McGurn was told he was under arrest.

Smoothly, he asked if he could finish his round. McGillen, knowing McGurn couldn't get anywhere, granted the request. McGurn's playing partner, Howard Holtman of nearby Beecher, Illinois, kept his cool, even after McGillen read the name on the warrant: "alias Machine Gun Jack McGurn." But McGurn double-bogeyed the 7th. His round was about to go sour.

Off McGurn, Holtman and the police went to the 8th tee, and after the tee shots, Mrs. Machine Gun couldn't contain herself any longer.

"Whose brilliant idea was this?" she beefed.

By now, reporters were making their way out from the clubhouse. Leader Macdonald Smith was almost an afterthought. This was news: A gangster in the Western!

McGurn played as if already handcuffed, taking a 7-over-par 11 on the 8th hole. On the green, he went after a photographer whose shutter clicked away while he was putting.

"You've busted up my game," McGurn growled, grabbing the lensman by the shirt.

McGurn settled down, to a degree. He finished the front side in 45, the back in 41 for 14-over 86. His two-day total of 169 was 14 strokes over the cut line. Not that McGurn would be back for the final two rounds on Sunday. He suddenly had other business.

The gallery tittered as McGurn finished on the 18th, his wife close behind.

"The heat must be off between the mobs or McGurn wouldn't bring her out here," McGillen mused. "If the Touhys were after him, they could shoot both him and the wife with a rifle, like sparrows, from here."

Michael Igoe, a Chicagoan and member of Olympia Fields who was also on the South Park District board and a former state representative, thought about the club's reputation first and the presence of McGurn behind bars second.

"What's the idea?" he bellowed at McGillen. "You're trying to pull a publicity stunt on this club. Who ordered this? What's the idea of arresting this man at his play? If you wanted to take him, why didn't you do it outside?"

Igoe was more ticked off than McGurn.

"I was out playing golf, so they arrest me," he told reporters. "Trying to suppress crime, hey? It's the punks out pulling stickups who shoot the policemen. Why bother me? I haven't done anything for a year.

"Just put it down that I'm booked for carrying concealed ideas."

He was off to the slammer, where men from the FBI had a few questions for him. And peace returned to the Western Open. ❏

Jack "Machine Gun" McGurn and his wife Louise, participant and onlooker, respectively, in the 1933 Western Open at Olympia Fields Country Club.

CHAPTER

7

CADDIES TO COLLEGE?
OF COURSE!

The notation is, at first glance, rather cryptic. It appears on the first line in the last page of the Western Golf Association's 1923 ledger book. It reads "May 8, 2 sets, J.W. Busch, $10.00."

The page is dedicated to the "Chick" Evans Caddie Foundation, but that one line is the only entry. It referred to the purchase of two sets of Chick Evans phonograph record albums—his recorded golf lessons. Joe Busch, the WGA's secretary at the time, had purchased the discs as a symbolic gesture to boost a public campaign for the Evans fund.

This was seven years after Chick Evans became a national golf hero by winning the 1916 U.S. Open and

U.S. Amateur and three years after his victories in the Western Amateur and U.S. Amateur, which resulted in his recording a series of lessons on 78s. Evans had received a $5,000 advance for the recordings and designated the money for his proposed caddie scholarship fund.

Had the WGA ledger book listed more purchases such as Mr. Busch's, the Chick Evans Scholarship Program might have started sending caddies to college in the mid-1920s. Unfortunately, sales of the records slumped.

It would be seven years before the first Evans Scholars would be selected and enter Northwestern University.

Evans, an amateur, had remained an amateur after winning the U.S. Open despite numerous lucrative financial offers. His mother, Lena, not only had

Bruno Varnagaris (left), the third Evans Scholar, welcomed to Northwestern by the originals, Harold Fink and Jim McGinnis.

Everything starts somewhere. The first recorded donation to the original Chick Evans Caddie Foundation was $10, in 1923.

Chick Evans himself teaching you how to play golf on a 78! The wonders of modern (1920s) technology!

advised him against turning professional, she suggested a use for any money Chick might receive through his success in golf.

"My mother wouldn't think of accepting any money unless we could arrange it to be trusted to furnish educations for deserving, qualified caddies," Evans recalled in 1971. "And this was what my mother and I tried to do from 1916 through 1919. Being both the National Open and National Amateur champion, I took it up with the United States Golf Association. But they didn't seem to want it or couldn't do it.

"Anyway, when I defended my Open and Amateur titles in 1919 and lost both of them, the caddie-scholarship idea was practically dead."

Hardly. The idea not only was sound, but revolutionary. Perhaps that is why the USGA bluebloods, always cautious in their dealings, failed to embrace the idea when Evans approached them in 1917. Still in its infancy, the USGA had yet to inaugurate its Public Links Championship and still had not granted public courses full membership. Now, with the country embroiled in a world war, here came the U.S. Open champion with a scheme that would require the USGA to administer scholarships for caddies. Caddies!

Evans finally decided his caddie plan was a bit much for the USGA to accept, especially after he beat Bobby Jones in 1920 en route to the Western Amateur title and defeated Francis Ouimet on the way to the U.S. Amateur championship that same year.

"I knew it was silly to talk to them again," said Evans, who also felt that Jones and Ouimet both had favored status with the USGA's leadership.

It would not be silly to talk to the Western Golf Association. Evans and the WGA had already collaborated on the Red Cross exhibition series of 1918, which raised over $300,000. Chick was one of Chicago's most recognized athletes and, in 1920, the year the Black Sox scandal broke in the papers, he was untainted by scandal. The WGA was Chicago-based. Evans had gone to Northwestern University in Evanston. The combination seemed a natural partnership.

"My mother and I were convinced that the American caddie would be able to hold his own in all educational institutions," Evans wrote in 1975. "We remembered that caddie boys all over the nation were

Charles O. Pfeil believed in Evans' caddies-to-college concept, and pushed the WGA to back the program.

the same as those of old Edgewater, who wanted to be rich like the members of their clubs. We always felt that caddie scholarships would gain for the game of golf a new popularity through a most wholesome undertaking."

Sentiment is one thing, action another. Between Mr. J.W. Busch's plunking down $10 for two sets of Evans recordings and caddies going to school, however, there would be plenty of work to do and obstacles to overcome. Years later, Evans recalled that WGA President Charles Pfeil of Memphis and former presidents Albert Gates and Charles Thompson were the men who first supported Evans' caddie scholarship plan. It hadn't hurt that Evans' win over Jones in the Western Amateur had come at Pfeil's Memphis Country Club.

The first written mention in the WGA's records of what is known today as the Evans Scholars Foundation is found in the minutes of the WGA's 25th annual meeting, held in the Congress Hotel in downtown Chicago on January 20, 1923. After it was noted that the WGA's bank account had grown to $7,770.42 and that the new director James K. Wadley, a Texas oil tycoon, had offered to donate a trophy for the Western Open, the Evans plan was discussed, and enthusiastically so. A Mr. Ray of the Briergate Club stood and said that he would take $1,000 of the Evans recordings.

A committee was appointed to, in the words of the minutes, "work out means and ways of putting over a successful selling campaign for the 'Chick Evans Foundation.'"

Perhaps Briergate's gung-ho Mr. Ray should have been on the committee. It had been decided that selling the Evans records should be the primary thrust of a fund-raising campaign for the new caddie scholarship fund. The set of records would give the donor a tangible asset—the golf instructions of Evans himself—along with the intangible plus of contributing to a worthy charitable cause.

Brunswick-Balke-Collender, the record company

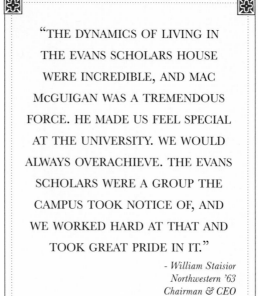

"THE DYNAMICS OF LIVING IN THE EVANS SCHOLARS HOUSE WERE INCREDIBLE, AND MAC McGUIGAN WAS A TREMENDOUS FORCE. HE MADE US FEEL SPECIAL AT THE UNIVERSITY. WE WOULD ALWAYS OVERACHIEVE. THE EVANS SCHOLARS WERE A GROUP THE CAMPUS TOOK NOTICE OF, AND WE WORKED HARD AT THAT AND TOOK GREAT PRIDE IN IT."

- William Staisior
Northwestern '63
Chairman & CEO
Booz, Allen Hamilton

that had paid Evans $5,000 to record his golf lessons—was all for the plan. Sales of the discs had stalled. "Arias" by Caruso and Tin Pan Alley dance tunes by Paul Whiteman for a half-dollar were proving more popular than Evans' recorded lessons.

Busch and Evans hit the road, visiting Midwestern WGA clubs to rally support for the scholarship fund. In April, some 300 golfers turned out for a gala dinner in Cleveland, watched Evans demonstrate every club in his bag, and heard Busch's pitch offering the record albums.

Pfeil, with the response of the Briergate's man fresh in his mind, believed that a representative at each WGA member club could be enlisted to sell records to fellow club members on the WGA's behalf. Originally, Brunswick had sold the record albums for $7.50, a hefty sum in that era. With some 5,000 sets of Evans records at the warehouse and another 1,000 albums at record shops still unsold, Brunswick was ready to deal. It would sell the warehouse sets to the WGA at $2 each, as needed. The WGA would resell them for $5, pocketing the $3 difference, less expenses. And Brunswick would ask dealers to drop their price to $5, to be fair to all parties.

Ideally, those 5,000 albums at the warehouse could bring in $15,000 for the Evans fund, if every last set was sold.

They didn't. By May 8, when Busch bought his albums, WGA Treasurer A.C. Allen said a check for $5,541.50 would be coming in the next day. Instead, the WGA received a check for $4,700.50, and a bill for $2,000, the latter covering Brunswick's expenses for advertising the records.

By the end of May 1923, it seemed that the net from the promotion would total only $2,700. Add in Evans' original contribution of $5,000 from the advance for making the recordings several years earlier, and other golf-related money he had made from an autobiography and other ventures, and there was, by Evans' recollection, about $14,000 available.

By October 2, 1923, it was clear the record-selling

campaign had run its course dry. The WGA executive committee discontinued work on the Evans fund, settled up with Brunswick and, after consultation with Evans, kept the $14,000 sitting in the bank.

It sat there for more than five years, earning interest, as WGA officials engaged in an occasional debate on how to implement the Evans caddie-college concept.

Finally, on December 6, 1928, President Robert Cutting, a member of Hinsdale Golf Club, reported to the 31st WGA annual meeting that the money had been placed in formal trust, and that the WGA would select one caddie and award him a scholarship to Northwestern University in the name of the Chick Evans Trust Fund.

If the WGA could not pick a worthy caddie, Northwestern would make the selection. And in the unlikely case of neither finding a likely candidate, that year's award would be presented to the Community Trust of Chicago.

At last, Chick Evans and his mother, Lena, were seeing their idea grow into a concrete plan. By the following May, it was decided that each WGA member club could nominate a caddie for the Evans award. With 531 member clubs, there would be no shortage of candidates.

By now, events were moving quickly, inside and outside the WGA's domain. The October 1929 stock market crash heralded the Great Depression. Prohibition was about to be repealed.

Even the caddie business, so to speak, was changing. Evans was a member of a committee appointed to study caddie employment issues. The WGA bylaws still held that any child who caddied beyond his sixteenth birthday was a professional.

That took kids out of the loop, literally, some two years before they were eligible for college, if they wanted to remain amateurs. The WGA, Evans wrote, would have to change that rule, if only to keep caddies working until they graduated from high school.

"We favor the increase of two years to the time now permitted young boys to caddie because we believe that such increase is at the easily formative period during which a boy may play his best game," penned Evans, "and we believe that America has found its best golfers by encouraging the young player, and the additional two years of outdoor playing will be of inestimable value in building up a young player's game."

More than anyone else, Carleton Blunt worked behind the scenes to establish the Evans Scholars Foundation and build it into the nationally respected organization it is today.

Evans spoke from experience here. His continuing ability to play at Edgewater, courtesy of the members and staff, went a long way toward building his championship game. The proposal that he, J. D'Esposito, and H.H. Bishop advanced was approved on January 16, 1930, and the WGA's bylaws were amended immediately. Caddies could caddie until they were eighteen and not be "branded" as professionals. (Today, of course, caddie status has nothing to do with professionalism.)

All of the pieces were in place for the first Evans Scholarship to be awarded. The first student would enter Northwestern in the fall of 1930. There was, however, a complication. Interviews with prospective candidates in the summer ended in a deadlock. The WGA Executive Committee, supplemented by Northwestern Dean of Men James W. Armstrong, couldn't pick between Harold Fink, who caddied at the Glen View Club in Golf, Illinois, and James McGinnis of the Indian Hill Club in Winnetka, Illinois.

So they sent both to Northwestern, with full rides. There would be two Evans Scholars, walking the same ground that Evans had walked over 20 years earlier.

A careful reading of the annual reports and surviving documentation indicates that, at first, the Evans Scholarships were not intended to be the renewable four-year grants that they are today. Rather, they were simple one-year scholarships, designed to help a caddie begin his college education. Indeed, as Fink and McGinnis undertook their freshman year of studies at NU, they had no idea how they would fund their education as sophomores.

When Bruno Varnagaris, a caddie at Butterfield Country Club, was awarded an Evans grant in the fall of 1931, the WGA board faced a dilemma. McGinnis and Fink had received high marks as freshmen. Northwestern had endorsed the program's concept. But the money the Evans Trust was earning wasn't sufficient to pay for three scholarships.

McGinnis and Fink would keep their scholarships, anyway, the WGA decided. Quoting the minutes of the December 11, 1931, annual meeting: "The two boys we sent last year, however, had made such creditable records during their freshman years that the committee decided to continue them one more year. So we are now carrying three scholarships at Northwestern University, and any deficit arising from the additional scholarship will be made up out of the general funds of the association."

That solid endorsement of the program marked a turning point in the course of the Western Golf Association. The Evans Scholarships had started as an adjunct to the WGA's role as a leader in golf; now the WGA was making a financial commitment to the program. Eventually, that commitment would become the driving force behind the WGA's activities on and off the golf course.

In 1931, a scholarship at Northwestern was valued at $300, while the Evans Trust was generating about $100 annually. The arrangement the WGA made with Northwestern was for each party to pay half of the tuition. With McGinnis and Fink enrolled, the WGA was responsible for $300 of the $600 total. The annual report noted that, among the expenses for the 1931 fiscal year was $199.30 for scholarship expenses over and above what the Trust generated.

By 1932-33, the third academic year of the program, there were six Scholars, some on full scholarships, some on partial rides, all attending Northwestern. In all, the WGA was writing $1,100 in checks, and at least one club, Chicago Golf Club, had contributed matching funds for its caddie. About $650 came from the WGA's general fund. Clearly, the directors and board had caught Evans' spirit.

For several years, the scholarships would be funded by proceeds from interest derived from the phonograph records, proceeds from WGA events and, on more than a few occasions, by the WGA directors reaching into their own pockets, sometimes quite deeply. Eventually, as the program grew, the original funds were tapped directly. This increased the number of "caddie-scholars," as Evans was fond of calling them, but depleted the coffers.

As a result, even as expenses were rising, money was short. It was the heart of the Depression. At a time when the scholarships were most needed, the WGA found it that much more difficult to fund them. Unless fortunes turned around, the WGA's attempt at educational philanthropy would end abruptly. Chick Evans' dream would die.

The WGA needed an idea man, someone who could turn a concept into cash. Such a man would be found in the person of Carleton Blunt.

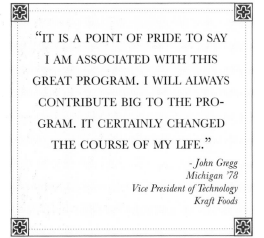

"IT IS A POINT OF PRIDE TO SAY I AM ASSOCIATED WITH THIS GREAT PROGRAM. I WILL ALWAYS CONTRIBUTE BIG TO THE PROGRAM. IT CERTAINLY CHANGED THE COURSE OF MY LIFE."

- John Gregg
Michigan '78
Vice President of Technology
Kraft Foods

THE FIRST EVANS SCHOLARS

Harold Henry Fink and Ralph James McGinnis didn't know each other before the fall of 1930, when they enrolled at Northwestern University.

It is likely they never would have known each other, and perhaps not have been able to go to any college, much less Northwestern, without an Evans Scholarship.

Fink and McGinnis were the first Evans Scholars. Each excelled in high school, and again in college. Each succeeded in business after college. Each knew how important the scholarship was.

Both Fink and McGinnis grew up in families that had endured financial difficulties. That, along with the two young lads' caddie duty, solid academics, and good character, made them prime candidates for the first scholarship. Indeed, they were so closely matched, the committee could not pick between them, choosing instead to send both to Northwestern.

Fink's case was typical of what the selection committee would find as it started to search for worthy Evans Scholars candidates. Fink had an older sister and a younger brother. He worked after attending Evanston Township High School. His father, who had been a successful contractor, had fallen from a building, suffering severe injuries. He wouldn't be able to work again.

To make ends meet, the family took in boarders. Fink chipped in with his earnings as a caddie at Glen View Club in the summer and from his after-school work. There wasn't much money.

Both of McGinnis' parents worked, and his four brothers and sisters all were going to Northwestern's night school while working. He was going to try to do the same after graduating from DePaul Academy, if there was money to do so, but his parents couldn't spare any money, and the $147 he had saved from caddie fees over the summer at the Indian Hill Club wouldn't be enough for college.

"I would caddie all day and average $2 a day," McGinnis told the *Chicago Daily News* in 1968. "Does that answer your question about Northwestern?"

Fink remembered the process of elimination that culminated in their selection.

After a tour of duty in the Navy during World War II, Harold Fink moved up through the ranks of Rand McNally to a vice president's post.

"When I heard about the program, I wrote letters to Western members. I submitted my scholarship records," Fink told the *Daily News*. "Then about 12 kids, including Jim and me, were interviewed at the Western headquarters downtown. When there were two of us left, they said, 'You can both go to Northwestern.' I owe everything in the world to that decision."

And to the one that made Evans Scholarships renewable.

"I always felt that when they extended it for a second year they really didn't have the money," McGinnis said. "The Western just dug into its pocket for some money."

Which is about how it happened. In so doing, the program began to grow, very slowly at first, and far more quickly after World War II, when the Bag Tag and Par Club fund-raising programs were started.

McGinnis lettered in baseball at Northwestern and also played on the basketball team. He joined the Petrolager Company in Chicago as traffic manager after graduating and, when World War II broke out, joined the Army and moved up to lieutenant colonel by the war's end.

Golf, though, was on his mind during the war. In April 1945, he wrote Chick Evans from somewhere in Southeast Asia, saying that British soldiers "certainly try hard to simulate British home life. You'll see a flat, drab piece of land with a bare spot to indicate a green, with a stick in the hole. Any self-respecting caddie at home wouldn't look once at the balls these fellows use."

McGinnis, who earned a commerce degree, became a commodities broker on LaSalle Street after the war, eventually owning W.J. Kamp and Company. He was eighty-three when he died on January 30, 1996.

Fink, who was on Northwestern's golf team, took a job at Rand McNally after graduating in 1934. One of the Glen View members he had caddied for was Fred McNally, proving that relationships forged on the golf course between player and caddie are often remembered years later.

Aside from a stint in the war as a Navy lieutenant, Fink worked at Rand McNally for 40 years, rising to a vice presidency in 1959. He was in charge of road maps and atlases. Among his other achievements, Fink devised the system of symbols for expressways and toll roads that every mapmaker, not to mention the government, uses.

He also became a trustee of the very Evans Scholars Foundation that enabled him to earn his way in the world, and he became close friends with Chick Evans.

"He was always calling me his No. 1 boy," Fink once said of Evans. "He was in his late eighties and I was approaching seventy, but he still called me that. The scholarship was like a miracle. It was the Depression, and it didn't seem possible to be able to go to college."

Fink was seventy-four when he died on September 26, 1985, just four months after speaking about Evans when Chick was the posthumous honoree of Jack Nicklaus' Memorial Tournament at Muirfield Village. ❑

Jack Nicklaus, winner of three WGA championships, honoring Chick Evans at the 1985 Memorial Tournament at Muirfield Village.

8

BUILDING THE
EVANS DREAM

As the 1930s dragged on, the Depression at home and turmoil in Europe made for anything but pleasant times. Unemployment and the specter of war conspired to ensure an excruciatingly slow economic recovery, even in the early years of Franklin D. Roosevelt's administration.

Business faced a prolonged bust, rather than the boom experienced in the 1920s. The golf business was no exception, as evidenced by the Western Golf Association's diminishing funds to administrate the nascent Evans Scholars Program at Northwestern University in Evanston, Illinois. The WGA, by increasing

In the fall of 1941, the growing group of Evans Scholars at Northwestern University posed in front of the original Evans House at 1935 Sherman Avenue in Evanston, Illinois.

the number of Scholars it was sending to college, had drained the original $14,000 that Chick Evans contributed to the scholarship fund through his proceeds from golf-related recordings, books, and the like.

The program, however worthy of support, was surviving through the kindness of strangers.

One stranger became not just an acquaintance but a dear friend of the Evans Scholars. Taciturn on the outside, warmly dedicated to Evans' concept on the inside, and always looking ahead, Carleton Blunt was that stranger.

Blunt, an Evanston native who graduated from Dartmouth in 1926 and was subsequently first in his class at Northwestern's law school in 1929, happened to be the secretary of the Glen View Club in 1932, the story goes, when the bill for Harold Fink's scholarship ended up in the club's lap. According to legend, the

This portrait of Carleton Blunt hangs in the Directors Room of the WGA headquarters in Golf, Illinois.

At the same time, from the start, clubs with caddie-scholars often matched the WGA's payment with one of their own. Even Blunt said in 1957 that he had simply checked on a payment that Glen View Club made toward Fink's scholarship, not that the bill had gone to the club as a last resort.

Regardless, Blunt knew of the Evans Scholars fund because Fink caddied at Glen View Club in the summer, and he knew Chick Evans, who often played at Glen View. After meeting Evans Scholars advisor James Leslie Rollins, then in Northwestern's personnel office, Blunt began to take a personal interest in the program. By 1936, Blunt was the WGA's general counsel. He would be associated with the WGA and Evans Scholars Foundation for the rest of his life, eventually serving as WGA president in 1957 and as an Evans trustee from 1944 until his death on May 6, 1988.

Rarely quoted, Blunt was nonetheless a major force inside the WGA, almost always concentrating on the Evans Scholars side of the organization. Blunt didn't worry about tournament activities. He worried about how to pay the bills that resulted from the growing caddie scholarship program.

And there were bills.

WGA couldn't afford its half of the $300 tab (Northwestern was picking up the rest), the school sent the bill to Glen View, and Blunt arranged for the club to pay the excess $150.

That is more myth than reality. Minutes of WGA meetings for 1932 indicate that the WGA awarded, and presumably paid for, $200 of Fink's scholarship. In all, the WGA had issued $1,100 in checks for the scholarship program, with some of the money coming from the original Evans fund and the rest from WGA investments. The WGA ledger for 1930-1934, which mirrors Fink's tenure at Northwestern, finds regular payments from the WGA's general account, supplementing the interest from the Evans fund, beginning September 24, 1931.

WGA officials Jerome Bowes, Carleton Blunt, James O'Keefe, and Chick Evans delight in another donation to the Evans Scholars, circa 1956.

There was good news from Washington the day the Internal Revenue Service ruled contributions to the Evans Scholars were tax-deductible.

A rare collectible today, Evans Scholars Golf Balls were sold by Carson Pirie Scott. And what ball today boasts of having an oil center?

By August of 1939, the situation was so desperate that at a special meeting of the WGA board, it was reported that the net proceeds of the Western Amateur and Western Open, held the previous month, "were sufficient to support the Evans Caddy Scholarships at Northwestern for the first semester of the school year."

After that, well, who knew?

It was resolved to trim expenses to the bone. Longtime executive secretary Ray W. Fruit, the WGA's only paid employee, and one who had already seen his pay halved at the onset of the Depression, was let go, thanked for his 15 years-plus work with a $250 bonus and a commemorative plaque. That saved $3,000 annually. President L.L. Cooke volunteered to take over the day-to-day administrative work.

With no staff to occupy an office, the WGA's suite in downtown Chicago was closed, and the WGA rented a smaller office on the city's north side. It cost only $15 a month. Director T.C. Butz contributed some used furniture for it.

It also was reaffirmed that WGA officers and directors would, as they had been doing, continue to pay their own expenses for any and all association-specific activities.

A month later, the combined WGA/Evans fund totaled about $3,500, with $800 more expected from Medinah Country Club, which had hosted the 1939 Western Open. The directors now were confident enough that on September 6, a week after Hitler ordered the German army into Poland to set off World War II, two new Evans Scholars were selected, bringing the total to 19.

Despite the trimmed expenses, the WGA/ESF still was a hand-to-mouth organization, and this at a time when, aside from tuition, the other expenses of college life were increasing steadily. The students had to live somewhere, and dorms were, for them, a considerable cost. There were textbooks to buy and lab fees to pay.

At least the WGA didn't worry about their charges eating. From the start of the Evans program, it was realized that if it was tapped for the meals of hungry college students, the fund would soon be bankrupt. Scholars had to work for their meals and still do today. Likewise, Scholars purchase their own textbooks.

The Western Open, with a $3,000 purse in 1939, remained solvent because the purse was annually funded by a host organization, usually a city's civic or

The term faculty advisor wasn't used yet, but James Leslie Rollins, Dean of Men at Northwestern, was the first to serve in that advisory role for the Evans Scholars.

John G. Searle's letter helped raise the funds for the Evans House at Northwestern.

tourism group. In 1940, the Houston Lions Club, eager to place the growing oil city on the golf map, offered to put up a Texas-sized sum of $5,000. The Western's officials were so concerned about setting a precedent for higher purses, they took pains to explain that the new $2,000 was coming from the Lions Club, over and above the traditional purse. Actually, it was all coming from the Lions Club.

That surplus of funds prompted the WGA board to send the $5 entry fees for the Western Open, not needed to support the purse, straight to the WGA's scholarship fund. The move brought in $950 in Houston, which was a help. What wasn't a help was a two-day downpour that delayed the start of the tournament for a similar length, making the River Oaks Country Club live up to the first half of its name and cutting into the weekend gate revenues.

That was how the WGA, like most golf operations, survived in those lean years. During the Depression, the WGA membership dropped from over 500 clubs to

less than 200. Tournament revenue fluctuated due to occasional poor weather. Individual contributions came in sporadically. Despite the financial challenges, the directors managed to improve the WGA Scholarship Fund's balance from $42.93 on October 31, 1938, to $1,474.94 two years later.

Sometimes, money came from unexpected sources, such as the day early in 1941 when a representative of Carson Pirie Scott and Co., the Chicago retailer, approached the WGA with the idea of marketing an Evans Scholars logo golf ball. It meant two things for the WGA: some much needed publicity and guaranteed revenue at a time when money was tight. The Evans Scholars Program was still little known outside of the WGA's inner circle, a situation that the directors realized but had yet to rectify.

By August of 1940, it had become obvious that the most pressing need for the Evans Scholars was housing. From the start, the Scholars had been on their own in finding a place to stay. That proved to be a hin-

Adding coal to the furnace was one of the many house maintenance duties facing early Evans Scholars.

drance to the desired camaraderie among the Scholars, to say nothing of the cost.

"There was just Jim McGinnis and myself and there was no organization as we see it today," pioneer scholar Fink recalled in 1982. "We rarely even saw each other because I lived in Morton Grove and Jim lived somewhere on the South Side of Chicago. On one of the few occasions we were together, someone asked where we ate, and I said 'The Davis Street L station' and Jim said 'And we sleep there too.' Well, it wasn't quite that bad, but it was a matter of survival."

James Leslie Rollins—the liaison between the university and the WGA and by now the school's assistant dean of men—was well aware of the need for housing. He scouted the immediate neighborhood and found a house close to campus that would allow all of the Evans Scholars to live under one roof. The house, at 1935 Sherman Avenue in Evanston, was selling for $12,500.

Often, WGA directors, all men of means, had literally thrown money on the table to fund scholarships. A recent outside fund-raising effort, the first in WGA history, had raised some $1,200, with 120 golfers contributing $10 each.

Now, much more was needed. A fund-raising letter was written. Dated August 28, 1940, and signed by WGA Secretary John G. Searle, the letter contained a collection of the most polite phrases ever devised to twist arms and to make those arms reach for a checkbook.

"It is two blocks from the campus and one-half block from Willard Hall, where most of the boys work for their meals," Searle wrote. All the recipients had to do was to contribute the money needed to buy the house and make needed repairs. The total estimated cost: $15,000.

Searle noted that $4,000 already was accounted for, a way to prime the pump among those who might believe the goal could not be reached.

"Here is truly a realization of something very fine," Searle penned. "It means our boys will live together, work and help one another and derive considerably

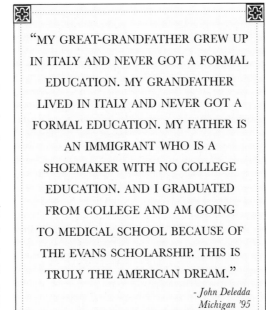

"MY GREAT-GRANDFATHER GREW UP IN ITALY AND NEVER GOT A FORMAL EDUCATION. MY GRANDFATHER LIVED IN ITALY AND NEVER GOT A FORMAL EDUCATION. MY FATHER IS AN IMMIGRANT WHO IS A SHOEMAKER WITH NO COLLEGE EDUCATION. AND I GRADUATED FROM COLLEGE AND AM GOING TO MEDICAL SCHOOL BECAUSE OF THE EVANS SCHOLARSHIP. THIS IS TRULY THE AMERICAN DREAM."

- John Deledda
Michigan '95
Student, University of Michigan
Medical School

more benefit than they have in the past."

By October 7, $5,200 was in hand, enough for the required down payment, with another $1,400 promised. Some of the arms had been twisted by Blunt, who, because of his Evanston upbringing and Northwestern connection, took a special interest in the project.

Suddenly, 1935 Sherman Avenue was a beehive of activity. The Scholars made a raft of improvements to the building: a coat of paint for the windowsills, a remodeled second floor to make four bedrooms into five, and a shower in the basement where a laundry had been.

Finally, the hammers were put down and the paint brushes cleaned. Where previously Evans Scholars had to live in someone's basement or an attic, or beg a couch from friends in the area, they now had a place to call their own. It was the fall of 1940, 10 years after Fink and McGinnis had entered Northwestern.

The Scholars, however, still did not receive a completely free ride. They had to pay house dues, which essentially took care of utilities, housekeeping and served as nominal rent. The fee was low enough to be affordable, yet high enough to impart a sense of responsibility to the residents. The same applies today.

The Evans House, as it quickly became known, turned out to be more than a home for the Scholars. It also became a showplace for the Evans program, garnering national publicity, such as an article in the June 28, 1941, edition of *The Saturday Evening Post*, then one of the country's foremost weeklies.

"It's quite a thing," an unnamed caddie, marveling at the concept of a scholarship program along with a place to stay, told the *Post*. "One day you're a caddie. You're 99 percent behind the eight ball, and the next day you're in. That's the way they treat you—you're in."

Eventually, the Northwestern Evans House would become a model for similar houses at other universities. That expansion, however, would have to wait until the conclusion of World War II.

This group of Evans Scholars, well-dressed for the cameraman, gathers 'round the house piano to work on their musical talent.

THE HOUSE ON SHERMAN AVENUE

A large gathering of Evans Scholars at the original Evans House before the 1953 move to new quarters.

In 1933, seven years before the Western Golf Association bought the Northwestern Chapter House at 1935 Sherman Avenue in Evanston, the WGA's select group of Scholars had organized the first Evans Scholars Club.

When word spread in 1940 that the dream of a single residence for the caddie-scholars was about to become reality, the young men were ready to become caddie-scholars-handymen. Since then, Evans Scholars have focused on scholarship, leadership, group living, and house maintenance as the four cornerstones of their collegiate experience. Today, most Evans Scholars attend one of the 14 universities where the Evans Scholars Foundation owns and operates a Chapter House.

In the early days, many of the Scholars came from families whose parents were born overseas, who had come to the United States seeking freedom and fortune, and who had found the former but not the latter. An open house one day in 1941 found one of the Evans Scholars' parents chatting with Chick Evans and a correspondent for *The Saturday Evening Post.*

"All the time I look, I only see now what I come for to this country," a father said in broken, eloquent English. "This is America."

The Evans House, technically leased by the WGA, housed Evans Scholars exclusively for only two years before it was turned back to Northwestern for military housing during World War II. When the program resumed in 1946, there were soon 20 caddie-scholars living in the house once again.

The Evans Scholars moved into this Chapter House on the University of Wisconsin campus in 1971.

The success of the program meant that the house at 1935 Sherman eventually would be outgrown. The Northwestern Scholars moved to nearby 1822 Sherman in 1953, then halfway back to the original residence in 1964, when 1900 Sherman became the flagship house of a program that by then had seven other chapters in the Midwest.

Finally, in 1969, a house was purchased at 721 University Place in Evanston. The purchase was made possible by a contribution of $125,000 by Mrs. John E. McAuliffe in memory of her late husband, who founded Triangle Conduit & Cable Co., Inc., in Newark, New Jersey.

The famous house at 1935 Sherman had been torn down years before, making room for the expansion of the Northwestern campus. But the spirit lives on at the current Evans House, itself remodeled and refurbished in recent years. In 1997, the Chapter House library was remodeled and named in honor of Bruce Goodman, an Evan Scholars Foundation trustee and WGA director and former president. ◘

The recently-refurbished Missouri Chapter House, home to the Evans Scholars since 1968.

In 1971, the new Chapter House at Northwestern was named the McAuliffe House, honoring John McAuliffe. Carleton Blunt and Mrs. McAuliffe were present for the dedication.

Scholar Norman Donato (left) with Dr. George Simonian and Chick Evans.

9

MAC AND THE
EVANS SCHOLARS

*D*uring the 1930s the Evans Scholars Program was confined to Northwestern University and, as a result, to benefiting caddies from the Chicago area.

For a fledgling program, that seemed sufficient. After all, the funds available to send deserving caddies to college were limited, and so was the amount of time that volunteer directors could spend on the program's affairs.

The need for scholarships, however, continued to grow. If the program were to expand, the Western Golf Association would need a more dependable revenue stream than proceeds from the Western Open and the

Roland F. "Mac" McGuigan, a long-time ESF educational director, celebrates his birthday in 1963 at a surprise party organized by Evans Scholars Alumni leaders Roger Mohr (left) and Jack Sauer (right).

Western Amateur, and directors digging into their own pockets. Also, WGA clubs from outside the Chicago area were beginning to nominate scholarship candidates.

By 1938, eight years after Harold Fink and Jim McGinnis began their freshman year at Northwestern University, Scholars had been selected from Los Angeles and Seattle. In 1940, two came from Cleveland, with the Cleveland District Golf Association paying half their tuition. And in 1941, Avron Greene, a caddie at Hillcrest Country Club in Los Angeles, was awarded an Evans grant for his junior year at UCLA. He was the first non-Northwestern Evans Scholar.

With the program growing in both size and scope, someone eventually would be needed to take charge of the day-to-day operations. At Northwestern, the WGA was fortunate to have an interested party in James Leslie Rollins, who later became the school's dean of men and also acted as the Evans Scholars' faculty advisor. In the summer, in his spare time, he also ran the Western Junior.

Then World War II erupted. The Evans program was essentially shuttered for the war, with the Evans House at Northwestern taken back by the university for military housing. While five new Scholars were named for 1942, only one was selected in 1943, and none were picked in 1944. In the fall of 1945, a foursome of new faces joined returnees from the war, and the incoming class of seven in 1946 was the largest since before Pearl Harbor.

During the war, Scholars fit for the armed services either volunteered or were drafted, with the guarantee that their scholarships would continue after the war. Those in the 4-F category, or studying in defense-related fields, continued school.

While the war was on, the WGA board conducted a scholarship fund-raising campaign, which helped boost the balance to $65,000 and assured a healthy transition to a full-scale operation.

Additionally, in 1942 Rollins left Northwestern to become assistant dean of the Harvard Business School. Northwestern professor Leon Kranz did what advising had to be done for the duration of the conflict.

As the program was beginning to expand once again, Roland F. McGuigan entered the Evans Scholarships picture. McGuigan had worked his way through school at the University of Wisconsin in Madison. He waited tables, worked in a theater, and even worked in a furnace room. He also served as president of three campus organizations. Academically, he compiled a 3.3 grade point average in pre-med and was admitted to the Harvard Medical School. Because of financial need, however, he was unable to attend.

In 1948, after four years of service in the Navy, McGuigan returned to Northwestern as the dean of men. He also agreed to serve as faculty advisor to Northwestern's Evans House. In 1950, McGuigan—

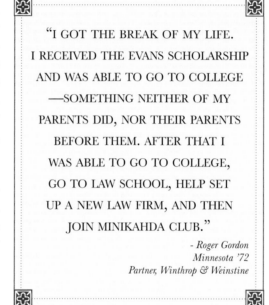

"I GOT THE BREAK OF MY LIFE. I RECEIVED THE EVANS SCHOLARSHIP AND WAS ABLE TO GO TO COLLEGE —SOMETHING NEITHER OF MY PARENTS DID, NOR THEIR PARENTS BEFORE THEM. AFTER THAT I WAS ABLE TO GO TO COLLEGE, GO TO LAW SCHOOL, HELP SET UP A NEW LAW FIRM, AND THEN JOIN MINIKAHDA CLUB."

- Roger Gordon
Minnesota '72
Partner, Winthrop & Weinstine

everybody called him Mac—was named the Evans program's first educational director, serving initially on a part-time basis and later full-time.

"All my training had been for university administration," he told *Golf Journal* in 1966. "I was sold on the philosophy that grades alone are not the only criteria, that the boys are placed in a house where they also work and live together, that it is not a 'free ride,' because the boys share the operating expenses of their houses and that there is concern for the individual's overall development and not solely at the academic level."

McGuigan, like program founder Chick Evans and fund-raiser and visionary Carleton Blunt, would prove to be vital to the long-term success of the Evans Scholars.

It was one thing to have a concept for a program, as Evans and his mother had. It was another to be able to call on friends at clubs across the country for donations, as Blunt and other WGA directors were able to do, to fund the program. Without a solid foundation for the program, however, the idea was just an idea and the money was just money.

McGuigan provided the foundation and the framework for virtually every enhancement to the program for more than 40 years. He began advising the Northwestern Scholars in 1948, was named part-time educational director in 1950, and accepted the position full-time in 1955. McGuigan continued to direct the program until his 1989 retirement. In his time, the number of chapter houses on university campuses went from 1 to 14, and the number of Scholars from 10 to more than 850. And McGuigan, amazingly, knew them all by name.

"Mac took the science of education and brought it into golf," Evans said. "Mac's presence is the most fortunate thing ever to happen to caddie-scholarship progress. His personal interest in the boys is a major reason why the boys do so well in school, and in later life."

"After the war, the program, and the economy, exploded," said James E. Moore, who succeeded McGuigan as educational director in 1989 after 22

Richard Femmel (left), the first postwar Evans Scholar, accepts congratulations from WGA President James Garard.

years as his assistant. "Mac liked the idea of giving guys a leg up on life. He had a great personality, a sense of concern. He was a great father figure to the Scholars."

McGuigan's shift to full-time educational director in 1955 followed a decision by WGA officials to establish permanent, organized fund-raising campaigns. The WGA leadership recognized that a reliable stream of revenue would be needed if they were to expand the program to campuses beyond Northwestern.

In typical WGA fashion, two revenue streams were fashioned, both beginning as McGuigan became involved in the program. Each continues to this day.

The first, the Bag Tag Program, was conceived by former WGA President Theodore Butz in 1946. During Butz' first term as president, the WGA switched from a club membership to an individual membership basis on the theory that contributions to the Evans Scholars

would increase exponentially. World War II ruined the experiment and, while club membership was resumed, Butz still believed that golfers would be willing to contribute to the scholarship program individually.

For a $5 donation, a golfer would receive a WGA/Evans Scholars bag tag as a memento, rather than a membership card. In short order, Butz arranged for each member at Exmoor Country Club, his home club, to be billed the $5 automatically. For a member of a country club, a $5 donation was painless. Jerome Bowes, the WGA's president in 1950 and 1951, convinced WGA directors to encourage their clubs to implement automatic billing.

The Bag Tag program spread quickly to virtually every Chicago-area club, then throughout the WGA membership. By 1954, there were 20,771 individuals contributing to the WGA.

Northwestern professor Leon Kranz, who followed James Rollins as the advisor to the Evans Scholars, has the close attention of three of his charges in the Evans House library.

Directors Ed Stegner (left) and Ells Widerman (right) look over a list of candidates with Mac McGuigan.

Bowes also believed that, with the cost of college increasing, more than small donations were needed. In 1950, he began to look for people, golfers and otherwise, who were willing to donate $100. Those who did so would become members of what Bowes was planning to call the $100 Club. Golf writer Herb Graffis came up with a better name: the Par Club.

Bowes had no trouble selling his fellow directors on the idea, perhaps because he guaranteed that by the end of the 1950 fiscal year, the Par Club would have 100 members, enough to bring the Evans Scholars $10,000.

Considering that Bowes only announced the idea in early March and didn't begin to press the campaign until after Labor Day, and that the fiscal year ended on October 31, finding 100 to give $100 was a tall order. Through the end of August, there were only 13 Par Club "members," among them Bing Crosby and Chick Evans.

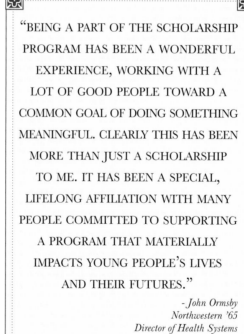

"BEING A PART OF THE SCHOLARSHIP PROGRAM HAS BEEN A WONDERFUL EXPERIENCE, WORKING WITH A LOT OF GOOD PEOPLE TOWARD A COMMON GOAL OF DOING SOMETHING MEANINGFUL. CLEARLY THIS HAS BEEN MORE THAN JUST A SCHOLARSHIP TO ME. IT HAS BEEN A SPECIAL, LIFELONG AFFILIATION WITH MANY PEOPLE COMMITTED TO SUPPORTING A PROGRAM THAT MATERIALLY IMPACTS YOUNG PEOPLE'S LIVES AND THEIR FUTURES."

- John Ormsby
Northwestern '65
Director of Health Systems
Dietary Products, a division of
Alliant Food Service

Then the checks began to pour in. On October 30, there were 67 members. On October 31, Bowes' self-imposed deadline, the original Par Club ledger lists 33 more checks received for a total of 100. There are 33 different names listed against as many $100 donations, but the long-held suspicion has been that Bowes wrote many of the checks himself, paying for the memberships of his friends to fulfill his guarantee and boost the following year's campaign.

The next year, 116 people joined; the year after, 187. By 1955, there were 297 Par Club members.

The gross income to the WGA and Evans program—$29,556 in 1946 when the Bag Tag program was just beginning—rose to $197,788 by 1955. By that time, the Bag Tag and Par Club programs were in full swing, contributing 73 percent of the total.

The growth paid off in diplomas. In 1949, there were 58 Scholars in school. In 1955, 259 were attending classes. Many of the new Scholars came from outside the Chicago area, as the WGA convinced local golf associations to join them in the caddie scholarship concept.

The Wisconsin State Golf Association was the first to join, in 1947, followed by the Detroit District, Pacific Northwest, Illinois Women's, and Minnesota golf asso-

He would also play a leading hand in finding places for them to live. As with the early years at Northwestern, Scholars attending other universities sometimes struggled when it came to finding adequate housing. The answer was the Chapter House system.

The first chapter to follow Northwestern was at Illinois in 1951. In quick succession came Michigan a year later, McGuigan's alma mater of Wisconsin in 1953, Michigan State and Marquette in 1955, and Minnesota in 1958.

"The directors think that such residence is an important part of the total education experience, since it means learning to live and work and get along with others," McGuigan said in 1959. "The chapter organization is sort of a human relations laboratory."

It was McGuigan who, with the help of WGA directors, selected the faculty advisors at each school. Most of all, he would fine-tune each and every application from potential Evans Scholars, giving every caddie who qualified the best chance at actually winning the scholarship.

Theodore Butz, a former WGA President, came up with the fund-raising Bag Tag program in 1946.

For just $5 in 1946, a golfer could both support the Evans Scholars and brag about it on his bag.

ciations, all by 1950. Today, 23 local and regional associations from Syracuse and Buffalo, New York, to the West Coast are co-sponsors of the Evans Scholars Foundation. Selection meetings, always with WGA directors and staff on hand, are held throughout the country to choose Evans Scholars.

The human avalanche of new Scholars gave McGuigan plenty to do. He would spend the year screening candidates for new scholarships, giving current Scholars advice and, more and more as the years went on, advising the Evans Scholar Alumni.

WGA President Jerome Bowes supported automatic billing for the Bag Tag fund-raiser, and in 1951 began what would become known as the Par Club.

The first Par Club membership card. Precisely 100 were issued.

And it was McGuigan who actively encouraged the Scholars to not only go to class and learn but to become involved in their college community. That had always been done on an individual basis, but the increase in the number of Scholars and the growing number of Chapter Houses made possible fund-raising efforts for local charities and leadership roles on campus.

He and a battery of secretaries did the entire job until 1967, when James E. Moore joined as his assistant. Moore took over as educational director when McGuigan retired in 1989 and has directed the scholarship program's continued development and growth during the past decade.

McGuigan and Moore both encouraged Alumni involvement, not just in donating to the program—donations have totaled over $1 million annually since 1992—but in mentoring current Scholars and networking among one another.

McGuigan, who briefly worked for a weekly newspaper as a young man, insisted that the Alumni keep in touch with him and with one another. He provided them with a vehicle—his famous and award-winning *Alumni Newsletters*. The newsletters, as they were named, were really massive paperback books. If a Scholar or Alumnus dropped Mac a line with some news, or included a photo, it made the *Newsletter*. Everything made the *Newsletter*, from baby pictures to vacation tales to job changes to clips about Scholars from newspapers.

Stanley Van Dyke, Scotty Fessenden, and Gordon Kummer (right) salute Jerome Bowes at the end of his 1950-51 term as WGA president.

The charter class of Evans Scholars at Michigan State University gathered for a group portrait in front of their rented house at 327 M.A.C. Avenue in 1955.

There was nothing else like it. Today, a slimmed-down, twice-yearly glossy magazine is entitled *The Mac Report,* in honor of McGuigan, who died in 1991 at age seventy-five. More importantly, the Evans Scholars Endowment Fund—started in 1981 and named in his honor when he retired—had more than $12 million by the end of 1997, ready to be used if the need ever arises.

"Before the endowment," said Moore, "our philosophy was we're a grass-roots organization. We'll raise the money each year to pay the bills."

Faced with escalating tuition and housing costs in the 1970s and early 1980s, the WGA leadership recognized the need to establish an endowment fund to give the Evans Scholars Program, and the hundreds of Scholars who attend college each year, a safety net in case the economy turns downward or the usual

The McGuigan-produced Alumni Newsletters were really trade-sized paperback books in disguise.

avenues of financial support erode.

"We are prepared to enter the twenty-first century with the assurance that we will be able to continue to provide deserving caddies with the opportunity to attend college as Evans Scholars," said Moore, a former school teacher who McGuigan recruited to strengthen the program's services. "We have interviewed record numbers of candidates for scholarships in recent years, and our programs at our 14 Chapter Houses are thriving. We are very optimistic about the future. The Evans Scholars are living proof that the American Dream can be realized through hard work and the support of many caring people."

Today, Moore and his associate educational director, Jeffery C. Harrison, provide the Evans Scholars with the same support and direction McGuigan offered Scholars for more than four decades. Their devoted commitment to the program is an even further guarantee that the Evans Scholarships will continue to be the largest, and most successful, privately funded scholarship program in the nation well into the twenty-first century.

Current educational director Jim Moore, who joined the WGA in 1967, is as tireless as McGuigan, his mentor.

CARLETON BLUNT AND THE NEW WGA HEADQUARTERS

The artist's rendition of the Western Golf Association headquarters, drawn up in 1954. Only the addition of a post office annex and awnings have changed the look since.

In 1954, the Western Golf Association was, as it had been for most of its 55-year history, headquartered in rented offices in downtown Chicago. Over the years, the WGA had made its home in the Grand Pacific Hotel, in a cubbyhole office at 7001 North Clark Street during the Great Depression, and finally back downtown at 8 South Dearborn Street, in the heart of the Loop.

Carleton Blunt, a WGA director and Evans Scholars trustee, envisioned a suburban office, one owned by the WGA, preferably near a golf course.

He knew the perfect place: in the tiny village of Golf, Illinois, not far

from the Glen View Club, where the first Western Open and Western Amateur were held. Blunt and Chick Evans were members of the club, and one of the first two Evans Scholars had caddied there.

There were two problems: Golf was strictly a residential community, and the WGA coffers had no money for a headquarters building. Blunt would see to it that both problems were overcome, and he would do so in less than a year.

Former WGA President Theodore Butz, who inaugurated the Bag Tag fund-raising program, had died in September 1953. His will made provisions

A 50s style photo opportunity: Chick Evans and pals take the carriage from the train station in Golf, Illinois, to the new WGA/Evans Scholars headquarters building, a short pitching wedge away.

for a Butz Foundation, with proceeds to benefit the WGA and Evans Scholars. Blunt was on the Butz Foundation board. On January 6, 1954, he proposed that a WGA headquarters building be built in Golf on a parcel of vacant land adjacent to the railroad station, with the Butz Foundation funding the major portion of the cost.

He and fellow board member Jerome Bowes had already canvassed key Golf residents, telling them the building would have room for a village hall. The residents were in favor of the idea, especially since it would cost them nothing.

Blunt made sure his plan had no loopholes. A committee was appointed to go forward on the matter. Blunt was on it. He was the only person who needed to be on it. By August of 1954, the lot had been purchased, an architect had been engaged, and bids had been taken on the building's construction.

The Butz Foundation had pledged $50,000. Blunt and Chick Evans would seek backers for

the balance of the project's approximate $100,000 cost.

They found them, donors who gave $1,000 each, the minimum eligible for inclusion on the "Evans Scholars Honor Roll," a list of the building's backers, which included the United States Golf Association. The building went up quickly, a handsome structure that has since been expanded with the addition of a post office annex. It was open by April 1955, dedicated in Butz' honor and christened by Evans in a ceremony that attracted the attention of local newspapers and *Sports Illustrated.* Evans rode to the building's dedication from the train station, some 50 yards distant, in a horse-drawn carriage.

It was typical of Blunt's dedication to the Evans program that, once he said something was going to happen, it happened, and in a big way. The headquarters building was not only paid for upon completion, but the maintenance of the building was also endowed.

Blunt was a behind-the-scenes guy. He wasn't someone newspapermen would approach for a quote. Upon the end of his one-year term as WGA president on December 6, 1957, however, Blunt spoke to the audience at the WGA's 59th Annual Meeting.

"Enough has been said of the past 25 years and of the 59th year," Blunt said. "It is the next 25 years which are really of interest. Our real assets are the 40 of you here today and those not present who share the responsibilities of the future. We have Chick Evans, the greatest real amateur of all time, as our spearhead and our inspiration. We are no longer 'sectional' in any sense of the word. Our possibilities are unlimited." ◻

Carelton Blunt had reason to be proud on that 1955 day the new headquarters building was dedicated.

CROSBY AND HOPE

Bob Hope, Bing Crosby and Chick Evans attracted 25,000 spectators for this 1947 celebrity match at Tam O'Shanter Country Club.

Think of Bing Crosby and golf, and visions of the Monterey Peninsula and the annual clambake come to mind.

Think of Bob Hope and golf, and memories of Hope's antics with Crosby, as well as his own Desert Classic, are in the forefront.

There's more to the involvement of Der Bingle and Ol' Ski Nose with the royal and ancient game than schmoozing with pros or kidding around during the "Road" pictures. Much of it involves the Evans Scholars.

Crosby became interested first, becoming a WGA director before World War II. He pulled Hope in after the war. Hope even worked as a starter on the first tee at the 1950 Western Open in Los Angeles. Eventually, the two—alone and together radio and motion picture superstars when that term had some meaning—were named honorary vice-presidents.

Along with fund-raising—Crosby annually sent a check ticketed for the Evans Scholars from the proceeds of the Crosby National Pro-Am—their big project together was "Honor Caddie," a 22-minute movie short made in 1949 with almost every golf star of the day, including Ben Hogan, Sam Snead, Patty Berg, Babe Didrikson Zaharias,

Bing Crosby, Chick Evans, Bob Hope, and Ben Hogan gather with actors playing caddies during the filming of "Honor Caddie" in 1948.

In 1956, with the Western Open in San Francisco, Crosby and Hope were the headliners in a special exhibition match at Presidio Golf Club the day before the championship commenced. Crosby's team, which included local amateur E. Harvie Ward and pros Doug Ford and Mike Souchak, beat the foursome of Hope, defending Western Open champ Cary Middlecoff, big-hitting George Bayer, and Ken Venturi, like Ward a Bay Area amateur sensation. The prize: the Crosby-Hope WGA Oscar. The appearance of Hope and Crosby helped draw large crowds to Presidio and made the Western a financial, as well as an artistic, success.

In the late 1950s, Crosby helped produce another film, "Your Caddie, Sir," a 20-minute film highlighting correct caddie procedures. Crosby, Chick Evans, and pros Horton Smith and Walter Burkemo were featured, along with two caddies from Detroit's Plum Hollow Golf Club. It took the premise of "Honor Caddie" a step further in terms of instruction. ◘

The sheet music to "Tomorrow's My Lucky Day," the featured song in the WGA movie, "Honor Caddie."

Byron Nelson, and, of course, Chick Evans. Crosby even prevailed upon Hollywood songwriters Johnny Burke and Jimmy Van Heusen to pen a tune, "Tomorrow's My Lucky Day," to croon along the way.

The idea for a pro-caddie movie came from WGA Executive Vice-President John Kennan. President Maynard "Scotty" Fessenden whispered it in Crosby's ear late in 1948, and Bing took it from there, donating his time, as did Hope and all the professionals. Crosby arranged for the filming at the Riviera, Bel Air, and Los Angeles country clubs.

The first caddie training film, it was well received by WGA member clubs across the country. It even had a "world premiere" of sorts, a showing at the Chicago Athletic Club on March 29, 1949. The production also went overseas, receiving rave reviews from the Golfers' Exhibition in London, and brought in thousands of dollars in donations from here and abroad. Hope and Crosby even carried their own prints of the movie to screen to business groups.

Der Bingle's team won this prize bauble at an exhibition match at Presidio Golf Club in San Francisco, the prelude to the 1956 Western Open.

CHAPTER

10

SELECTING SCHOLARS

*I*t is the dead of winter in the northern suburbs of Chicago. A light snow has fallen overnight, a picturesque coating made blinding by the low sun, the sheer white contrasting with the clear, blue sky.

The scene may be Currier and Ives on overdrive, but it is not a good day to play golf no matter how willing the spirit, unless a flight to a warmer climate precedes the trip to the first tee. This late January day is meant for pulling the chair a half step closer to the fire.

It is also, contrary to outside appearances, the start of Chicago's golf season. Not on the course, certainly, but rather in a well-appointed room at the Knollwood Club in Lake Forest. There, nearly 50 directors of the

An Evans Scholar candidate addresses the scholarship committee.

Western Golf Association will gather to consider candidates for what is both a precious gift and a distinct honor: an Evans Scholars award.

The WGA's famous logo consists of crossed golf clubs in front of the lamp of knowledge—a lamp undoubtedly burning the midnight oil. Adopted in 1953, the logo explains at a glance that the WGA is all about golf and scholarships through golf. It all comes together on days like this at Knollwood.

Before the day ends, the Evans Scholars Foundation —the educational arm of the WGA—will have granted tuition and housing scholarships to 25 Evans Scholars candidates. The scholarships, to major universities, are renewable for four years. The 25 high school seniors receiving the scholarships will have walked into the meeting room, stood at the lectern, looked out upon the directors, gulped, and explained who they were and what they wanted to become.

For each of the candidates, all of whom hope to join the more than 800 Scholars in college, the story of how they have come to this setting has a common theme, one rooted in the rich tradition of the century-old Western Golf Association and its nearly seven decades of support for the Evans Scholars Program.

Every candidate is a caddie at a WGA-member country club or public course, as was program founder Charles "Chick" Evans, Jr., the leading amateur player of his era. Evans remained an amateur in the face of lucrative offers to turn professional after winning the 1916 United States Open. He dedicated most of his adult life to promoting caddie scholarships.

Every candidate has excelled in academics at his or her high school. Scholastic achievement has been a criterion for receiving the Evans award since the first two Evans Scholars, Harold Fink and Jim McGinnis, enrolled at Northwestern University in Evanston, Illinois, in 1930.

Every candidate is of outstanding character, as attested to in letters from the club president, caddie master, head professional, school officials and others.

Every candidate, finally, needs the financial assistance. The Evans Scholars Foundation exists to aid qualified young men and women who require a helping hand, who probably would not go to college—and certainly not to a major university—without aid. Financial eligibility is determined on a case-by-case basis. Factors considered include the size of the family, income, medical expenses, the number of children in college and other potential financial burdens. One thing not counted against caddie-candidates is how much money they have earned themselves, either looping or working after-school jobs. That is considered a plus.

An Evans Scholarship provides for full tuition and lodging. Scholars are expected to work for their meal money, or for the meals themselves, and for their

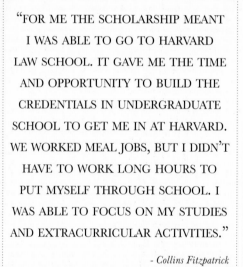

"FOR ME THE SCHOLARSHIP MEANT I WAS ABLE TO GO TO HARVARD LAW SCHOOL. IT GAVE ME THE TIME AND OPPORTUNITY TO BUILD THE CREDENTIALS IN UNDERGRADUATE SCHOOL TO GET ME IN AT HARVARD. WE WORKED MEAL JOBS, BUT I DIDN'T HAVE TO WORK LONG HOURS TO PUT MYSELF THROUGH SCHOOL. I WAS ABLE TO FOCUS ON MY STUDIES AND EXTRACURRICULAR ACTIVITIES."

- Collins Fitzpatrick
Marquette '66
Circuit Executive
Judicial Council of the
7th Circuit, Chicago

books. While the program is national, most of the Scholars are concentrated at 14 universities from Ohio to Colorado which have an Evans Scholar Chapter House on the campus.

The first Chapter House, opened at Northwestern University in 1940, proved so beneficial to knitting the Scholars together that when the program expanded beyond Northwestern after World War II, Chapter Houses became the norm. They also have helped cut housing costs dramatically.

The all-for-one concept extends into the classroom. The graduation rate for Evans Scholars is over 90 percent, astounding compared with the national four-year collegiate average of less than 50 percent. Scholars graduate in all fields, from education to business, from the social sciences to the physical sciences. There even have been Evans Scholars on the PGA Tour and LPGA Tour, though it's the ability to caddie, not to play the game, that earns the scholarship.

It is to fill the Evans Scholars Chapter Houses with the bright and eager minds of young men and women—the program has been coeducational since 1954—that the WGA directors and staff have gathered at Knollwood on this frigid day in 1997. The assemblage is one of over a dozen selection meetings held in the Midwest, Colorado, and Pacific Northwest in the course of the year. At the meetings, the candidates are interviewed by directors of the WGA and, depending on the location, by directors from one or more of the 23 regional golf associations that co-sponsor the Evans program. Following the interviews, the directors and their guests vote on each candidate individually, deciding whether the candidate should be granted a prestigious Evans Scholarship.

To ensure that the candidates all have the opportunity to pass with flying colors, WGA Educational Director James E. Moore reviews each candidate's qualifications at a briefing for the directors and guests. Meanwhile, Associate Educational Director Jeffrey C.

WGA directors take their work seriously, going over the profiles of all scholar candidates carefully.

Harrison, himself an Evans Alumnus, prepares each candidate in a room adjacent to the meeting room. Since the candidates, if successful, will be living in a Chapter House, they're expected to know precisely what their responsibilities will be. Harrison reviews those duties with them and also tries to put them at ease. After all, the directions their lives will take depend upon the next 12 minutes.

"Those meetings are just terribly important," says the ever-ebullient Moore, who joined the WGA staff in August 1967 as an assistant to Roland F. "Mac" McGuigan, the first educational director. "It's an exciting day because the people who support the program are there, and they get a chance to meet these young people.

"There's a tremendous amount of time that goes into preparing files and in interviewing. I feel a great sense of responsibility in making the selections. I want to make sure that we select the

WGA Director and Scholarship Committee Co-Chairman Rich Peterson interviews candidate Bryan McNulty at an Evans Scholars Selection Meeting. McNulty earned a scholarship to the University of Illinois.

right people, make sure we didn't leave out someone who deserved to be in."

Even in a booming economy, there are more applicants than ever before. Once the final cut is made, the successful candidates are invited to a selection meeting. After getting the final instructions from Harrison and a few current Scholars, they are escorted one by one into the meeting room. The escort is Donald D. Johnson, the WGA's executive director since July of 1988. Usually, Johnson spends his days concerning himself with the big-picture aspect of the WGA and Evans operations. Meeting the candidates is a welcome change of pace from looking at budgets and mulling over contract details.

"I try to make them more relaxed," says Johnson. "I chat with them, ask them where they caddie. I tell them who in the room they might know, a director

from their club, perhaps their caddie master, and that we all want them to succeed. I remind them that more than 6,800 caddies just like them have gone before them."

Johnson escorts the first candidate into the room, handing him off to the co-chairmen of the scholarship committee, John P. Hanna and Richard E. Peterson. Hanna is an old hand at selection meetings, having chaired them since the early 1980s. Peterson's father was a WGA director before him, and he, too, has taken an intense interest in the process.

That is true of all the directors. They are volunteers, their only reward being the satisfaction that comes with a job well done. They take their jobs seriously, not at all bashful about asking questions.

Candidate No. 1 fields the first question: "What's the single most important thing you've learned in being a caddie?"

Chick Evans with his favorite people, caddie-scholars in school because of the scholarship program he began.

Evans Scholars at Northwestern take notes in class.

what they actually do?" The answer brings the house down, a combination of laughter and applause.

There are several other WGA staff members on hand for the selection meeting, including Tournament Director Gregory T. McLaughlin—who is in charge of on-course operations during the Motorola Western Open, Western Amateur, and Western Junior.

McLaughlin, who joined the WGA in 1994, first learned of the Evans program when he was attending Ohio State in the early 1980s. Two members of the rugby team he was on were Evans Scholars. His next contact was after he joined the WGA, following stints running the Los Angeles Open and Honda Classic.

"When I went to my first selection meeting, I had no idea what would go on," he said. "The thing I noticed is that you have one boy or girl going into the room, and unless they really mess up, they've got the scholarship, and most of them are from really, really difficult home environments. They might have a 10-year-old car. They might come from a broken home. Their parents may have immigrated to the United States from another country."

"These kids have to cling to certain things. These kids are workers. Without that paycheck, without

"Dealing with people," the answer comes back. "Sometimes you get lucky and get a light bag and a great guy. And sometimes..."

Candidates are asked if they would accept a scholarship to a different school if necessary, who has influenced them, what they believe the challenges of college are, and what the particular responsibilities of an Evans Scholar are. Each candidate asked easily comes up with "scholarship and leadership." The other two cornerstones, group living and house maintenance, usually come to mind after some friendly prodding.

One candidate says she wants to be a lawyer, and is asked the question, "What do lawyers do for a living?"

She responds without missing a beat, "What they're supposed to do, or

Jeff Harrison, the associate educational director and an Evans Scholar Alumnus, preps a candidate on what will happen in the interview room.

being a caddie, they might not be able to pay the rent," McLaughlin said. "And they're high on education. They have no money and you're laying a four-year education on them. They're getting the greatest opportunity in the world, and most of them don't forget that. It's more than just a scholarship, it's a way of life. It's kind of who they are."

As Moore says, "We don't want couch potatoes, we want leaders," and the group at Knollwood seems filled with them. Says one candidate, quizzed about his part-time winter job and the amount of time he spends on extracurricular school activities, "I've learned you should never underestimate yourself."

The day at Knollwood has been long but fruitful, all business except for a lunch break. One of the last candidates to be interviewed is asked about the time she'll have to devote to house maintenance.

"I don't hear any of the kids complain about it," she says. "How could you when you get this?" How, indeed.

The 25 candidates leave Knollwood not knowing whether they have been granted a scholarship. While rejection of a candidate by the directors is rare, Moore remembers it happening.

On this day, there are no rejections. Everyone in the room can vote on prospective candidates, either an unqualified yes, a probable, a doubtful, or an outright no. A majority of yes and probable votes is needed for selection. All 25 win overwhelming majorities.

Within a week, every candidate will receive a letter on WGA stationery, the envelopes postmarked Golf, Illinois. Those letters, from Jim Moore, will begin, "I am pleased to advise you that the WGA Scholarship Committee has awarded you an Evans Scholarship," then will name the university and note that the scholarship will begin that fall. And through that letter, the new Evans Scholars' lives will have changed.

In those earnest and simple words, Chick Evans' dream will have come true again. Twenty-five lives will have been made better. They will have received a college scholarship from a group of almost complete strangers who believe that caddies who demonstrate excellence on the golf course and in the classroom, but who are financially limited, deserve an opportunity to move forward in their lives.

Scholarship Committee Co-Chairman John Hanna greets a candidate.

The midnight oil burns not only on the WGA's logo, but in the rooms in every Evans Scholar Chapter House at exam time.

A quintet of Evans Scholars on the move at Northwestern.

HISTORY: FOUNDING OF EVANS SCHOLARS CHAPTERS

▶ **First Chapter**

Northwestern University

1933 First Evans Scholars Club organized

1940 First Evans Scholars Chapter House,
1935 Sherman Avenue, Evanston

1953 New Chapter House, 1822 Sherman Avenue, Evanston

1964 New Chapter House, 1900 Sherman Avenue, Evanston

1969 New Chapter House, 721 University Place, Evanston

1987 Chapter became co-educational

▶ **Second Chapter**

University of Illinois

1951 Evans Scholars Chapter organized:
112 E. John St., Champaign (temporary housing)

1953 404 E. John St., Champaign (temporary housing)

1954 206 E. Green St., Champaign (purchased)

1969 Construction of new house completed:
1007 South Third St., Champaign

1991 Chapter became co-educational

▶ **Third Chapter**

University of Michigan

1952 Evans Scholars Chapter organized:
819 E. University Ave., Ann Arbor (temporary housing)

1953 1026 Oakland Avenue, Ann Arbor (purchased)

1960 1004 Olivia, Ann Arbor (purchased)

1975 1800 Washtenaw, Ann Arbor (purchased)

1981 Chapter became co-educational

▶ **Fourth Chapter**

University of Wisconsin

1953 Evans Scholars Chapter organized:
614 Langdon St., Madison (temporary housing)

1954 Evans Scholars Chapter House:
422 N. Murray St., Madison (purchased)

1959 234 Langdon St., Madison (purchased),
609 Howard (purchased as annex)

1971 141 Langdon St., Madison (purchased)

1985 Chapter became co-educational

▶ **Fifth Chapter**

Michigan State University

1955 Evans Scholars Chapter organized:
327 M.A.C. Ave., East Lansing (temporary housing)

1956 215 Louis St., East Lansing (temporary housing)

1957 243 Louis St., East Lansing (purchased)

1966 237 Louis St., East Lansing (purchased)

1967 Completed one-story lounge connecting 237 & 243

1981 Chapter became co-educational

1988 Construction of new house completed:
831 E. Grand River Ave., East Lansing

▶ **Sixth Chapter**

Marquette University

1955 Evans Scholars Chapter organized:
807 N. 12th St., Milwaukee (temporary housing)

1956 2923 W. Highland Blvd., Milwaukee (purchased)

1968 2920 W. State St., Milwaukee (purchased as annex)

1986 Construction of new house completed: 1318 W. Wells St.,
Milwaukee & Chapter became co-educational

► **Seventh Chapter**

University of Minnesota

1958 Evans Scholars Chapter organized:
1300-5th St. S.E.-Minneapolis (temporary housing)

1960 1115-5th St. S.E.-Minneapolis (purchased)

1968 1120-6th St. S.E.-Minneapolis (purchased as annex)

1978 Construction of new house completed:
929-5th St., S.E., Minneapolis

► **Eighth Chapter**

Ohio State University

1962 Evans Scholars Chapter organized:
1909 Waldeck Ave., Columbus (temporary housing)

1964 1945 Indianola Avenue (purchased)

1978 Scarlet & Gray Dormitory, 52 East 14th Avenue,
Columbus (purchased)

► **Ninth Chapter**

Purdue University

1967 Evans Scholars Chapter organized:
1253 Terry Courts, West Lafayette (temporary housing)

1969 117 W. State St., Lafayette (temporary housing)

1971 Tower Acres - A.E. Pi (temporary housing)

1975 Pemberly Court Apts. (temporary housing)

1976 Townehouse Apts. (temporary housing)

1979 221 Littleton, West Lafayette (purchased)

1983 Chapter became co-educational

1990 Construction of new house completed:
1001 Hilltop Dr., West Lafayette

► **Tenth Chapter**

University of Colorado

1967 Evans Scholars Chapter organized:
1135 - 11th St., Boulder (temporary housing)

1969 1029 Broadway, Boulder (purchased)

1982 Chapter became co-educational

► **Eleventh Chapter**

University of Missouri

1968 Evans Scholars Chapter organized:
923 Maryland, Columbia (purchased)

► **Twelfth Chapter**

Indiana University

1969 Evans Scholars Chapter organized:
Brown Hall, Woodlawn Complex, Bloomington
(temporary housing)

1974 1075 N. Jordan Ave., Bloomington (purchased)

► **Thirteenth Chapter**

Miami University

1974 Evans Scholar Chapter organized:
219 E. Church St., Oxford (purchased)

1998 Construction of new house completed

► **Fourteenth Chapter**

Northern Illinois University

1987 Evans Scholar Chapter organized:
901 Greenbrier, DeKalb (purchased & rehabbed)
co-educational ◻

11

CHICK EVANS
AND HIS FRIENDS

Perhaps a more thorough search would turn up someone who held a grudge against Chick Evans. Perhaps there once was someone out there whom Chick Evans beat in a long-ago match, a disgruntled golfer who never forgave Chick for a particularly lopsided defeat.

That person, should he exist, has not been found. It appears that everybody who knew Chick Evans liked Chick Evans. Everybody.

And almost everybody knew him, to one degree or another: everyone in golf, everyone in Chicago sports, most everyone in the educational field and many in business, especially in the milk sales industry, where Evans spent decades making sales and friends.

The smile of Chick Evans glows through the ages.

Here is one measure of how unforgettable he was. Dorothy Ellis—the young girl who raced with Chick across the Midlothian Country Club grounds in 1914 in an impromptu race that cost him a sprained ankle and perhaps a U.S. Open—never forgot that day. When she died in 1961, she left much of her estate to the Evans Scholars Foundation. The bequest was $65,000, at the time the largest single gift in WGA/Evans Scholars history.

Chick's name was in the headlines for over 50 years after his last Western Amateur win. He played in 49 U.S. Amateurs. He won the Chicago City Amateur in 1944, at age 54, his second triumph in that event coming 37 years after the first, and won it again the following year.

He played in the Western Open at age 77, scoring

93-87 in the first two rounds at Beverly Country Club in 1967, and he surely will always hold the record of being the oldest competitor in the championship.

In 1975, when the 85-year-old Evans was inducted into the World Golf Hall of Fame, then in Pinehurst, North Carolina, he wowed the crowd, remembering a North and South Amateur he had played in over 60 years previously.

"Actually, I was the first on this spot," said Chick, decked out in a WGA blazer and a bow tie. "I hit a shot over the green at the fourth hole (of the No. 2 course) here in the North and South."

He was instrumental in getting the right people together to start the PGA of America in 1916, then helped establish several senior golf organizations in the 1950s. He received honorary degrees from every university that has an Evans Scholars Chapter House, including Northwestern, where he was unable to finish his own schooling as a young man.

Closest to his heart, of course, was the Evans Scholars Foundation, which went from an idea in his mother's thoughts to a cause he championed on and off for seven years before the Western Golf Association rallied to his side in 1923.

The reverse was true as well. Evans Scholars corresponded with Chick regularly.

"They held him in reverence," Evans Educational Director Jim Moore said of Evans' relationship with his Scholars. "Every year, we have the 'Golf Ball' in the winter. It used to be at the M and M Club in the Merchandise Mart. Chick would dress in this velvet black-and-white dinner jacket. You could tell he reveled in the whole atmosphere."

"It was more than recognition," said former WGA Executive Director Marshall Dann. "It was almost like he was a holy person."

While Chick and Esther, his wife of 40 years, never had children, he had a huge family in the Evans Scholars.

As always, the connection between the old player and the young student was the scholarship, and the connection to the scholarship was the game and the role of the caddie. Evans, of course, always took a caddie when he played, preferably a young caddie, someone to whom the game was fresh, as it once was to him.

Evans was worried that the rise of the golf cart would eliminate the need for caddies, especially the young preteen lads who would have no other chance to learn the game except by carrying a bag. He advocated fewer than 14 clubs and lightweight bags to carry those clubs in.

"If we adopt something like this we would have the caddie again greatly in the majority," he told a gathering in Detroit in 1961. "I want him back with his thousands of mannerisms trudging along and bringing a sense of close comradeship between the player and the young man. Then again they would be allowed to observe early in life the ways of successful men."

Jack Atten, who lived a block away from Evans on North Damen Avenue, adjacent to Edgewater Golf Club, was one of those kids. The first time he caddied, in 1935 at age nine, it was for Chick Evans.

"He'd just practice, hitting back and forth," Atten recalled. "We'd be on the 14th hole at 5:30 in the morning. He'd hit every club in the bag. I'd put a dozen balls down, he'd hit them, then he'd go and hit them back to me. Back and forth, for about an hour. He'd pay me 50 cents, and that was good money in 1935.

"He was great from tee-to-green, especially his irons. Just perfect. He'd knock 'em stiff, where he could barely miss a putt, and I mean mid-irons. And he'd never take a divot. He'd sweep 'em."

At first, Evans was just the golfer down the block to Atten. He eventually realized that this was not just any

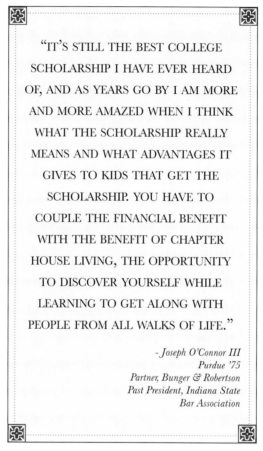

"IT'S STILL THE BEST COLLEGE SCHOLARSHIP I HAVE EVER HEARD OF, AND AS YEARS GO BY I AM MORE AND MORE AMAZED WHEN I THINK WHAT THE SCHOLARSHIP REALLY MEANS AND WHAT ADVANTAGES IT GIVES TO KIDS THAT GET THE SCHOLARSHIP. YOU HAVE TO COUPLE THE FINANCIAL BENEFIT WITH THE BENEFIT OF CHAPTER HOUSE LIVING, THE OPPORTUNITY TO DISCOVER YOURSELF WHILE LEARNING TO GET ALONG WITH PEOPLE FROM ALL WALKS OF LIFE."

- Joseph O'Connor III
Purdue '75
Partner, Bunger & Robertson
Past President, Indiana State
Bar Association

"He had a temper," Atten recalled. "When he'd go bad, he'd really start cussing. But not in front of people. He was a perfectionist. One day, we're on the 18th hole at Tam O'Shanter, and he hit his second shot in the water. He grabbed his clubs and he was going to throw them into the river."

Evans also had his quirks. One involved Atom, the Pomeranian dog Chick and Esther owned.

"Atom was part of the family," Atten said. "He'd take Atom to the movies. He'd wear an overcoat and put the dog under his coat, hold him under, walk in, sit down and the dog would sit on his lap and be real quiet. If he did it once, he did it 25 times.

"I remember when Atom died, he called me. We went to the back of the 14th green at Edgewater, behind the green, and buried Atom in one of the silver cups Chick won. I remember digging the hole. Chick had a plaque

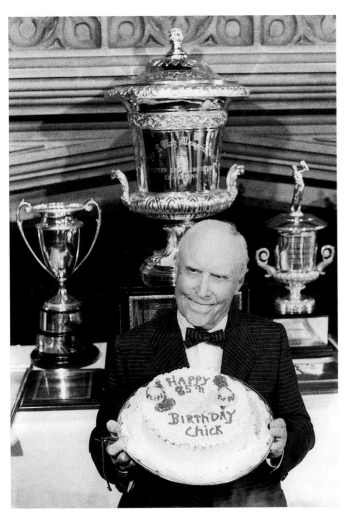

Chick, always ready to ham it up, poses with his 85th birthday cake for photographers in front of the WGA's trophies.

Evans was the recipient of honorary degrees or awards from every school with a formal Evans Scholars chapter, in this case, Marquette University.

golfer. By the time Atten was in high school, he had taken up the game and was playing with Evans. They became fast friends, and even competed in the same Western Amateur on a few occasions.

"I remember 1947 at Wakonda in Des Moines, it was the first day of qualifying. I was about to tee off, and Chick came up, scheduled a half-hour behind me. There were quite a few people around the first tee, and they were saying, 'Here comes Chick!' He was great with people. He should have been a politician."

Atten is quick to point out that while Chick Evans was like a father to him, Evans was not a saint. When he muffed a shot, he would get as mad as the next golfer.

Chick with Evans Scholars and Cincinnati-area WGA officials at Kenwood Country Club in 1962.

made and I'm sure it's still there, because the east end of Edgewater is still there (as the Robert A. Black public course)."

Away from golf, Evans dabbled in the financial markets without success, but made his niche as a milk salesman. As if it were a Hollywood script commissioned by Frank Capra, this career amateur—one who advocated college educations for caddies—would sell the most wholesome product on the market. And ice cream, too.

"He was with Beloit Dairy, the largest wholesale

dairy, and he got all the big accounts," said Atten, who joined Evans at the company in 1951. "Fields, the big hotels, all of those. He'd take the managers to lunch and he'd come back with the account. There was nothing to it."

Business was business, and Chick worked at it well past retirement age, but golf remained Evans' sporting passion until the end.

The day he turned 80, July 18, 1970, Evans fired an absolutely spectacular 79 at the Chicago Golf Club, where he had caddied in one U.S. Amateur and lost in

Jack Atten first caddied for Chick Evans, then competed in the same Western Amateurs.

the final of another. Seven-over-par, yes, but one-under-age!

"That's the best I've seen Chick play in 10 years," marveled Jim Miller, one of Chick's old pals, to *Chicago Today* golf writer Tommy Kouzmanoff, who set up the round and noted that Evans had made up for his loss of length off the tee with an uncanny short game.

Even after he ended his formal tournament career, Evans was a fixture at the Western Open, shaking hands, posing for pictures, talking with the pros, and always talking up the Evans Scholars Foundation.

While he never helped decide who would and would not get an Evans grant—he wanted others to handle that burden, not having the heart to turn someone down—he did all he could, even when his own finances were low, to encourage donations to the program.

In 1971, on "Chick Evans Day" at Indiana University, Evans played a full round on the Indiana course before a fund-raising dinner at which he was the honored guest. At one point during the day, he was asked, "What if you had to do it today? Would you turn pro now?"

July 2, 1969

Mr. Charles Evans, Jr. V.P.
SIDNEY WANZER & SONS, INC.
8 South Michigan Avenue
Chicago, Illinois 60603

Dear Chick:

Yes, I shall see you on July 18th and I want to tell
you that anytime I'm in your presence I'm not lessen-
ing my rank. You're a wonderful man, not only in
golf, for you've brought a lot of sunshine into many
lives and I'm proud to know you. There must be a lot
of boys grateful to you - boys who will go on in this
world to be fine citizens because of your charitable
soul.

I did play with Del Webb the other day and he used
that 48 inch driver and hit the ball a long way. It
cost me money; however, I'll not hold it against you.

I understand there will be a great crowd at your
dinner and I'm happy I shall be able to be there for
it will be a pleasure to be with you.

                    Regards,

                    Bob

BH:mh   Bob Hope

There aren't too many milk salesmen in Chicago with whom Bob Hope exchanged letters.

Evans took a few seconds, mulled it over, and complimented reporter Paul Borden for his query.

"That's a good question," he said. "I think what I'd do, I'd let them call me anything they want—pro, amateur, whatever. But I think I still would turn the money over for a scholarship foundation. There's nothing any better."

Evans' last round of golf ended on a high note. It was at Glen View Club in 1978. Playing with friends Ken and Harle Montgomery, Evans was 25 yards from the final green in two. Said Harle Montgomery, "Chick, let's see one of your patented chip shots."

Wrote Gordon "Joe" Ewen, a former WGA president and a close friend of Evans: "Chick smiled, took his wedge from the caddie, waggled briefly, and lofted a lovely pitch that bounced twice and disappeared into the cup. What a fitting finish to the golfing career of a man who gave far more to the game than he took from it."

Chick Evans died on Tuesday, November 6, 1979. He was 89. The memorial service for him the following week at Evanston's First Presbyterian Church was attended by several hundred Evans Scholars and Alumni, including the presidents of each chapter. Evans Scholar Alumnus and WGA Director Roger Mohr, a 1953 Marquette graduate, noted that Evans never wavered in his interest in the Scholars.

"Chick Evans liked nothing more than to hear about these successes, perhaps because they, more than his golf accomplishments, were his greatest contribution to the game of golf," Mohr said. "We know Chick was symbolic of the men—many of them here today—who made our education possible. But he was the man who started it all."

Yes, career amateur Chick Evans is in the PGA of America's Hall of Fame, not only for his on-course success, but for the Evans Scholars. Plus, Evans helped found the PGA of America in 1916.

In 1968, what is believed to be the putter Chick Evans used in winning the 1916 U.S. Open turned up in Los Angeles. Milwaukee's Frank Woodside (right) grabbed it and returned it to Evans with the help of Wisconsin Governor Warren P. Knowles at a fund-raiser.

ALUMNUS
ROBERT ALSTEEN

Robert Alsteen has heard the question before. He is still wary of the answer.

"I'd hate to guess where I'd be without the Evans Scholarship," he said. "The opportunity for the education, that's such a big ticket to the ball game." The ball game of life, of course.

Alsteen, who grew up in the Milwaukee area and caddied at North Hills Country Club, says he might have signed a pro baseball contract with the old minor-league Brewers, or perhaps earned a baseball scholarship at Texas had he not listened to the venerable Scottish pro at the country club.

"George Calderwood was very instrumental in my getting the scholarship," Alsteen recalled. "I didn't apply until July, after my senior year in high school. That's the rump meeting these days. And under today's criteria, I would have been borderline."

He won the scholarship and made the most of it. One of the first graduates from the Evans Scholar Chapter at Wisconsin, matriculating in 1958, Alsteen has been a success in business, notably in printing, and in life. He was also the first Scholar to ascend to the post of president of the Western Golf Association. Alsteen, a director since 1980, was WGA president in 1992-1993.

Well before then, in fact, when applying for the scholarship, he pledged to never forget who gave him the "ticket." He wrote: "If I am granted a scholarship, I will always remember what has been done for me. And I will try all through my life to help others, to show my appreciation."

Alsteen is most proud that he and his fellow Alumni have contributed to the program that has given so much to them. In recent years, the Alumni have written checks totaling more than $1 million annually. Alsteen, while he doesn't like to talk about it, has been very generous personally.

"Whatever I give back, it wouldn't be enough," he says. "I come from a pretty good family background, and my wife Janet and I, we enjoy doing this. I like to do it and not be in the limelight."

He prefers talking about his fellow Alumni and the prospects for the future.

Bob Alsteen was the first Evans Scholar to become the WGA's President.

"It's really a very young Alumni Association," he says. "We have nearly 7,000 Alumni, and 5,000 of them are just beginning to get into the mainstream of life." Alsteen believes that as the Alumni grow older and more secure in their own lives, their contributions to the program will steadily increase. That will help ensure the Evans Scholarships will remain on solid financial footing.

Bob Alsteen's energy would put a kid to shame. His activity seems to have increased since his term as president. Among other things, Alsteen has been a leader in the renovation of the Wisconsin Chapter

128

House—a house far larger than the one he first entered in the fall of 1954—and in the fortunes of the Northern Illinois Chapter. He wrote the check for that house. Wherever he goes in the Evans community, he finds the Scholars impressed that someone has cared enough to finance their education and takes a continuing interest in them.

"They're very appreciative," he says. "Appreciative to see people putting money on the line for their futures."

Alsteen, like all the Scholars of a certain age, had the opportunity to meet Chick Evans.

"To see the look on his face when he met with the Scholars, he knew he was on to something," he recalled. "And Mac McGuigan, he was our direct link to the Evans program and Western Golf. He would make the rounds of every chapter; he came around every quarter." And not just to check on grades and see that the floor was polished. McGuigan made sure the Evans program was about more than going to class.

"It's a requirement that every chapter has a philanthropic fund drive," Alsteen said. "We tell them, 'We expect you to put something back here.'"

In later life, the message is the same.

"I tell Scholars, 'If you have the finances, you've got to give back. Don't turn your back.'"

Those Scholars, present and future, owe Alsteen a pat on the back at the least. ❏

Jim Ashenden and Bob Alsteen, WGA Presidents in 1990-91 and 1992-93, respectively.

ALUMNUS ROBERT McMASTERS

Thanks to an Evans Scholarship, everything fell into place for Robert McMasters.

"What I wanted to do was go to school, get an education, play on the golf team, and after graduating, begin selling technical products," McMasters recalls. "That's exactly what I did."

McMasters might have gone to the University of Michigan anyway, or to Michigan State, on a golf scholarship. He played the game that well.

Or, if the golf scholarship didn't come through, there was Michigan Tech, located in the state's upper peninsula, near his grandfather's house. But the Evans Scholars program? McMasters didn't even apply until the July after he graduated from high school.

"The golf coach at Michigan, Bert Katzenmeyer, saw me in a junior tournament and asked if I had applied to Michigan, and told me about the Evans program," McMasters said. "I didn't know about it. My family didn't know about it. I came from a loving family, but we weren't tuned in. My club had no knowledge of the program, either."

McMasters found out he might be eligible for the scholarship by virtue of his many years of caddying at Red Run Golf Club in Royal Oak, Michigan, near Detroit. McMasters had started caddying at age eight, but he was unaware of the Evans program because it hadn't expanded yet to Michigan.

McMasters applied for and received the scholarship. He picked Michigan and joined the school's charter Evans Scholars class.

"If I got a scholarship today, I would have been the Lucky Strike extra," he kids.

As a golfer, McMasters was good enough to become the number one player and captain of the Wolverine team in 1955-56, his senior year in Ann Arbor. But the Evans grant assured him of more than a way to get into the classroom.

"Finding a place to sleep was the big thing," McMasters remembered. "It would have been a lot more difficult otherwise. Then, the housing part of the scholarship was worth more than the schooling."

There was also something else. The fellowship in the James Standish House was priceless.

"We started the chapter at Michigan," he said. "All of us living together helped in getting jobs. I got a job at the campus bookstore

Evans Scholar alumnus Bob McMasters was the WGA's President in 1996-97.

through the athletic department, and then got four or five jobs for others in the house. We networked. We bonded quickly.

"It gave me a chance to have a leadership role."

That's a role McMasters has always held, in school, as exemplified by his captaincy, and in the years since in business—the McMasters-Koss Company, formed with Michigan State Evans Alumnus Marty

Koss, sells seals, O-rings, and the like—and in his work with the WGA. A director since 1982, McMasters was the WGA's president in 1996 and 1997, the second Evans Scholar to hold the post.

Having a business rather than working for someone else, as McMasters did prior to 1977, has given him a chance to do something golf-related that involved more than putting a tee in the ground. What's more, he was able to do it close to home. He joined Red Run in 1974 and eventually became club president. He also moved up the ranks in the Golf Association of Michigan and was in line to become the GAM's president when the same post beckoned with the WGA.

"If you can't sell youth, education, and the work ethic, you might as well get out of the business," McMasters said of promoting the Evans

program. "It's a proven concept, it works and it's timeless."

McMasters, like almost all the Scholars from that era, knew Chick Evans, and stayed in touch with the legend.

"He looked after us kids on the golf teams," McMasters remembered. "He was the honorary starter at the Big Ten championship in 1956, and said when I came to the tee with my opponent (Minnesota Evans Scholar Tom Hadley), 'You can't tell me how good this feels to have two of my guys in the tournament.' Neither of us knew the other was an Evans Scholar."

"Chick sent me a nice note the day he was inducted into the World Golf Hall of Fame. I can't imagine why he thought of me on that day. I've got pictures of him in my office at home. He's with me all the time." ◻

Among the many Evans Scholars Alumni who contribute to the strength of the Evans Scholars Program are six WGA Directors who serve as officers of the Western Golf Association/Evans Scholars Foundation. From left, in front of WGA/ESF headquarters in Golf, Illinois, are: Dan Coyne, Roger Gordon, Roger Mohr, Bob Alsteen, Bob McMasters, and David Shaw.

12

HOGAN AND SNEAD

S am Snead and Ben Hogan. From the end of World War II through the mid-1950s, it was impossible not to think of one of those players without thinking of the other. Rivals with personalities as different as day and night, one with a natural swing, the other a master of swing mechanics, Snead and Hogan, alone and together, both symbolized and fueled the first postwar golf boom.

The Western Open was one of their great stages. Each won a pair of Western Opens in a five-year span immediately after the war. Snead's first Western Open title came in 1949 with a record-setting performance, a stunning 20-under-par shootout at Keller Golf Course in St. Paul, Minnesota. Hogan's win at Sunset

Sam Snead and Ben Hogan: genius born and genius developed.

Country Club near St. Louis in 1946 not only marked the return of the Western Open from the wartime hiatus, but at the time was considered his first major championship, a feat overlooked by most today.

The triumphs of the taciturn Hogan and ebullient Snead proved to be the Western Open's high-water mark for a decade. The Western Open championship, long considered one of golf's major titles, provided yearly thrills but was about to gradually lose its status as one of golf's revered majors even as the Western Golf Association expanded the Evans Scholars Foundation, building it from a local to a national institution.

In the 15 years from Hogan's win at Sunset to Stan Leonard's triumph at Western Golf and Country Club in Detroit in 1960, much changed in golf. The definition of the majors began to change markedly.

Television quickly grew from a novelty into a force. The distinction between club professional and touring professional grew. The touring professionals sought more control of their tournaments.

The WGA was affected by all of the above.

Consider, for instance, the Western Open's major tournament status. Today, the professional majors appear to be carved in stone, set there by everything from public opinion to tradition. However, the four majors—the Masters, U.S. Open, British Open, and PGA Championship—have not always been such an inseparable, highly esteemed foursome.

Byron Nelson won not only the Western Open in 1939, but the U.S. Open and North and South Open as well. All three championships were then considered majors.

Until the 1960s, few American professionals played in the British Open, the time and expense of the travel making the trip less than worthwhile. It was, on this side of the Atlantic, a curiosity more than a major, especially after Bobby Jones retired and Walter Hagen's star faded.

From its 1934 start, the Masters had special advantages, aside from Jones' presence, that made it more than another golf tournament, but it wasn't immediately considered a major.

The Western Open was a major championship. Other majors of the past included: the North and South Open at Pinehurst (although that title's status had faded even before Hogan won it twice), the New York area's Metropolitan Open and, in the eyes of some, the year's first tournament, the Los Angeles Open, and the World Championship at George S. May's Tam O'Shanter Country Club in Niles, Illinois.

The Met Open and North and South succumbed to rising purses. The big-money World disappeared at May's whim after a dispute with the PGA over control. The Los Angeles Open, the first tournament with a huge purse, goes on today, albeit usually played at Riviera Country Club, but as just another event, one with the name of a car maker having supplanted the traditional sobriquet.

The year 1939 is a good reference point in considering the Western Open's place in golf's firmament. Byron Nelson was in his ascendancy. He had won the Metropolitan Open in 1936 and the Masters in 1937. He went without a major in 1938, but in 1939, broke out by capturing the U.S. Open on the Spring Mill course of the Philadelphia Country Club, the Western Open at Medinah Country Club, and the North and South Open at Pinehurst. The triple vaulted him to the top of the profession, both in stature and monetary rewards.

"Had I won the PGA, it would have been considered a kind of grand slam," Nelson, runner-up to Henry Picard in the 1939 PGA's match-play final, said a few years

When this picture was taken at Augusta National in 1937, Sam Snead (left) was the hottest rookie in years, "Light Horse" Harry Cooper was still going strong and Ed Dudley was settling in as Augusta's head pro. All three won the Western Open in its days as a major. At right is Bobby Jones, whose Masters tournament at Augusta National grew in stature in the years following 1937.

ago. "One reason the Western was called a major was that we got a bonus (from equipment sponsors) for winning the (U.S.) Open, a bonus for the PGA, a bonus for the Western, and a bonus for the North and South."

One key to the respect shown the Western Open was obvious. It, like the U.S. Open, was administered by a golf association and was open to anyone in the world. Likewise, the PGA Championship, run by the professionals' own organization, immediately was considered a cut above the average tournament among professionals, its match-play format differentiating it from the U.S. and Western opens. And, while Jones was active and for years thereafter, the U.S. Amateur was at the level of the PGA, drawing national interest.

Summer was essentially reserved for the association championships, including the Canadian Open, administered by the Royal Canadian Golf Association.

As Nelson noted, Western Open winners would get bonuses from their sponsoring equipment manufacturer. They would also get national press and a place in history. Old PGA of America record books list the year-by-year details of the U.S. Open, PGA, Masters, and Western Open. Any other tournament results must be looked up under a player's biography.

That the Western Open's star began to slip just as the Masters moved up a notch was a product of synchronization rather than cause and effect.

When the Masters commenced in 1934, the WGA embarked on a series of decisions that resulted in the erosion of the Western Open's status as a major. At first, it was a matter of inferior geography. In 1934, the Western Open was played in Peoria, Illinois. In 1935, South Bend, Indiana, was the port of call. In 1936, Davenport, Iowa, was the destination.

Record crowds—62,300 for the week—attended the 1962 Western Open at Medinah Country Club, making the permanent return of the Western to Chicago a wise and lucrative decision.

That started a pattern that continued until the early 1950s. The USGA usually took its Open to a major city with a great course. The PGA, the same. The WGA too often went to lesser known courses in smaller cities because a course was available and a civic group was putting up the prize money. That practice escalated in Houston in 1940, when the Lions Club wrote $5,000 in checks, a Western Open record.

As a result, for every Medinah or Canterbury or Olympia Fields, there was a Miami Valley or Peoria or Davenport, fine courses that held dramatic championships—it took 108 holes for Harry Cooper to triumph over Ky Laffoon at Peoria in 1934—but nonetheless lacked the grandeur of a Medinah.

In 1951, for instance, the Quad Cities Civic Golf Association funded the $15,000 Western Open purse, and the championship visited Davenport for the second time in 15 years. The WGA and the group split the net profits.

Such decisions benefited the bottom line of the Western Open and the ever-expanding Evans Scholars Foundation—in 1951, overall receipts totaled $99,068.36, a record which enabled 94 Scholars to attend college. In the long-term, however, the Western Open's reputation suffered. The WGA, rightfully concerned with sending deserving caddies to college, became hostage to the whims of groups willing—or not willing—to financially support the Western Open. The consideration of what course the championship would be played on came second.

At the same time, the Masters began to grow in stature. The invitational concocted by Jones and Clifford Roberts made Augusta, Georgia, an attractive springtime playground for the top professionals. As the championship matured, Augusta National received worldwide fame for its Southern hospitality, the zealousness of its course manicuring, and the excitement produced on its beautiful yet bedeviling back nine.

The Western Open remained a major in name but began to receive less in-person coverage by the national media than the Masters, U.S. Open, or PGA.

That trend changed for a time after World War II, when larger metropolitan areas began to host the Western Open. St. Louis, with area businessman and well-connected premier amateur Hord Hardin doing much of the negotiating, welcomed the Western Open three times in eight years, starting in 1946 when Hogan won at Sunset. (Hardin, eventually a WGA director, played as an amateur in the 1953 Western Open. He would go on to serve as USGA president and eventually take the reins of Augusta National and the Masters.)

The championship went east to Buffalo in 1948 and west to Los Angeles in 1950 and San Francisco—at the picturesque Presidio course—in 1956. Still, there was the Western Open in Davenport again in 1951, and in 1955 the championship traveled to Portland, Oregon, at the time less than a metropolis.

If the sites selected allowed more people to be exposed to the Western Open and the professional tour by the 1950s, the professionals were becoming less attracted. The championship's purse sat still for years, while other, lesser tournaments awarded more and more money.

In the 1948 Western Open, when Hogan clobbered Ed "Porky" Oliver with an overwhelming victory in an 18-hole playoff at Brookfield Country Club, just outside of Buffalo, the Hawk took home $2,500 of the then-record $15,000

purse. That matched the third-largest purse of the year, behind only the $30,000 May put up for the All-American Open and $25,000 offered by the Reno Open. The Western Open's purse was underwritten by the J.N. Adam & Co. Sports Foundation, the philanthropic arm of Buffalo's big department store. In comparison, the Masters and U.S. Open each paid $10,000.

In 1954, the Western Open purse still was $15,000. Lloyd Mangrum toured Kenwood Country Club in Cincinnati with a cool 5-under-par 66 in the final round to force a sudden-death playoff with Ted Kroll, and then dropped a birdie putt for the win on the first overtime hole. He pocketed just $2,400. By then, George May's World Championship was offering the first $100,000 purse in golf, the Masters was at $33,500, and the U.S. Open, $23,280. Only nine tournaments paid less than the Western Open and one of them was the Mexican Open.

By 1960, when Stan Leonard won in Detroit, the Western's purse was just $25,000. Leonard earned

Presidio Golf Club, which hosted the 1956 Western Open, puts up a good argument for the Western Open's most spectacular site. It's certainly the only one with the Golden Gate Bridge as an attractive distraction.

Stan Leonard, at forty-six the oldest Western Open champion, earned just $5,000 for winning the 1960 championship.

$5,000. In comparison, Arnold Palmer collected $17,500 from an $87,050 purse at Augusta National for winning the Masters, and snagged $14,400 of the U.S. Open's $60,720 purse for coming from behind at Cherry Hills Country Club in Denver. In all, 16 of the 42 tour stops, including most of those surrounding the Western Open on the summer schedule, paid more than the Western. The week after the Western Open, the PGA Championship was worth $63,130.

The theory that the professionals would play in the Western Open because they knew the tournament benefited caddies proved incorrect. The lower purse made the Western an optional tournament among those touring professionals who, while they didn't have

to return home to a summer club job, nonetheless simply wanted a week off. The week to take off was the one with the smaller purse, never mind tradition.

In the 1950s, the tour went from part-time status in the summer to a full-time operation. There was a tournament nearly every week, sometimes two, and a season which once went from November to April then took time off before the summer titles were on the line, began to go year-round. Venerable status or not, Evans Scholars or not, the Western Open was no longer a must-play event.

It was different in 1946, when the WGA resumed the Open after a three-year wartime hiatus. At Sunset, 88 pros, many of them from the St. Louis area, and 87 amateurs played in the Western Open. No more than 20 of the professionals were regulars, and almost all of them had club jobs of one fashion or another. Even Hogan registered out of Pennsylvania's Hershey Country Club.

By the time he was through at Sunset, the course was in proverbial tatters. Short even for that time at 6,270 yards, Hogan opened with a 4-under-par 68, four strokes off Jim Ferrier's brisk pace. He tied Ferrier at 10-under 134 with a 66 on Saturday and went into Sunday's 36-hole finale—this was the final Western Open to schedule a 36-hole final day, incidentally—as the favorite.

Snead was out of the picture, having disqualified himself for having too many clubs in his bag after an opening-round 69. Nelson, three strokes back at 7-under 137, was a threat but wouldn't make a move. The other notables were farther back. It seemed to be Hogan against Ferrier.

By the start of Sunday's afternoon round, it was Hogan against the course and himself. His morning 5-under 67 opened a three-stroke lead on Lloyd Mangrum. Nelson was another shot back. Ferrier skied to a 74. On a chilly, rainy day, all Hogan had to do was hit fairways and greens and battle the flu he had been fighting all week.

He hit the fairways and the greens, and he got well in the process. A smooth 2-under 70 was good enough for a record-setting total of 17-under-par 271 and a four-stroke victory over Mangrum.

It was only that close because Mangrum had holed out from 100 yards on the home hole in the final round and Hogan had triple-bogeyed the par-4 17th. Hogan closed with a birdie, his 22nd of the championship to go with an eagle.

And what was he thinking about?

"Gee, I don't recall ever taking a seven before any place," said Hogan after receiving the J.K. Wadley Trophy.

His playoff win over Oliver at Brookfield two years later was so one-sided, even Oliver was shouting "Get in!" at Hogan's birdie attempts down the stretch. Hogan's 8-under 64 was a course record. He beat Oliver by nine strokes and became the first player to win the U.S. Open,

PGA Championship and Western Open— "the three major titles," according to the Associated Press writer at the scene—in the same year.

Programs from Ben Hogan's first Western Open win are priceless.

Snead, second or third in three of his first four Western Opens, reasserted himself at Keller Golf Course in St. Paul in 1949. The first public course to host the Western Open was torn apart by Slammin' Sam. His total of 20-under 268, constructed via four rounds in the 60s, has never been surpassed in the Western Open and has been equaled but once, by Chi Chi Rodriguez at Tam O'Shanter in 1964. Cary Middlecoff was four strokes behind as

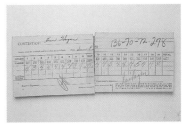

Ben Hogan's final-round scorecard from the 1941 Western Open.

Snead, cheered on by the record final round crowd of 15,000, became the first player to win the Masters, PGA, and Western Open in the same year.

Snead had a bigger fight on his hands at Los Angeles' Brentwood Country Club in 1950, even though he shared the lead after 18 holes. He fell off the pace at the halfway point, posted a 2-under 69 in the third to take a three-stroke lead, then lost that on the first 13 holes of the final round, and was tied with Dutch Harrison and Jim Ferrier, already in at 1-under 283.

A birdie on the par-5 14th put Snead back into the lead, and pars on the final four holes allowed him to repeat, the first to do so in the Western Open since Ralph Guldahl's three-year streak in the 1930s.

Ben Hogan and Sam Snead had won four of the five Western Opens since the end of World War II. A similar streak of superstar dominance wouldn't be seen again in the championship until the 1960s. By then, the Western Open was attempting to recover its former glory.

Crowds lined the ropes at the 1953 Western Open at the original Bellerive Country Club course in St. Louis.

Sam Snead, seen here in his rookie appearance in the 1937 Western Open, posted two victories, two seconds, and 14 top-10s in 20 appearances.

This rare on-course color photograph of Ben Hogan was taken during the Bing Crosby National Pro-Am at Pebble Beach, probably in 1948.

Ben Hogan with the winner's spoils from his forgotten 1948 Triple Crown: the trophies of the PGA Championship, United States Open, and Western Open.

SNEAD CONQUERS KELLER

Sam Snead jumped onto the golf scene in 1937.

Twenty under par! Even today, in an era of low scoring occasioned by the combination of advanced agronomy, technically advanced equipment, generous pin placements, and precise professionals, 20-under in a tournament is impressive.

Imagine, then, what a sensation it was in 1949, when Sam Snead scored 20-under 268 at Keller Golf Course in St. Paul, Minnesota.

Western Open scores had started to fall following World War II. Hogan won at Sunset Country Club near St. Louis in 1946 by scoring 17-under 271, setting records for total strokes and deepness into the red. The next year, at Salt Lake Country Club, Johnny Palmer did Hogan one better, scoring 18-under 270.

Now, with the field at Keller, the first public course to host the Western Open, low scores were expected again. Henry Ransom had won the 1946 St. Paul Open at Keller with 20-under 268. All that was standing between the players and bright red numbers on the scoreboard were par-72 Keller's 6,557 yards.

Snead was an obvious favorite. He already had won the Masters, the PGA Championship, and three other tournaments in 1949, doing so with a putter left in his locker accidentally by fellow pro Stan Kertes in Tucson. His opening-round 69 was two strokes off the pace, and he was still two strokes behind Lloyd Mangrum and Chick Harbert with 36 holes to play.

On Saturday, as over 10,000 fans flocked to the course, Snead turned serious, going out in 5-under-par 31 and coming home in 2-under 34 for 7-under 65, with a three-round total of 15-under 201. That matched the three-round record established by Hogan three years earlier and, more to the point, set a new 54-hole standard at Keller.

He would need a final-round 69 to match Johnny Palmer's total of 270, scored in 1947 at Salt Lake Country Club. A 68 would beat it.

Snead shot neither 69 nor 68. Snead shot 5-under 67, sprinting home with a 4-under 32 on the back nine to douse the hopes of hard-charging Cary Middlecoff, who closed with a 65.

Snead was 20-under-par. He was the Masters, PGA, and Western Open champion. And he was $2,600 richer.

The WGA was celebrating its 50th anniversary when the stylish sage of White Sulphur Springs, West Virginia, made a mockery of par. In the nearly 50 years since, nobody has matched Snead's under-par standard.

Chi Chi Rodriguez scored 268 at Tam O'Shanter in 1964, but Tam was a par-71 layout, and thus his score in relation to par was 16-under. Nick Price had a chance on Cog Hill's Dubsdread layout in 1993, when he lapped the field, but finished at 19-under 269. He birdied the 15th hole in the final round to get to 19-under, but couldn't get any lower.

Some day, Snead's scoring record will be surpassed, no matter how tough the course. Until it is, it is fitting that the lowest total in Western Open history was authored by the man with the sweetest swing. ◘

Snead's silky putting touch puts the wraps on his first-round 69 at the 1949 Western Open with Johnny Palmer and amateur Skee Riegel watching.

THE WESTERN OPEN AND TELEVISION

The latest equipment was used in 1951 to bring residents of the Quad Cities live television coverage of the Western Open over WOC-TV.

The WOC-TV mobile unit, about the size of a milk truck, seems lost among the trailers and telephone trucks behind the Davenport Country Club clubhouse in 1951.

A logical thinker would believe the appearance of the Western Open on television would hold great benefits for the touring professionals. The exposure and attendant publicity would make them more widely known. Offers to play exhibitions and earn easy money from endorsements would result.

Today, that obviously is the case. It has been for nearly 40 years, since budding agent Mark McCormack helped Arnold Palmer cash in on his newly found fame after winning the Masters and U.S. Open in the same season. Palmer, exciting in person and on the small screen, became not just a golfer, but a star.

In the beginning, not everybody saw the potential benefits. More than a few professionals viewed television as an unwelcome intruder.

Such was the case in 1950, when the Western Open was held at Brentwood Country Club in Los Angeles. There being no coast-to-coast connections in that era, the TV rights were picked up by KECA-TV, the local ABC station. Coverage of all four days was beamed to the Los Angeles basin via Channel 7.

Viewers did not see Ben Hogan, one of golf's leading stars. Recovering in 1950 from his near-fatal car accident, Hogan had planned to play in the Western Open. Essentially, he would be defending the championship he had won in 1948 but could not defend in 1949 due to the accident.

However, Hogan, Sam Snead and other leading players weren't pleased with the television coverage of the Los Angeles Open earlier in the season on KTTV. They hired a lawyer to look into the legality of the shows, and they wanted a share of the TV rights fee. Curiously, no such argument had been made the year before, when NBC televised the U.S. Open from Medinah Country Club. Also, George S. May's 1949 World Championship at Tam O'Shanter Country Club had been televised.

Snead showed up at Brentwood to defend his title, and did so successfully. Hogan stayed home. According to the May 31, 1950, issue of *Golf World,* Hogan wired the Los Angeles Junior Chamber of Commerce, the local sponsor, and said he wouldn't play if the Western Open was televised. Then he caught a case of the flu anyway and stayed home in Fort Worth, Texas. Jimmy Demaret, one of the most popular professionals and the Western Open's winner in 1940, also stayed away.

The absence of Hogan hurt the gate, and the championship endured a $1,300 deficit. WGA officials suggested that the successful televising of the event locally also had cut attendance, contributing to the deficit.

The red ink didn't stop local coverage of the Western Open. To name two examples, the 1951 championship was televised in the Davenport, Iowa, area, with action from all four days seen on WOC-TV, while Detroit's WXYZ was on hand for the 1957 Western at Plum Hollow.

With the exception of 1987, CBS Sports televised the Western Open from 1976 through 1998, bringing fans nationwide drama from Butler National and Cog Hill.

Portable cameras, unheard of in 1951, bring fans at home close to the action, as in this bunker shot by Ben Crenshaw during his 1992 victory.

When the Western Open returned to the Chicago area permanently in 1962, WGA officials set out to arrange a national TV deal, similar to those of the Masters, U.S. Open, PGA, and Bing Crosby National Pro-Am. The Crosby, because of its host and picturesque Pebble Beach setting, was the first nonmajor aside from May's World Championship to gain television access. The WGA succeeded in 1963, when the Western Open at Beverly Country Club was televised by entrepreneur Dick Bailey's Sports Network Inc., which also televised the NCAA Basketball Championship in the early 1960s.

In that era, both independent stations and affiliates of ABC, CBS, and NBC had plenty of air time to fill on weekends, so SNI's Western Open telecasts, with notables such as Chris Schenkel, Jim Simpson, Ray Scott, and Jim Thacker in the towers, were seen virtually everywhere. From the start, the Western Open was a hit on TV. The 1963 Western Open's 18-hole playoff between Arnold Palmer, Jack Nicklaus, and Julius Boros had fans glued to their seats, even though Palmer had wrapped up the title by the time TV coverage began on the 16th hole.

Over the years, the sophistication of the SNI coverage improved. In 1965, the Western Open was seen for the first time in color, a year the Masters and PGA were still seen in black-and-white. SNI's financial terms were so favorable, the WGA rejected a bid from CBS to televise the Western Open beginning in 1966.

In 1976, the Western Open would move to CBS, after a tumultuous series of conflicts between the WGA and PGA of America Tournament Bureau, which took over television rights administration in 1969.

In 1971, the PGA sold tournament rights en masse, but SNI, by then known as Hughes Sports Network—having been bought by billionaire Howard Hughes—didn't include the Western Open in its package, and the 1971 Western Open was not televised. Eleventh-hour negotiations with WGN-TV, SNI's Chicago outlet, for a local showing proved impossible because of the PGA's rights fee demands. A yearlong scramble resulted in WBBM-TV handling the 1972 Western Open, much as it had in 1962, when the championship returned to Chicago.

The Western Open was on Hughes Sports Network for two years beginning in 1973, and was scheduled to be televised by Hughes again in 1975, but the horrible thunderstorm that struck Butler National on Friday afternoon and forced a delay in the tournament prompted Hughes to cancel its coverage to avoid a Monday telecast.

That was the end of the Western Open's "off-Broadway" years. In 1976, CBS was on hand and would cover every Western Open through 1998 with the exception of 1987 (when ABC handled it, and nearly got flooded out in the process). Early-round coverage began with a second round telecast on the USA Network in 1983. By 1989, the first and second rounds were on USA. Beginning in 1999, under the PGA Tour controlled television contract, the Western Open moves back to ABC for at least four years. ◻

13

STRANAHAN ROLLS UP
HIS SLEEVES

Today, the notion that a golfer with enough talent to make money via his play would remain an amateur seems an anachronism, as distant a concept as a Western Union messenger on a bike or a nickel phone call across town. Even Jay Sigel, the most successful career amateur of the 1980s, finally turned professional at age 50.

Once upon a time, there was an era when excellent players remained amateurs because they wanted to, because they could.

Chick Evans never turned professional, serving instead as the founder and guiding spirit of the Evans Scholars Foundation.

Frank Stranahan, the most successful amateur of the postwar era.

Bobby Jones never turned professional, winning the Grand Slam as a part-time golfer and then retiring to write, make movie shorts on how to play golf, open a legal practice, and help create Augusta National and the Masters Tournament.

Then there was Frank Stranahan. In the years immediately after World War II, nobody made as important an impact on the amateur scene as Stranahan, and no amateur since Jones had as much success against the professionals.

Stranahan wanted to become the best golfer in the world and wasn't bashful about saying so.

The son of an automotive tycoon, blessed with good looks that would have taken him far in Hollywood, Stranahan was no rich kid on a spree. He meant what he said. Notably, he indulged in weight training and working out, which gave him distance off the tee and the stamina to play the 36-hole matches common to the era.

He experimented, changing his swing abruptly on two occasions, winning with not only his original swing, but with both subsequent versions.

And, because he could afford to, he played the professional tour almost exclusively, finding the competition—the likes of Ben Hogan, Sam Snead, and Byron Nelson, to name three—far superior to that on the amateur circuit.

Nobody in golf had ever lifted weights. Swing changes were generally gradual, small adjustments, not wholesale revisions. No amateur played virtually the entire tour circuit, and there had been those who could afford to.

Stranahan did all three.

Curiously, he never won the U.S. Amateur, the title he most coveted, though he was many times the favorite. But Stranahan won four Western Amateurs in six appearances, captured two British Amateurs, was twice runner-up in the British Open and also came in second in the Masters. He set an amateur scoring record in the 1947 Western Open that still stands. And he beat the professionals four times before finally turning pro himself.

"When you shoot for the moon, you pick up a lot of stars," Stranahan said in a reminiscence.

Nobody since Chick Evans had as much success in the Western Amateur. Nobody since has won the Western Amateur more than twice.

The most famous amateur of his day, he also played in—and won—a match in the 1946 Western Amateur against the most infamous amateur of the time.

The opponent was thirty-seven-year-old Smiley Quick, who came out of California as the U.S. Public Links champion of that year. Quick, who also owned an eclectic assortment of regional and local crowns, not only had plenty of game, as proven by his surprise 26th-place finish in the U.S. Open the same year, but an overabundance of raw toughness. A resident of Inglewood, California, a suburb of Los Angeles, Quick may or may not have been from the wrong side of the tracks, but he'd certainly visited there in his travels since growing up in Centralia, Illinois.

Stranahan, who turned twenty-four the first day of the championship, was the opposite of Quick, almost always cool where Quick was hot, considerably more polished where Quick was rough. But beneath Stranahan's usually placid, seemingly aloof exterior beat the heart of a fierce competitor, one tempered by his upbringing as much as Quick was influenced by his surroundings.

Frank Stranahan was fortunate enough to have been born into a wealthy family. His father, R.A. Stranahan, Sr., was chairman of the family-owned Champion Spark Plug Company. Frank Stranahan was often identified in stories of the day as a rich kid. He was also called "the Toledo strong boy," thanks to his working out and the fine physique that resulted.

Quick came to Northland Country Club in Duluth, Minnesota, site of the 1946 Western Amateur, in quest of a title and, he made sure all knew, Stranahan's scalp. For some reason, Quick disliked Stranahan.

A Navy veteran of battles in the Pacific Theater during World War II, Quick made references during the week to his war injury, an ugly leg wound. Another service-related injury was a broken left hand that had been caught under a pile of falling lumber.

Perhaps not knowing that Stranahan had served in the service as well, as a stateside flight instructor for three years, he needled Stranahan relentlessly whenever they crossed paths. They had played before in informal matches, and Quick had won four of five times. They had not yet met in a tournament.

Quick also tried to promote the rich vs. poor angle. And he did all this from the start of the championship, not knowing whether either would make the 64-man match-play field, though that was assumed. His talk soon had won the gallery over to his side.

Quick and Stranahan advanced to match play with ease, scoring 3-under-par 141s to share co-medalist honors with Marvin "Bud" Ward, a two-time Western Amateur and U.S. Amateur champion.

As it turned out, Stranahan and Quick met in the semifinals, a 36-hole double-round that would produce several verbal confrontations and a dramatic conclusion.

"He was a tough guy," Stranahan recalled in 1997.

Stranahan remembers much about Quick, including his 3-0 record over Quick in formal competition, a series of matches that began at Northland.

"He did some disgusting things," Stranahan remembered of that windy day in Duluth.

The match started on a unfriendly basis, without a

For Frank Stranahan, practice made perfect.

birdie putts of 42 and 16 feet. But the gallery, almost exclusively in favor of Quick at the start of the match, had started to turn on the sixth, and it was Quick's fault.

After Quick sank his 42-footer on No. 6, he said to Stranahan as Frank addressed his five-foot birdie putt, "All your millions won't help you now."

Stranahan missed.

Loud enough for Stranahan to hear, Quick said, "That's the worst choke putt I've ever seen."

Quick led 2 up at the morning turn, and still had a 1-up lead on the 15th green, where tempers flared again. Stranahan bunkered his approach on the par 4, then knocked a sand wedge 10 feet past the pin. His par putt ran 18 inches past the hole, where he marked only after Quick, waiting to attempt a four-foot par putt to win the hole, made him do so.

Here was a chance for Quick to apply the spurs. First, though, he conceded Stranahan his bogey putt by picking up his coin and throwing it at him. Then Quick managed to catch himself with the spur, missing the par putt to halve the hole.

They also halved the 16th, but Stranahan won the 17th and went to lunch even.

The duo traded the first two holes of the afternoon round, halved the third, and Stranahan won the fourth to go 1 up. Quick figured to even the match on the par-3 fifth when Stranahan missed the green, but wanted to make sure. After Stranahan got on the green with his chip, Quick began to whistle. It wasn't a songbird's whistle, but rather a close-to-quiet whistle, one Bill Carlson of the *Minneapolis News* termed "nonchalant." Stranahan knew what was up and was upset. He missed his putt and the match was even again.

Quick would win the seventh and eighth holes when Stranahan was wayward off the tee and led 2 up at the final turn. Then, his game began to deteriorate. Stranahan won the 10th with a bogey, lost the 11th, but won the 12th. He was 1 down with six holes to play, and

handshake on the first tee, but the first major point of friction came on the fifth green.

Stranahan, doing his best to ignore Quick, refused to concede an 18-inch putt for a halve on the par 3, then walked off the green before Quick could hole out.

That prompted this verbal joust from Quick: "From here in, boy, I'm going to put the spurs to you."

"You'll have to," Stranahan said.

"With that golf swing of yours, I wonder if I will," Quick retorted.

Quick delivered, winning the next two holes with

Smiley Quick, Frank Stranahan's nemesis, notably in the 1946 Western Amateur.

evened the match with a birdie on the par-5 14th when Quick three-putted for the second time in three holes.

Now they marched in lockstep down the final holes, Stranahan ignoring Quick's whistling on the 18th to hole a difficult 10-footer for an up-and-down par that assured extra holes. It had been emotional and tense golf, but it hadn't been great. Both Stranahan and Quick went around par-72 Northland in 73 in the morning and 76 in the afternoon.

The sudden death playoff was hardly anticlimactic. The sun, absent much of the day, was out now, and it was boiling. After a pair of regulation pars by both players, Stranahan hit the rough off the tee on the uphill third hole, then hit a low punch to within 12 feet of the pin. Quick was short of the green with his second, then chipped to three feet. He needed that for par. Stranahan could win with a birdie, a sidehill putt

that broke to the left.

Quick wasn't whistling now, just watching. He saw the ball disappear and heard a roar from the gallery of perhaps 3,000. Stranahan, after 8 1/2 hours and 39 holes, had won the match and the gallery. *Chicago Tribune* golf writer Charlie Bartlett wrote of the hand-shake between the two that it "would not qualify either as a loyal member of any lodge or fraternity, but it will suffice until they meet again."

In the other semifinal, Ward was easily dispatching George Victor by a 5 and 4 margin. When he heard of Quick's antics, he told Stranahan, "That's the most disgraceful thing I ever heard of."

With the perspective of over 50 years, Stranahan says of Quick now, "I always liked him. But he did some terrible things. He lost the gallery because of that."

The next day, Stranahan was forced to the 38th hole by Ward before triumphing via a par in a match devoid of controversy but filled with sublime golf. Both players were 7-under-par for the regulation two loops, Stranahan winning with an up-and-down par on the second extra hole.

The 1946 Western Amateur was, aside from the North and South captured earlier in the year, Stranahan's first major amateur title. The wins would come with regularity, especially in the Western Amateur, for a number of years. He would lose the 1947 Western Amateur to Ward when the pride of Spokane, Washington, chipped in from here, there and everywhere in the final at the Wakonda Club in Des Moines, Iowa. But he came back to capture the 1949 edition, and take back-to-back Western Amateur titles in 1951 and 1952.

Stranahan's 1951 triumph at South Bend Country Club is notable for the history of his opponent. WGA records have Stranahan beating James Blair III, which is technically correct. But Blair was better known to one and all as Jim Tom Blair, the son of Missouri's lieu-tenant governor and Stranahan's caddie in 1946 when he won the Kansas City Open.

"He'd thumbed his way to Kansas City," Stranahan recalled. "He was just a little kid, just 14, but by the time I saw him in South Bend, he was 6 foot 3 inches tall, 230 pounds, and he was a real good player."

No matter. Stranahan administered a 7 and 6 whip-ping. The following year at Exmoor Country Club in Highland Park, Illinois, Stranahan beat Blair in the quarterfinals, en route to a final match win over Harvey Ward, Jr. in which he never trailed.

For Stranahan, four Western Amateur titles were enough. He never played in the Western Amateur again, concentrating on playing the professional tour as a warm-up for his chase of the U.S. Amateur title. After turning pro, he played in the Western Open through 1964. His best finish was a tie for seventh at Red Run Country Club near Detroit in 1958.

"The Western was always my favorite golf association," Stranahan said. "I thought I was treated so much better with them. Things happened with the USGA, but the WGA, I really liked."

For all his amateur success, his WGA and R&A titles, and his wins over professionals, Stranahan didn't plan to remain an amateur as long as he did, nor did he want to. It was his quest to win the U.S. Amateur, and the wishes of his father and mother, that kept him from taking a check for the last four summers of his amateur career.

"I always told my dad I wanted to be a professional," Stranahan said. "He said, 'No, you can't.' And my mom didn't want me to. I finally told my dad I would turn pro after the 1954 U.S. Amateur in Detroit, regardless.

"The pros didn't treat me properly. Snead would say, 'I'm glad Frank won, because I get all the money.' If I turned pro, I'd be able to play at their own game and take money out of their pockets."

Ironically, even after turning pro, Stranahan could not receive purse money for six months, thanks to PGA of America rules in force at the time. He won twice as a professional, including the Los Angeles Open of 1958. His best finish on the money list, 15th, also came in 1958.

Success in investments eventually took him from the tournament scene, but his interest in fitness never waned. Rather than play golf, he ran marathons.

Never, though, did he have a tougher track to master than the obstacle course created by Quick in the 1946 Western Amateur.

A massive gallery follows Frank Stranahan (dark shirt) and Jim Tom Blair in the 1951 Western Amateur final at South Bend Country Club.

GEORGE S. MAY AND THE WGA

WGA President James M. Royer, Tam O'Shanter impresario George S. May, and WGA official W.F. Souder congratulate each other on another donation to the Evans Scholars Foundation.

It's hard to say if Bill Veeck was the George S. May of baseball, or if George S. May was the Bill Veeck of golf.

Whichever is correct, they were birds of a promotional feather, attracting attention to their game by promoting it like nobody had before.

Memories of Veeck's two stints as owner of the White Sox, during which visitors to Comiskey Park were introduced to exploding scoreboards and major-leaguers in shorts, are still strong, but those of May have receded somewhat. Owner of a Chicago-based management consulting business, May loved golf so much he bought the Tam O'Shanter Country Club in Niles, Illinois, a suburb just north of Chicago, and applied his management efficiency principles to it.

This was the foundation: "You've got to spend money to make money."

May did both. In 1941, to draw attention, and members, to Tam, May started a golf tournament and unabashedly called it the All-American Open. Byron Nelson beat Ben Hogan in the inaugural and won again in 1942.

Then, in 1943, when virtually no tournament golf was played, May not only held the All-American, but added an event called the World Championship of Golf to his schedule. War or no war, May was going to put on a show.

And what a show. May had professional and amateur divisions for men and women in both tournaments. He invited champions from across the globe to the World Championship.

To make sure spectators would be on hand, May hired airplanes to fly over the Loop and drop free tickets on the unsuspecting public. He charged those without free passes a dollar to get in and made money on the food and beer they bought.

May's galleries were huge, often over 20,000 for the final round in an era when 7,500 was a mob.

May's purses were equally huge. In 1949, when the Western Open's purse was $15,000 and the U.S. Open paid just $10,000, May paid a total of $60,900, with $20,000 in the All-American men's division, another $4,000 in the women's division, and $35,200 the following weekend for the men's side of the World Championship, with $1,700 more for the ladies.

He also spent about $55,000 in advertising, including a live telecast of the World Championship on the Dumont Network, which stretched from Chicago and St. Louis to Boston and New Haven.

And his purses went up and up. In 1953, when Lew Worsham's 104-yard wedge shot won the World Championship, May ran onto the green in celebration, then announced that the $25,000 first prize Worsham had just won would be doubled to $50,000 the following year, with another $50,000 to the winner for 50 exhibitions. Bob Toski cashed in on that.

Eventually, May's purses so dwarfed the rest of the professional tour, the PGA of America stopped considering them as official money, because they threw the season-long money list out of whack.

That was the start of several disputes with the PGA over how May ran his tournaments. Finally, after the 1957 tournaments, May and the PGA split, which meant there were no tournaments in 1958. The purses for the tournaments that replaced May's for those two weeks were $41,000 smaller.

In 1949 May also began to aggressively promote the Evans Scholars Foundation to his membership. The members responded each year by enrolling in the Bag Tag program almost en masse. Then May and wife, Alice, would match the membership's donation. In the first 10 years, the Tam O'Shanter/May family contribution totaled nearly $120,000.

May was a WGA director from 1956 to 1960, and after his death in 1962, the connection between May and the WGA became even stronger. Alice May offered the WGA Tam O'Shanter's massive championship trophy to serve as an overall trophy for the Western's three championships, provided that the winners of the All-American and World tournaments were not forgotten.

The offer was gratefully accepted, and a base nearly as large as the trophy itself was fashioned. The sterling silver trophy, always a show-piece, became news itself when it was stolen in 1980, when silver prices were at their peak. It never turned up.

Next, Alice May offered the Tam O'Shanter course for the Western Open. It was played there in 1964 and 1965. For a time, the WGA also considered purchasing Tam O'Shanter, using the course as a perma-nent site for the Western Open, Amateur, and Junior while also running the country club operation. A feasibility study was made, but no action was taken.

At the same time, reversals in the George S. May Company's over-seas operation caused a need for quick cash, and Tam O'Shanter was sold to developers, effective after the 1965 Western Open. A small part of the original course was retained and turned into a nine-hole munic-ipal layout. The rest of the one-time tournament showplace became an industrial park. ◘

Alice May and WGA President Tom King inspect the George S. May Memorial Trophy prior to the 1964 Western Open at Tam O'Shanter Country Club.

THE TEAM TANGO

The big scoreboard for the First International Four-Ball Championship. An artistic success but financial flop, there was only one more.

I n the mid-1920s, the WGA settled on a schedule of three championships—the Open, Amateur, and Junior—and except during World War II, they were played without fail.

In 1954, a new tournament was added to the menu, a concoction called, somewhat presumptuously, the First International Four-Ball Championship. Held at the Highland Golf and Country Club in Indianapolis, site of the 1926 Western Open, the Four-Ball featured two-man teams in a match-play elimination format.

The idea of a team championship had been considered by the WGA for a couple of years before Highland came forward to host the event as the centerpiece of its 50th anniversary celebration. Expectations were high.

In actuality, Highland's Hoosier hospitality aside, the championship was something of a bust. Amateur golf's heyday was passing. It was the professional tour that was growing. Even Frank Stranahan, who skipped the Four-Ball, was about to turn pro.

Hillman Robbins (left) of Memphis and Eddie Merrins of Meridian, Mississippi, captured the 1955 Four-Ball title the same year they battled for the Western Amateur title. (Merrins won in 37 holes.)

When the Four-Ball was announced, Highland officials said they hoped for 300 two-man teams to try to qualify for the 64 match-play slots. Only 47 teams entered, with 42 playing, making the stroke play simply an exercise in who would get first-round byes.

The championship was won by the team of Dale Morey of Martinsville, Indiana, a member of Highland, and singer Don Cherry of Wichita Falls, Texas. They beat Chicago's Art Hoff and Jack Culp 6 and 5 in the 36-hole final, knocking 10 strokes off par in the 36 holes they played. For the week, the Morey-Cherry team was 46 under over 156 holes. They were clearly the best duo on the field. Morey was winner of the 1953 Western Amateur and the runner-up in the U.S. Amateur. Cherry won the 1953 Canadian Amateur winner and was co-medalist in the 1952 Western Amateur's stroke-play qualifying.

Their effort made the Four-Ball, in which the play was described as "spectacular" by Wayne Fuson of the *Indianapolis News,* an artistic success. It was not, however, a financial winner, losing $1,061. Nor did it attract national attention.

One outing does not make a success or failure, the WGA board concluded in deciding to hold the International Four-Ball again in 1955. First, however, the name was changed to the Western Amateur Best-Ball Team Championship. The date was shifted from July to October in an effort to increase participation. Switching the format from match-play after stroke-play qualifying, which took seven days to play, to four rounds of stroke play, was also expected to boost the field.

Memphis Country Club took the revamped event and saw the team of hometown favorite Hillman Robbins and Eddie Merrins of Meridian, Mississippi, triumph with a score of 272, a stroke ahead of Jim Mangum of Shreveport, Louisiana, and future tour professional Johnny Pott of Brookhaven, Mississippi. There were 46 teams in the field.

Said WGA Vice President Cameron Eddy at the annual meeting that December, "The field, although not large, was studded with name players, with the South predominating in the number of contestants."

Left unsaid was that the Best-Ball was a money-loser again, that it wasn't pulling in all the name amateurs, that it didn't draw a huge gallery—some 1,000 watched the final round—and that it wasn't a headline-grabber outside of Memphis.

With the 1956 calendar featuring the traditional Western Amateur slated for Nashville and the Western Open set for October in San Francisco, there was no room for the fledgling championship on the WGA's autumn docket. The Best-Ball was announced as suspended for 1956. It never was revived, joining the Marshall Field Trophy, Tom Morris Trophy, Olympic Cup, and Western Senior Amateur as a former WGA competition. ◘

CHAPTER

14

THE RETURN HOME –
TO OPEN ARMS

arshall Dann, the Western Golf Association's executive director in 1960, remembers the telephone call as if it came yesterday.

"It was New Year's Eve, 1960, and Scioto Country Club was on the phone," Dann recalled. "We had an agreement with Scioto to hold the 1961 Western Open there, through James Rhodes, a club member who would eventually become governor of Ohio. Now they were calling and said, 'We have to withdraw.'

"They didn't say why. I think they got scared of raising the money."

Celebrities such as Anita Bryant helped team up with Chick Evans to publicize the return of the Western Open to Chicago in 1962.

Raising the money to pay the purse and to finance tournament operations was the club's job in that long-ago era. In return, the host club shared in tournament profits.

Now it was Dann who, if not scared, was at least concerned. He had joined the WGA in 1959, replacing Milt Woodard, who left after 10 years to join the front office of the fledgling American Football League. Dann, like Woodard and John Kennan before him, had been a sportswriter. Dann had covered golf and hockey for the *Detroit Free Press* and had covered the several Western Opens held in the Detroit area in the 1950s.

Suddenly, as 1960 became 1961, the WGA had to find a new site for the Open, its oldest, most prestigious and most visible championship. The dates were June 22-25, and they weren't going to change.

In his nearly 30 years as executive director, Marshall Dann saw the Western Open grow from a vagabond championship financed by clubs to a Chicago-based showcase with year-round WGA guidance.

The WGA scheduled an emergency meeting for February 11, giving Dann six weeks to find a club interested in the 1961 Western Open. After talking with 37 clubs in 21 cities, he found several receptive, of which the most attractive was Blythefield Country Club in Grand Rapids, Michigan. With little other choice, the WGA executive committee voted to accept Blythefield's bid. For the first time in years, the financial risk of staging the championship would rest on the WGA's shoulders.

Scioto's withdrawal came as professional golf was changing from a money sport to a big-money sport. Blythefield's coming forward was most welcome. With purses on the rise and the financial gamble becoming more dangerous, however, the club's insistence on not being responsible for the finances would become the

norm for future Western Opens.

Dann remembered that at the February meeting one board member suggested suspending the playing of the Western Open after Blythefield. The member argued that finances dictated such a decision and that conducting professional golf tournaments and sending caddies to college were becoming mutually exclusive endeavors.

That drastic step would never be taken. Previously, Clifford Domin of Medinah Country Club had intimated that his club, absent from the big-time tournament scene since the 1949 U.S. Open, might be convinced to host the Western Open. Domin, the chairman of the WGA's Tournament Sites Committee, was in a position to make sure Medinah's position was known to the WGA and viceversa.

The decision to stay in the professional golf championship business was made with the confidence that at least one of Chicago's leading clubs would be willing to step forward as the host club the following year. It was decided, on May 8, 1961, that the Western Open would no longer travel the country, but would stay in the Chicago area. With the WGA headquartered in nearby Golf, with the majority of the directors in the area, and with hands-on operation now necessary, logic dictated that the Open move around to those Chicagoland clubs willing to host it. That was step one.

The Future Open Committee, headed by former WGA President Stanley McGiveran, announced its belief the Western Open should continue, then addressed the long-standing failure of the WGA to raise the purse at the same pace as other major championships. The purse would have to be raised to "regain lost prestige," McGiveran said. That was step two.

With the Western Open anchored in Chicago, the WGA now could oversee the entire tournament operation, including local media relations and course preparations. That was step three.

Success seemed assured, if attendance at tournaments elsewhere was any indicator. Galleries thronged to Augusta National annually for the Masters and filled Cherry Hills for the 1960 U.S. Open. Professional golf was booming, thanks in part to the popularity of Arnold Palmer, the game's first television star. With the Western Open still a prestigious stop on the golf calendar, the majority of the WGA's officers believed the championship could generate significant revenue

With courtesy cars for players came courtesy license plates.

for the scholarship program if it were held in the Chicago area.

Then McGiveran announced that not only was Medinah ready to sign up for 1962, but that Beverly Country Club was willing to sign a contract to host the 1963 Western Open. With that, the executive committee voted unanimously to continue the tournament's sponsorship.

The Western Open was not only off the chopping block but was poised to become more vibrant than ever. Soon Alice May, George S. May's widow, informed the WGA it could hold the Western Open at Tam O'Shanter whenever needed. Olympia Fields and Midlothian also became interested. It was clear that the Western Open wouldn't lack for a site.

"I even had one meeting where Beverly, Midlothian, Medinah, and Olympia Fields were all represented," Dann recalled. "They said they'd all hold one and they'd agree on the sequence."

Arnold Palmer, Julius Boros, and Jack Nicklaus approach a par 3 during their 1963 Western Open playoff at Beverly Country Club.

The anchoring of the Western Open in the nation's hottest golf market had several salutary effects on the entire WGA/Evans operation, not the least of which was the increased media attention, first in Chicago and then nationally, that the championship received. By 1963, the Western Open was on national television for the first time, the result of a three-year deal between the WGA and SNI, the leading syndicated sports telecaster. Finally, the Western joined the U.S. Open, Masters, PGA, and British Open on America's TV screens.

The exclusively-in-Chicago policy also made repeat ticket sales possible. Fans who came out once to see a favorite would come out again the next year, and while attendance fluctuated from year-to-year, depending on the weather and the quality of the field, crowds gradually increased.

Additionally, it became possible to begin a pro-am fund-raiser on the day before the Western, with all proceeds earmarked for the Evans Scholars Foundation. Wednesday, seen as a final tune-up by the pros, and a not altogether serious one, became a most important day in generating additional tournament proceeds.

Finally, the Western Open in Chicago meant that a great event and a city's savvy fans would remain together for good. And from the start, the gallery got

its money's worth. In 1962, many thought just walking around Medinah Country Club's grounds, punctuated by the most amazing clubhouse in golf, was worth the price of admission. As it turned out, the golf was also championship caliber from the start.

Jacky Cupit, hardly the biggest name in the field, was in front, either alone or with a partner, for the final 54 holes. He pulled away from leading challenger Billy Casper with birdies on the par-4 15th and par-3 17th to escape "the Monster" with a total of 3-under-par 281, a two-stroke victory and the first-place purse of $11,000 from the total payout of $55,000. Both money figures were records and both would be surpassed in future years, as WGA officials made good on their pledge to revive the Western Open in every way.

In terms of excitement, the 1962 Chicago-area renewal had nothing on the following year. The gallery at Beverly watched perennial runner-up Fred Hawkins dominate the first 36 holes, then fall back as fifty-one-year-old Sam Snead and crowd favorite Arnold Palmer took the lead going into the final round.

After the 72nd hole had been played, Palmer, who had won the 1961 Western at Blythefield, was still in front, but not by himself. This time he was joined by rising star Jack Nicklaus, via a final-round 5-under 66, the low round of the championship and, through a 67, veteran Julius Boros. There would be a playoff. And it would be an 18-hole playoff—the last one in Western Open history—one pitting Boros, the reigning U.S. Open champ, against Palmer, who had an Open, two British Opens, and three Masters crowns to his credit along with the Western title, and Nicklaus, who had proved his mettle a year earlier by defeating Palmer in the U.S. Open playoff at Oakmont.

This was what the Western Open was supposed to be about, the big names fighting it out down the stretch. And it would get better. A crowd of 10,200 poured through Beverly's gates on July 30, 1963, for the 12:30 p.m. tee off, proving once again that nobody works in Chicago when golf beckons.

Normally in that era, half the playoff proceeds went to the contestants, on top

Medinah Country Club's rococo structure dominates the center of the grounds.

Jacky Cupit bites his lip mulling over his victory speech while 1962-63 WGA President William F. "Fritz" Souder, Jr. (right) introduces Cupit as the 1962 Western Open champion.

his second Western Open title in three years.

Palmer's triumph, combined with Nicklaus' playoff presence, set the tone for the championship in the 1960s. Invariably, the biggest names in golf would rise to the top by the end of the week.

The following year at Tam O'Shanter, Juan "Chi Chi" Rodriguez met Palmer's final round charge with one of his own, blistering par with a total of 16-under 268 to edge Arnie and his Army, which turned out several platoons, by one. Nicklaus tied for third, with Billy Casper among those in sixth.

It would be Casper's turn next, and often after that. He took the 1965 Western Open at Tam by two strokes, then won the 1966 edition on Medinah No. 3 by three, the first back-to-back winner since Snead in 1949 and 1950. Big Billy, whose diet of buffalo meat might have re-endangered that species for a while, scored 270 at flat and open Tam, and 283 at hilly, tree-lined Medinah.

The Western Open was in the middle of a great run of champions. In 1967, Jack Nicklaus earned a place for his name on the Western Open's J.K. Wadley Trophy, playing the last three rounds in 11-under to beat Doug Sanders by two strokes at Beverly. The following year, Nicklaus threw a pair of 6-under 65s on the board at Olympia Fields to win by three. And in 1969, while the Cubs swooned, Casper rolled, scoring a four-stroke victory at Midlothian.

Casper played well at Midlothian, the oldest course the Western Open had been played on since the championship's early days. The course was basically the same in 1969 as it had been in 1914, when Walter Hagen beat Chick Evans by a stroke in the U.S. Open. When the Western Open returned to Midlothian in 1973, Casper won his fourth Western Open title, holding off Hale Irwin and Larry Hinson by a stroke.

By 1973, however, the Western Open's traveling days were ending. Several years of private talks had culminated in the building of a championship golf course in Oak Brook, one designed specifically to be the Western Open's permanent home.

of the regular purse. But early on Sunday evening, down in Beverly's locker room, Boros said, "Who needs tomorrow's money? It's honor enough to be in the playoff. I'm going to suggest to Jack and Arnie that we donate our share to the Evans Scholars fund." Naturally, Nicklaus and Palmer went along, enriching the Evans fund, it was estimated, by an extra $15,000 or so.

The donation was announced at the first tee. Then Palmer went out in 3-under 33, led by four strokes after 10 holes, only to see Boros tie him with a par on the 15th. Nicklaus couldn't make a move and, in fact, all three players moved backward, thanks to the diabolical 17th, a par-3 with one of mankind's most severely sloped and well-bunkered greens.

Nicklaus, two behind Palmer, three-putted it for a bogey 4. Boros, who had missed the green, chipped on and then three-putted for a double-bogey 5. That allowed Palmer, who was bunkered, a slight bit of breathing room. He got on the green, then two-putted for a bogey 4 and a one-stroke lead on Boros.

It was hardly picturesque, but it stood up when he and Boros parred the par-5 18th. Arnie had captured

Jack Nicklaus, Arnold Palmer, and Julius Boros shake hands before their 18-hole playoff to decide the 1963 Western Open.

The standard, and Arnie's sly smile, tell the story of the 1963 playoff.

Billy Casper won the first of four Western Opens by sinking putts like this at Tam O'Shanter in 1965.

THE KING AND HIS ARMY

It never fails. Find Arnold Palmer on a golf course, and autographs result.

Arnold Palmer arrived upon the Western Open scene already knowing how to win.

When he teed it up in the 1955 Western Open at the Portland Golf Club in Oregon, he was just nine months removed from his triumph in the 1954 U.S. Amateur. He quickly served notice that he would be a force in the professional game as well, scoring 6-under-par 66 in the second round of the Western Open. Palmer finished tied for 16th, a dozen strokes behind winner Cary Middlecoff, but he had set the stage

for better performances in the years to come.

That, in fact, is an understatement. Arnold Palmer, who broke into the professional winner's circle at the Canadian Open seven weeks after his showing in Portland, finished in the top nine in his next seven Western Open appearances. As he dominated the professional golf scene generally, he also dominated the Western Open for nearly a decade, helping to draw some of the biggest crowds in the championship's long history.

Invariably, Arnie was near or in the lead. In 1959 at the Pittsburgh Field Club in Fox Chapel, not too far from his home of Latrobe, Palmer was in the chase all week, leading outright at the halfway point and deadlocked with Joe Campbell after 54 holes.

Alas, the hometown crowd which had been rooting him on went home disappointed, for after Mike Souchak's closing 5-under 65 on the 6,625-yard layout had been posted, Palmer came to the par-3 18th needing a par to tie and a birdie to win.

He earned neither, settling for a bogey after failing to get up and down from a greenside bunker. It wasn't the bunker shot that hurt, but the missed 2-footer for par after a successful explosion.

As always, though, Palmer had given the crowd a thrill, and two years later, he gave himself one. He jumped out to a share of the lead with Al Geiberger in the first round of the 1961 Western Open at Blythefield Country Club and never fell out of that lofty spot. By the time 72 holes had passed, it was Arnie alone on top, able to add the Western Open title to the Masters, U.S. Open, and a large number of lesser crowns.

He annexed his 27th professional title by holding off the challenge of forty-nine-year-old Sam Snead, already ageless in 1961, who finished two strokes behind Palmer's total of 13-under 271. He wowed the gallery of 14,600 in the process. And, typically, he expected a little more of himself.

"I figure I missed about 15 birdie putts, but I'm satisfied," Palmer, who made 18 birdies along the way, said after accepting the J.K. Wadley Trophy.

A fortnight later, he used his success in the Western Open as a springboard to his first British Open title. And while he couldn't repeat in the 1962 Western Open on Medinah's famed No. 3 course, finishing seven strokes behind winner Jacky Cupit, he enjoyed the view. Arriving at the spacious west suburban club via helicopter, Palmer said, "Now that's the way you should lay out a golf course—and keep it."

The next year, with the Western Open, now anchored in the Chicago area, at Beverly Country Club on the southwest edge of the city, Palmer bounced back from an opening round of 2-over 73 to claw his way into the thick of the chase. Six strokes back after the opening salvos, Arnie was tied with Snead, even more ageless at fifty-three, with a round to play following two straight 4-under 67s on the Donald Ross creation.

Even more drama was in store for Sunday's final round. With a national television audience watching, Snead faded. Charlie Sifford made a run, then fell back. U.S. Open champion Julius Boros scored a 67 to finish at 4-under 280. Jack Nicklaus, just a week removed from annexing the PGA, matched him. Palmer stumbled with bogeys at the 15th and 16th—errors caused by comprehensive hooks into Beverly's heavily treed rough—and signed for the third 280 of the afternoon, forcing a playoff.

It would be an 18-hole playoff and, as fortune had it, the last such exercise in Western Open history. The tradition ended with a great cast, one that drew a gallery of 10,200 to Beverly on a sultry Monday, the majority ready to support Palmer.

The extra session hardly went according to form. Palmer, the great closer, went out in 3-under 33, with Boros at 36 and Nicklaus struggling to a 37. It would not, however, be a rout. Boros battled back by bagging a brace of birdies. Nicklaus warmed up. And Arnie, after a 6-iron to five feet on the par-3 10th for a cast-iron bird, cooled off. He failed to get up and down from a bunker at

Big Mike Souchak lifts the J.K. Wadley Trophy with ease after beating Arnold Palmer in the 1959 Western Open at the Pittsburgh Field Club.

It was all smiles after Arnie beat Sam Snead to earn his first Western Open crown at Blythefield Country Club in 1961.

the 13th, then three-putted from 50 feet on the stout par-4 15th.

Crowd favorite Arnie was tied with Boros with three holes to play, while Jack was two strokes in arrears. After the trio parred the 16th, the drama intensified.

Beverly's 17th hole is a 210-yard par-3. The green slopes severely from back to front, also falling off a shade to each side in typical Ross fashion. There are bunkers in all the right places. From the elevated tee, all the trouble is in view, which makes the hole seem even more

daunting. The club of choice on this day was a 2-iron.

Boros' tee shot crashed into the rough behind the green. Nicklaus hit his a mere five feet from the cup, prompting cheers. Palmer's try came up short, in the left front bunker. Nicklaus clearly had the upper hand, or so it seemed.

In short order, Boros was flubbing his chip shot, Palmer was slashing his bunker shot 35 feet past the pin, and Nicklaus was skidding his birdie putt past the target and down the slope. The damages: a dou-

Every player in the 1962 Western Open received a money clip.

ble-bogey 5 for Boros and bogeys for Palmer and Nicklaus. Arnie led Boros by one and Nicklaus by two with the par-5 18th to play. When both Nicklaus and Boros missed their birdie putts on the last, Arnie's second Western Open title in three years was assured.

Palmer nearly made it three championships in four years in 1964, when he put together four rounds in the 60s for a total of 15-under 269 at Tam O'Shanter Country Club, George S. May's old playground in Niles, just north of Chicago. But that was the year that Juan "Chi Chi" Rodriguez stole the show, his opening round 7-under 64 building the foundation for a 16-under 268 that tied the Western Open scoring record established by Sam Snead 15 summers earlier. Chi Chi edged Arnie by a stroke, giving Palmer the championship record for the lowest score by a nonwinner. Arnie still held that record in 1998.

Palmer, who is a life member of the WGA's Par Club in support of caddie scholarships, continued to post top-10 finishes in the Western Open in the 1970s. In 1974, the year the Western Open moved to ultra-tough Butler National Golf Club in Oak Brook, Arnie's total of 10-over 294, while ho-hum on the surface, was good enough for a share of fifth place.

Once again, however, he won the crowd. In the Western Open, Arnold Palmer always won the crowd. ◻

Be it from fairway or rough, Arnold Palmer never took an easy swing.

CHI CHI'S WESTERN OPEN

Chi Chi Rodriguez accepts the cheers of the crowd at the conclusion of the 1964 Western Open. He still had to wait for Arnold Palmer (on the 17th green in the background) to finish to assure his win.

In later years, when he was a consistent winner on the Senior PGA Tour, Chi Chi Rodriguez would always kid about his Western Open victory when he came through Chicago. "I remember before I won the Western, they said it was a major championship," Rodriguez would say. "Then I won it, and it wasn't a major anymore." The audience would chuckle, and Chi Chi would go on by saying, "After I won, Mrs. May gave me a lifetime membership to Tam O'Shanter. Then she sold the place." Another rim shot.

Truth is, back when Chi Chi was better known as Juan Rodriguez, he played some of the best golf of his life to win the Western Open, and in so doing, captured the biggest title of his career. To win the 1964 Western, Rodriguez would have to hold off a cast of characters that included defending champion and recent Masters winner Arnold Palmer, Jack Nicklaus, Billy Casper, British Open victor Tony Lema, Julius Boros, Gene Littler, and U.S. Open champion Ken Venturi, whose battle against heat and humidity at Congressional weeks earlier had

Thirty-four years after Ed Dudley won the Western Open, Chi Chi Rodriguez did the same, then started a caddie scholarship fund in Dudley's name.

Some of his fellow pros didn't like Chi Chi's habit of throwing his hat over the cup after a birdie, but the crowds loved it.

already become the stuff of legends. Rookie Ray Floyd was on hand, and, for nostalgia, so was Chick Evans.

Rarely had the Western Open featured a faster field, and it was clear from the start that fast would be the order of the week. Rodriguez and Casper opened with 7-under-par 64s on the 6,686-yard Tam O'Shanter course, good for a three-stroke lead on the field. The lead was Chi Chi's, but only by one stroke, after 36 holes. Palmer arrived in second place.

So it would be for the final 36 delightful holes, Arnie and Chi Chi, throwing birdies at each other from here, there, and everywhere at Tam. Palmer scored 4-under 67 on Saturday, Rodriguez 3-under 68, so they went into the final round knotted at 12-under 201, four strokes ahead of the crowd. Serious golf would be needed to catch them. Dead serious golf would have to be produced by the winner.

Rodriguez produced, authoring a sterling 4-under 67 to beat Palmer by a stroke. The key was Chi Chi's back nine of 4-under 32, including birdies on the 11th through 13th holes, and one more on the par-5 15th, a hole reachable in two. That birdie, a 40-foot two-putt, moved Chi Chi

ahead to stay at 16-under. However, even though Palmer bogeyed the 17th to drop two strokes behind, Chi Chi still had to sweat out the finish. After all, Lew Worsham had holed out from the rough adjacent to the 18th fairway to win the 1953 World Championship. No reason why Palmer, whose finishing kick was unsurpassed, couldn't do the same thing.

Except he didn't, settling for a mere birdie, and Rodriguez was the champion. A grateful one. There were no jokes at the awards ceremony. Instead, Juan Rodriguez cried. "I'm going to build another story on my home in Rio Piedros, Puerto Rico, for my mother and sister," Chi Chi said. "I also am going to start a caddie scholarship fund in Puerto Rico in honor of Ed Dudley."

In honoring one of his mentors, he also honored the Western Open's cause. He, too, came from an impoverished background, rising above it because he'd learned, and with rudimentary equipment, how to play winning golf. Playing in the sun sure beat working in it.

"Boy, when I was fertilizing that sugar cane, I never thought I'd ever have $11,000 in my whole life," he said. ◘

BACK-TO-BACK JACK

Jack Nicklaus lets loose with a big drive at Beverly Country Club in the 1967 Western Open.

When Jack Nicklaus stepped onto Beverly Country Club's first tee in 1967, he had done everything but win the Western Open. He had won two U.S. Opens, the second just a few weeks before. He had tried on the green jacket of the Masters on three occasions, snared a PGA Championship and, a year earlier, triumphed in the British Open at Muirfield.

Nicklaus had come close in the Western Open. He finished in the top 10 in his first three appearances as a professional, including a tie for second in 1963 when he lost in a three-way playoff to Arnold Palmer at Beverly Country Club in Chicago. A year later he tied for third, but the sweet taste of victory had eluded him.

Nicklaus had enjoyed a victory in another WGA championship, the

Western Amateur. In 1961, when he was ruling the amateur ranks and dominating college golf at Ohio State, Nicklaus won the Western Amateur, held that April at the New Orleans Country Club. He then swept all the major amateur championships that year, including the NCAA and the U.S. Amateur.

Two years earlier, when the Western Open was played at the Pittsburgh Field Club, the nineteen-year-old Nicklaus came over from Columbus, Ohio, made the cut, and finished tied for 52nd. His score of 12-over-par 292 earned him low amateur honors, a stroke ahead of Don Cherry.

Fast-forward to 1967. Nicklaus, Palmer, and Billy Casper were the favorites whenever they appeared together. All three were in the 64th

Western Open, and all were off the pace after 18 holes at Beverly. Nicklaus was a half-dozen strokes back after he carded a 1-over 72 that was triggered by a pair of three-putt greens. Then he started his move.

A second round of 5-under 66 kept Nicklaus in contact, and a third round of 6-under 65 moved him into a tie for second, a stroke behind Doug Sanders and in the next-to-last group in Sunday's finale.

On Sunday, Nicklaus birdied the first hole, then took the lead when Sanders bogeyed No. 4. When challenger Tom Veech faded, all Nicklaus had to do was par the 18th to finish at 11-under, forcing Sanders, 10-under through the 16th, to birdie either the par-3 17th or par-5 18th, tough propositions.

Instead, Nicklaus three-putted. "White Fang," the putter that he had

Runner-up Doug Sanders looks as happy as winner Jack Nicklaus at the 1967 awards ceremony. Looking on are WGA Director Joe Sheehan (left) and 1966-67 WGA President Adelor J. Petit, Jr.

Need someone to make a putt to save the day? Here's your man.

Two greats, Jack Nicklaus and Chick Evans, share a smile after Jack captured the 1968 Western Open. At right is WGA Director George M. Bard, who served as WGA President in 1972-73.

used to win the U.S. Open at Baltusrol by a record score, suddenly betrayed him, and Jack was in the house at 10-under 274, even with Sanders.

"I said to myself, 'Here we go again,' " Nicklaus confided to reporters later. "You know, I lost my last three starts by a total of four shots—the Canadian by one, the British by two, and the PGA by one."

Such is a measure of Nicklaus' dominance in 1967. He would not lose at Beverly. Sanders would, bogeying the 17th and 18th. He botched the par-3 by flying the green with his 4-wood, then pitching well past, which ensured a 4 on the slick surface. Now a birdie was a must for the flamboyant Sanders, but an errant approach set up an overcooked pitch. His must-make chip never came close, and Nicklaus finally had a Western Open title.

Somebody in the gallery of 21,200 yelled, "Now smile, Jack." Nicklaus, ever the gentleman, could not.

"I didn't, because I don't like to win a tournament through somebody else's misfortune. Doug played fine golf in this whole tournament until those last two," Nicklaus said. "It feels like coming in the back door."

Regardless of Sanders' finish, and of Jack's three-putt at the last, his last three rounds, in which he was 11-under, proved him the class of the field. And it was his putting, after everything else was considered, that made the difference.

"This is the best putting I've done in a couple of years, and I include the National (U.S.) Open in that," figured Nicklaus.

If the 1967 Western Open was a thriller, then the 1968 edition, when Nicklaus made a successful defense of his title, was more a coronation. Held at Olympia Fields Country Club, where the clubhouse is almost bigger

It was a stylishly slimmer Nicklaus who returned to the Western Open's battleground, by then Butler National, in 1981.

up close enough for an easy eagle that the longtime members at Olympia Fields still talk about. As with the year before, Jack credited the victory to putting. The short stroke had betrayed him a fortnight earlier at the PGA, so he went back to crouching, eyes behind the ball.

"It's the putting stance I grew up with," Nicklaus said. "And, if you're going to change your stance, you might as well change your putter, too."

So he did, using the putter with which he had won the 1966 British Open. That combination worked well during his two rounds of 65, then helped to steady him as he grew nervous down the stretch on Sunday. He hadn't won, after all, since a victory in the Sahara Invitational in October 1967, the longest drought of his pro career.

"When you haven't won for a while, you get a little excited out there," he smiled.

Of course, there was something to be said for Jack's length off the tee. He was 9-under on Olympia's three par-5s.

"That really surprised me," he told scribes. "I've never done much scoring on the par 5s—not the way I should for as long a hitter as I am."

Nicklaus' back-to-back titles followed a similar feat by Billy Casper in 1965 and 1966. Jack couldn't match Ralph Guldahl's three in a row when the 1969 Western rolled around, never getting untracked at Midlothian Country Club. The following year at Beverly, Nicklaus tied for third, five strokes behind Hugh Royer.

The Golden Bear didn't play in another Western until 1981, when his appearance at Butler National brought out the biggest crowds in the history of the championship, and yielded a seventh-place finish. He made one more appearance, in 1985, and while he didn't contend for the title, even that was not without its drama. He needed to make a 10-foot sidehill birdie putt on Butler National's ninth green late on Friday afternoon to play on the weekend. In characteristic Nicklaus fashion, he made it.

There was something about Nicklaus and the ninth hole at Butler. Four years earlier, play had slowed during the pro-am, and Nicklaus was waiting with his amateur partners to hit their approaches on No. 9. Suddenly, a young boy, no older than 5 or 6, waved a piece of paper from the edge of the gallery. Nicklaus spotted him.

"C'mon," said Jack, motioning him over a couple of times. The youngster trotted over to the center of the fairway, where Nicklaus gave him an autograph, a pat on the head, and talked to him for a couple of minutes. The gallery loved every second of it. As Jack walked up the fairway, two more kids ran out of the crowd and walked with him.

On that day, Jack Nicklaus, winner of two Western Opens, won considerably more hearts. ◘

than some courses, Nicklaus opened with a record-tying 6-under 65 on Olympia's famed North Course. After a 1-over 72 on Friday pushed him a stroke out of the lead, he stormed back with another 65, then a closing par 71 to finish at 11-under 273, three strokes ahead of Miller Barber.

Again, never mind that Nicklaus outdrove the field, or that his 1-iron approach from the left rough on the par-5 18th hole on Saturday snuggled

15

THE BUTLER DOES IT

*P*aul Butler made most of his fortune in paper, aviation, and cattle ranches. He also had an interest in real estate. Stating it that way, though, is like saying Frank Lloyd Wright dabbled in architecture, or that Picasso fooled around with painting in his spare time.

Butler bought the land and then developed Oak Brook, Illinois. He named it, too. He even named some of the streets. Jorie Boulevard is named after his daughter.

He envisioned Oak Brook as a community of plush homes, offices, and shops, and saw to it that Oak Brook's development matched his vision. He also made sure there were recreational facilities, including a golf

Butler National: beautiful and beguiling, but never benign.

club, polo fields, and more. But while the York Golf Club, a daily-fee course that Butler designed back in 1930, was good, he envisioned something better, a private country club with a membership that was prestigious and with a course that stood out from those at other area clubs.

He wanted a tough golf course, one that could hold a major tournament without major alterations.

Much of the land he needed for his dream course already was occupied by the York layout. The new course would take on a different routing, with a new clubhouse. He called on friends to join and help with the organization of the club, which had a working name of Oak Brook National Golf Club.

Before that, however, he called the Western Golf Association. As early as May of 1968, Butler and Irving C.

Millionaire developer Paul Butler and WGA past President Mark Cox take a close look at the plans for Butler National at the 1972 unveiling.

"Red" Harbour, Butler's construction guru, met with WGA President Boyd Simmons and Adelor "Bud" Petit, chairman of the WGA's Tournament Policy Committee, to see if the WGA was interested in holding the Western Open on the revamped York site, either occasionally or permanently.

Butler wanted an early answer so the course could be developed properly, from providing ample areas for spectators, to bringing in the right architect, to the installation of ancillary facilities for a tournament. In the next few years, it became evident that Butler was going to build a championship course, regardless of the

WGA's interest.

WGA officials let Butler know they were very interested. By 1971, with George Fazio as the architect, what is now known as Butler National Golf Club was nearing completion.

The clubhouse was small, without the requisite ballrooms or massive lobby that so many old-line clubs feature. But it was just the right size when the membership of the club—limited to about 150 men—was considered. As a men-only golf club, there was no need for largesse, or for swimming pools, tennis courts, or a ladies locker room. Butler, after all, had already provided for such amenities at the International Sports Core he had developed in Oak Brook. Butler National would be his getaway, a playground for him and his friends.

"This is ideal for the men golfers, because they do like to get away from all that noise and just play golf," Butler said even before the first tee was stuck in the ground.

In typical Butler fashion, this would be a no-punches-pulled project. Fazio beat Pete Dye for the commission to design Butler National on the strength of his Jupiter Hills, Florida, layout. He designed Butler National so it could be played as a member-friendly 6,559-yard course or a 7,463-yard long behemoth. From the back tees, the shortest par 3 measured 198 yards, the longest par 4 was at the limit of 475 yards, and the shortest par 5 was no less than 577 yards. Par was 71.

One par 5, the seventh, started out due north and finished going due east, with Salt Creek along the right side all the way, two trees standing sentinel in the rough on the right side just where a tee shot should be placed, and a patch of rough splitting the fairway where the big hitters would want to hit. Butler designed the hole, insisting on the rough bisecting the fairway and the preservation of the two trees. Fazio tweaked it.

Butler, who also insisted on keeping the famed tree in the middle of the double-dogleg 18th fairway, might have had a 17-hole golf course, one without a ninth hole, but for some actions that took place behind his back. A grove of trees—most of which are still in place—stood where the ninth hole was to be constructed. Butler couldn't bear to see them come down.

"We had to give a few big oaks 'Dutch elm' disease to get the fairway built," Bill Gahlberg, part of the Del Webb team that helped develop the business side of Oak Brook, recalled in 1984.

"We'd use a bulldozer to crack the tree and break up the root system, then dress down the area and wait a few weeks. The tree would start to wilt and I'd bring Paul out and point out the 'dying' trees. We had to take out 15 to 18 big oaks to make that fairway, and it's still one of the narrowest in golf."

Butler National was a course that would not treat favorably those who were either daring or foolhardy. Placed on a plot of land that rose and fell from east to west, the course would feature Salt Creek on six holes. A man-made pond, Teal Lake, would gnaw at three other holes.

Following two years of construction, Butler National opened to its select membership in the spring of 1972. A couple of months earlier, the announcement had been made that Butler would host the Western Open in either 1973 or 1974, depending on how quickly the course matured.

It would be 1974, after the rough had grown in sufficiently and the tournament infrastructure had been put in place. Paul Butler, whose invitation had started the process by which the Western Open was coming to Oak Brook in the first place, was slightly nervous about

At Paul Butler's insistence, the tree in the middle of the 18th fairway stayed.

Billy Casper grinned at Chick Evans' tales of days gone by after winning the 1973 Western Open at Midlothian. The next year, he wasn't smiling.

making a good impression.

"We had some feeling that in another year we would have been better prepared," Butler wrote WGA Executive Director Marshall Dann on October 15, 1973. "However, we seem to feel that the excitement and enthusiasm which your WGA has engendered into the matter by wanting to go ahead will more than make up for the other."

Closer to the event, he was more confident, but nobody really knew just how such a young course would be received.

The 1973 Western Open had been played at Midlothian Country Club, a charming par-71 course of 6,654 yards that dated to 1898. So little had changed, Chick Evans could walk around the course and tell admirers just where he and Walter Hagen had dueled for the 1914 U.S. Open title. Billy Casper won the 1973 Western Open, his fourth such crown, with a total of

12-under-par 272.

Midlothian and Butler National are about 25 miles apart. They might as well have been on different planets, so different was the 1974 Western Open from the 1973 model.

The PGA Tour's field staff—noting that the Chicago District Golf Association had rated Butler National at 76.2, the highest in the CDGA's realm—believed 7,002 yards would be long enough for the first Western Open. Even at that distance, the three par-5 holes weren't expected to be birdie territory.

The 1974 Western Open was played two weeks after the U.S. Open at Winged Foot Golf Club—which Hale Irwin won at 7-over-par 287 on what is still considered the toughest U.S. Open setup in modern times—and the week after the American Golf Classic at always-formidable Firestone Country Club was captured by Jim Colbert's score of 1-over 281.

The professionals were ready for a respite. They had heard that Butler National would be tough, but after a fortnight at Winged Foot and Firestone, how tough could it be?

Frighteningly tough, they found out. Butler in its larval stages would prove, in many ways, a tougher site than Winged Foot, with comparable scores. It most certainly wasn't Midlothian.

Butler National, simply put, was the most difficult golf course in Western Open history.

The Western Open arrived, and the pros arrived, in late June. The low scores were lost in transit. Even before the first ball was struck, the professionals were shaking their heads, not at the conditioning, which Butler was concerned about, but at the degree of difficulty.

"This is the second hardest course I've ever played from what I've seen," said Casper on Monday. "The toughest? Winged Foot."

And Casper had barely stepped on the back nine. He had picked up after 10 holes. A reasonably long hitter, long enough to win two U.S. Opens, including the 1959 edition at Winged Foot, Casper had hit driver and 4-wood to reach the green on Butler's uphill ninth.

"The greens are too small for the length of the course," big Billy griped. "The greens are going to putt tough, too. Courses like this and Winged Foot are going to drive guys from the tour. If the greens were a little larger I think it could be a real good course —a super course."

Such criticisms, tempered visions of the future, were commonplace.

"Don't make me a villain," said Dave Stockton. "This is going to be a great course. It is one of the most beautiful pieces of property I've ever seen. And it does have some really great holes now. But I guess I'm just not ready for this one. Some of the holes are impossible to play. If the USGA ever got its hands on this golf course, it would be all over. It would play as if it were 8,000 yards or something."

Which would have been fine with Tom Weiskopf, then playing the most consistent golf of his career.

"I hope we play it all the way back, but they'll probably put skirts on us again this week," Weiskopf said. "I've always felt courses on the tour are usually set up too easily. It's a helluva lot more exciting to know that if you can shoot 68, you'll pass up a bunch of guys. Besides, this course is designed to play long, so let's play it that way."

Tom Weiskopf wanted Butler National to play tough.

Arnold Palmer concurred.

"It's a tough course from the back, but not if they play it all the way up," said Arnie, fresh off an eagle of the 552-yard second in his Tuesday practice round.

Irwin doubted that.

"If we were playing from the back tees, some guys surely wouldn't finish," the reigning U.S. Open champion guessed.

All of that was said before the first round of the 71st Western Open, held on June 27, 1974.

In that round, nobody broke 70. Thirty-three players scored 80 or higher. Amateur Scott Webster scored 90. Nine players withdrew. The field average was 76.54, 5 ½ strokes over par. And the wind didn't blow.

"Why, this chicken-bleep course is so tough, you've got to close your eyes to hit the ball," said Charlie Sifford, whose 3-over 74 was good for a tie for 25th.

Casper? A 7-over 78. "And I played beautifully," he said.

Al Geiberger was on his way to a 3-under 68 but finished at par thanks to a bogey, double-bogey windup.

"There's just no way to play 18," griped Geiberger.

"It has the makings of a good hole, but not yet. I don't mean to criticize, but it's not fair. There's only about a 20-foot spot to drive."

Gary McCord, then as now an iconoclast, found an alternate route for the 18th. He hammered a high fade over the trees to the 10th fairway to get a favorable angle to the green on the double-dogleg. He, Butch Baird, and Bob Goalby led after 18 holes with 1-under 70.

"The only thing you have to worry about is the concession stand," figured McCord.

Then he was told that some Butler National members used that route regularly.

"Gee, I thought I was the first one to try it," he said.

The tone for the week was set. On Saturday, when the wind blew, nobody broke par, and only four players matched it. PGA Tour officials even shortened the par-3 fifth hole from an all-water carry of 220 yards to one of 168 yards. Didn't matter. It still was a torture test.

Tom Weiskopf, one of those four to match par 71 on Saturday, stood at 1-under for the first 54 holes and took a five-stroke lead into the final round.

Seen here as the low amateur in the 1968 Western Open, Tom Watson would break through at the 1974 Western with his first pro victory.

Normally, a five-stroke lead is safe. Not at Butler National. There, nothing was safe.

Tom won. Tom Watson, who was tied for third, six behind Weiskopf, when the final round began. Tom Watson, who had faltered under pressure in the previous two U.S. Opens, this time withstood the heat and surged to the front as Weiskopf unraveled on the back nine.

Watson shot 3-under 69, Weiskopf ballooning to 6-over 77, including a 6-over 41 on the back side. And still, Weiskopf almost won, taking a one-stroke lead into the final two holes. On the downwind par-4 17th, he hit a mammoth drive that sailed past the left-hand turn of the dogleg and ended up by a pump house next to a pond. The errant shot cost him a bogey and created a tie with Watson.

A final round of 2-over 73 was all Al Geiberger needed to win the 1976 Western Open.

Trying to be conservative, Weiskopf took a 1-iron on the 443-yard 18th, the double-dogleg finishing hole which required a fade off the tee and a drawn second shot for optimum results.

Watson, whose 15-foot birdie putt on the 14th hole would prove vital, was already on the home green, making par, when Weiskopf teed off. He pushed the shot well right, into the arm of Salt Creek that then ran for some 175 yards along the right-hand side of the fairway. It was a lateral hazard, so Weiskopf could drop there for his third shot, but he didn't have a clear approach to the green for what would have been a miracle up-and-down. He ended up with a double-bogey 6 and a tie for second with J.C. Snead.

Watson's total of 3-over 287 meant Butler National had produced the highest winning score in the Western Open in 34 years, since Jimmy Demaret scored 9-over 293 on rain-soaked River Oaks in Houston during the 1940 championship.

While the toughness of the course kept some players away, it did nothing to hurt the image of the Western Open, to say nothing of Butler National or those who won the championship there. Hale Irwin won the 1975 test, one interrupted by lightning that sent three players, including Lee Trevino, to the hospital, and scared the wits out of dozens more. Al Geiberger, at 4-over-par 288, won the 1976 Western Open when Joe Porter and Bob Dickson finished with 73 and 80, respectively.

The course was made easier numerically in 1977, when the par-4 12th was lengthened to 478 yards and turned into a par 5. It also matured, but it didn't really get easier. There was always a triple-bogey lurking in the weeds, ready to pounce on an unsuspecting player who allowed his mind to wander for a shot or two.

Other changes were eventually instituted, including a shift in the fairways from bluegrass, which occasionally produced "fliers," to bent grass, which was truer and produced crisper shots. The integrity of the course's design, however, stayed the same.

Paul Butler wanted a championship course and a worthy championship played on it. Hosting the Western Open at Butler National more than fulfilled that goal.

LIGHTNING!

The storm came so swiftly, and from the wrong direction, that it seemed more like a nightmare than a reality. It was both.

When lightning from a suddenly-developing thunderstorm above and to the east of Oak Brook hit Butler National Golf Club during the second round of the 1975 Western Open, golf was instantly lowest on the list of priorities.

It was 4:04 p.m. on June 27, 1975. Play had just been suspended. For a few terrorizing minutes, Lee Trevino couldn't help wondering if that date would be on his tombstone. He was hit by the first bolt of the previously placid afternoon, along with Jerry Heard and Bobby Nichols.

Trevino and Heard were huddled under an umbrella by the green on the par-3, 13th hole, adjacent to Teal Lake, when the bolt hit the water and flashed out in every direction. Nichols was several hundred yards away, walking up the fourth fairway. He

Jerry Heard and Lee Trevino a few minutes before lightning struck Butler National—and them.

was struck at the same time, perhaps by an offshoot of the same bolt.

Trevino and Heard were flattened, the bolt streaking across the water and through the putter Trevino was leaning on.

"I'm hit," Trevino yelled as he rolled around on the green. He got up, then fell, burned on his back.

Heard was hit in the groin and right leg. Nichols was hit on the head. They, like Trevino, suffered burns. In a matter of seconds, Butler National was in turmoil.

Ann Grassel of Libertyville was working the manual scoreboard at the 13th hole and ran to Trevino.

"He was conscious, but very scared and thought he was going to die," she told reporters. "He said his whole life was passing before him. I noticed a welt on his shoulder, then a doctor came and took his pulse."

Local caddie Ned Garmoe was working for Trevino that week. He

and Heard's caddie were sent to get hot dogs and pop when the sirens sounded the delay.

"We were coming back with them, maybe 50 yards from them when I heard the thunder and saw the bolt," Garmoe said. "Mr. Trevino was lying flat on the ground and I thought he was kidding around. He's such a great kidder. Then I heard somebody cry, 'Get an ambulance.'"

WGA official Joe Hill had already dispatched the ambulance on duty at the clubhouse.

At the time it was unclear who else might have been hit. All that was evident in the first moments was that Trevino and Heard were injured. Following the first lightning bolt, the sky was crackling, and it was pouring. Nobody knew about Nichols yet.

"I was standing near Jack (Tuthill, the PGA's head tournament official) and he hit the siren as soon as that first bolt hit," said J.C. Snead.

"I've never seen so many pops hit a golf course at one time."

Nichols never saw what hit him.

"There was a rumbling in the sky, but I thought it seemed a long way off," said Tony Jacklin, who was with Nichols on the fourth fairway. "Then ZAP! I felt tingling in my arms, like a cattle prod. The club left my hands. It landed 15 feet away. I don't remember throwing it. I looked over at Bobby. He'd been knocked clean over. He rolled over and was holding his head."

Nichols, it turned out, had a steel plate in his head because of an auto accident as a teenager. With no emergency crews in sight, Nichols walked back to the clubhouse as rain started to pour down. When he reached shelter he asked for a doctor and told Butler member "Red" Harbour, "I feel strange." Harbour said his breath smelled like burnt cork or burned wiring.

Jacklin wasn't injured, but a finger of the bolt also hit the portable

metal scoring standard being carried by fourteen-year-old Bobby Mortimore of Hinsdale. He was shaken up but unhurt.

Billy Casper was playing with Palmer on the 14th and couldn't believe what was happening.

"I've been playing golf for 20 years and we've had strikes on the course before, but nothing like yesterday," he said a day later. "It hit, and I hit the ground. Palmer was just ready to hit his second shot, and it scared the hell out of him. For anyone who was on the golf course—players and spectators—it's probably frightening for them to think that with all that lightning, it could just as well have been them."

Palmer grabbed his chest when the bolt hit, the club jumping out of his hands. When Arnie got to the clubhouse, the word was already out.

"What about Heard and Nichols?" he asked. "Is it true they got hit?"

It was. And Trevino as well, he was told. All three were sent to Hinsdale Sanitarium, the local hospital, and kept overnight in the intensive care unit despite being listed in satisfactory condition. The intensive care was a precaution, said Dr. Paul Fredrickson, because lightning strikes can cause heart trouble that doesn't appear immediately.

Trevino and Nichols were moved to private rooms on Saturday and were released on Sunday. Heard was released on Saturday, and when play resumed on Sunday, he was back on the course. Amazingly, he finished tied for fourth, five strokes behind winner Hale Irwin.

Fredrickson stressed that the trio was alive because they hadn't been directly struck by the lightning. "I don't think they'd be here today if they were," Fredrickson said.

Trevino was subdued by the experience.

"It completely lifted me off the ground," he said when released. "It straightened me out and my hands were up in the air shaking. I couldn't breathe. It was a sensation of somebody walking up behind you and hitting you as hard as he could on the left shoulder blade.

"At the hospital, I had little welts on my back. I couldn't see them, but they said they looked like little spiders," Trevino said. "And my legs, it was like I was having convulsions. The electricity had straightened me out. I told my wife for the first time I was 6-foot-2. I was finally tall once."

Jokes aside, Trevino suffered severe back trouble in the years after getting hit, and didn't return to the Western Open until 1981. In 1989, his final appearance at Butler National, he finished tied for fifth. Nichols and Heard played in three more Westerns at Butler. ◻

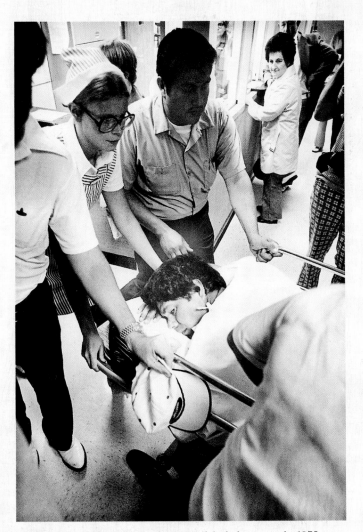

Lee Trevino in the hospital after being struck by lightning at the 1975 Western Open.

THE EVANS PRO-AM

The Chick Evans Memorial Pro-Am is the most prestigious fund-raiser in Chicago golf.

In a normal year, the most important single day to the Evans Scholars Foundation can be found right in the middle of Western Open week.

Not on Sunday, when the championship is decided, but on Wednesday, when the Chick Evans Memorial Pro-Am is held.

The Evans Scholars Foundation Pro-Am is the largest one-day fund-raiser staged by the Western Golf Association on the Evans fund's behalf. While there are exceptions—as when the appearance of Tiger Woods at the top of the leaderboard causes some 50,000 fans to appear at the gate on Saturday and Sunday—the pro-am's proceeds often exceed the net that the WGA returns to the Evans fund for the rest of the week. Tournament expenses being what they are, the other six days don't exceed the revenue raised when 208 amateurs play with 52 pros on Wednesday.

Those amateurs, generally businessmen who play weekend golf—and sometimes have swings to match—consider it a privilege to write their checks.

"I just like to have caddies, I guess," Bob Hammerschmidt said before the 1993 Pro-Am. Hammerschmidt, a west suburban businessman, and Jack Thompson, owner of a south suburban car dealership, were more than regulars. Hammerschmidt didn't miss an Evans Pro-Am until the mid-1990s, and Thompson played in every one of the first 35.

"I guess I'm sort of a golf nut," Thompson kidded. "Al Geiberger's one of my best friends. And Beverly's where I first met Arnold Palmer. We got to be buddies because we both had airplanes."

Beverly was the site of the inaugural Evans Pro-Am in 1963, which featured the 52 leading professionals in the field playing with 156 amateurs who had anted up $250 each. That meant the Evans fund was guaranteed $39,000 regardless of the rest of the week's profitability.

The Chick Evans Pro-Am attracts considerable repeat business, as evidenced by the continuing presence of Hammerschmidt and Thompson. Drawn by the chance of playing with a big-name profes-

sional and the worthiness of the cause, many play in it year after year. In 1998, it cost each of the 208 amateurs—fivesomes having been deemed proper to raise the charity take a few years earlier—$3,000 to tee it up, assuring the Evans fund of $624,000.

Soon after the first pro-am was established, a waiting list was started, and eventually another pro-am was added. The second pro-am, now called the WGA Pro-Am, is held concurrently on Cog Hill's No. 2 course and in recent years has been used by Motorola mostly as a client outing. There is still a waiting list for the Evans Pro-Am.

Part of the lure is the manner in which professionals and amateurs are paired. The defending champion normally plays in a group with the WGA president and a top executive from the Western Open's title sponsor, which has been Motorola since 1994. The rest of the professionals are assigned via a blind draw.

That means everyone has a chance to rub elbows with the big names, but it is fair to say that through the years, Bill Osborne, who played in his first Evans event in 1964, has been luckier than most.

"I got in it (at Tam O'Shanter) and drew Jack Nicklaus," he remembered. "It was a great thrill for me. He's a super guy. I had so much fun, I just continued to play in it. I've had unbelievable draws. Tom Watson, Greg Norman, Hale Irwin. In 1992, I played with Ben Crenshaw. A number of guys I've drawn have gone on to win."

Usually, on Pro-Am day the regular tour caddies work with their pros, but starting in 1997, on the suggestion of Illinois native (and 1987 Western Open champion) D.A. Weibring, Evans Scholars began carrying the bags of the professionals in the Chick Evans Pro-Am. The players donated their $7,500 purse to the Evans Scholars Foundation, a sum matched by PGA Tour Charities. It was a throwback to the years from 1962 to 1986 when the top-rated caddies from Chicago-area clubs carried for the pros during the Western Open proper.

While the main beneficiary is the Evans fund, the professionals can benefit from the day as well. Witness the day in the late 1980s when Curtis Strange came to the WGA headquarters trailer at Butler National. He wanted the names and addresses of each of his partners for the day. They comprised the best pro-am group he had ever been a part of, he said. Strange wrote each player a thank-you letter. ◻

In 1980, defending Western Open champion Larry Nelson found that playing in the Evans Pro-Am didn't guarantee an easy day.

Payne Stewart poses with his teammates-for-a-day during the 1996 Evans Pro-Am.

CHAPTER

16

THE 1980s – UNFORGETTABLE, UNPREDICTABLE OPENS

*P*erhaps it was an omen, Butler National Golf Club's greens dying just before the 1980 Western Open.

A little more than a week in advance of the Western, all but one of the greens became more dirt than grass, the result of a bacterial killer called red leaf disease that hit many private clubs in the Chicago area but left public courses untouched.

At the time, Butler National's fairways were being changed from bluegrass to bent grass similar to that on the greens. The fairways weren't hurt, but the putting surfaces became a topic of hot debate.

Tom Kite jumped for the sky after draining the putt that brought him the 1986 Western Open title in a four-way playoff.

"The (pros) who will cry about the greens will be those who shoot 80," said Errie Ball, Butler National's director of golf.

Not that the absence of grass bothered Scott Simpson. The former University of Southern California star dug his first professional win out of the dirt, leading the last three rounds en route to a five-stroke victory over 1978 champion Andy Bean.

If anything, Simpson's stoic effort—he was the first winner at Butler to match or better par in all four rounds, and just the fifth player overall—brought a pinch of normality to an edition of the championship that had longtime observers shaking their heads. That, though, was all that was normal. The rest of the decade saw the Western Open, fully revived from the doldrums of the 1950s, stage one wild championship after another.

As Bruce Lietzke can attest, trying to make a putt on Butler National's dead greens in the 1980 Western Open was an adventure.

Want a Monday finish? Come to the Western Open. How about an amateur winning? Visit Butler National. Or a four-way playoff? Oak Brook's the place to be. Or a flood causing a makeshift course to be devised? Paddle on over.

There were heartbreaking finishes, rallies and blunders, a death threat and a plane crash. There was even some golf.

Through it all, likely because of it all, the Western Open became a more popular gate attraction than ever. In 1974, when the championship was moved to Butler National, all attendance records were shattered by the 91,900 that gathered for the four rounds of the championship. The following year, the U.S. Open came to nearby Medinah and the fabled lightning storm forced a Monday finish. Attendance dropped by over 30,000.

Gradually, the crowds came back. By 1980 the four-round total—not a turnstile count but one based on cars parked, hot dogs eaten, and beer quaffed—was 92,600, a new record. The following year, when Jack Nicklaus and Lee Trevino were in the field for the first time in 11 and 6 years, respectively, the Friday, July 3, crowd was announced at midday as 32,700, a record for any round of any Western Open.

That announcement was made too early, considering that at one point—when Nicklaus, Trevino, and Tom Watson were simultaneously on the adjacent first, 10th, and 18th fairways—there wasn't a square inch of space to squeeze in another spectator. Later, PGA Tour officials told WGA officials they had never seen so many people on a golf course. It's very likely that well over 40,000 people, perhaps as many as 50,000, were at Butler National at some time during the day.

The crowds kept coming. Aside from the 1983 and 1987 championships—where attendance was trimmed by major rainstorms and, in the latter, a massive flood—the rest of the decade saw galleries of over 100,000 on hand for each week the Western Open was played.

Almost always, fans were treated to a fierce fight for the title. Every year from 1982 through 1989, the Western Open came down to action on the final green, and on four occasions, the competition continued into sudden death. The depth of the fields and the quality of Butler National, maturing into a first-rate layout that demanded pinpoint perfection, made for a perfect combination of action punctuated by acclaim and anguish on a stupendous stage.

Even a rare runaway would provide excitement. Ed Fiori's winning total of 11-under 277 in 1981 was a record for the Western Open at Butler.

"Really?" said Fiori. "This is such a tough course, maybe it'll stand forever. Or maybe somebody will break it next year."

Somebody did, by one stroke. That the somebody was Tom Weiskopf, and that he did so in most dramatic fashion, was fitting. Eight years earlier, Weiskopf had been in the driver's seat of the first Western at Butler when the wheels fell off and the engine fell out. In 1982, after Bob Gilder set the tone for low scoring with a course record 8-under 64 in the first round, Weiskopf revved up. He trailed rather than led down the stretch, but used a 7-foot birdie on the last hole—where he had made a double-bogey in 1974—combined with a three-putt bogey by Larry Nelson to effect a two-shot swing and take the title. Weiskopf had nearly holed out from the fairway with his 170-yard 6-iron approach.

"I usually try to force things, and today I didn't," said Weiskopf, who hit an astonishing 61 of 72 greens in regulation and saved par three of the four times he was bunkered. "I'm probably as excited as I can remember. It became evident to me that (a lack of patience) was my problem. I'm thankful I saw the light."

The Butler-Western record would fall again, but not until 1989, when Mark McCumber and Peter Jacobsen toured the grounds in 13-under 275. McCumber won the sudden-death playoff to take his second title in six years. He did so in the first million-dollar Western Open and, as in his first win, he captured the title on a Monday. Andy Bean also won in sudden death in 1978.

McCumber had edged Tom Watson in 1983, but Watson rebounded the following year to earn his third WGA crown in a dramatic playoff with Greg Norman. Watson sank a 20-foot birdie putt with two feet of break on the third sudden-death hole—Butler's 18th—while Norman's 33-foot effort stopped a turn short of the cup.

At the time, it was seen more as one in a long string of triumphs for Watson, one that added luster to both his resume and the stature of the championship. The ensuing years, however, have made that playoff loss by the "Great White Shark" the start of one of the Western Open's greatest hard-luck stories. Norman, by 1993, had wrested from none other than Walter Hagen the quixotic record of the most second-place finishes in the championship, with five. Hagen had finished second on four occasions.

Scott Simpson didn't care how dead the greens were. He won the 1980 Western Open by five strokes.

In 1982, Tom Weiskopf birdied the 18th hole he had double-bogeyed eight years before, then celebrated his Western Open victory with his children, Eric and Heidi.

The difference between the Haig and the Shark is obvious. Hagen also won five Westerns.

Norman, as has been the case throughout his career, has suffered bizarre strokes of misfortune in the Western Open. In 1984, Watson, with whom he was paired in the final round, saved par after hitting his tee shot adjacent to a concession stand on the par-3 11th hole. Watson, given a free drop, made the most of it by chipping onto the green with a 7-iron, then rolling in a 20-foot par putt.

"That was the best par I've ever seen," said Norman, elevating it above his own save that year on the final hole of regulation in the U.S. Open.

In 1987, Norman ran out of golf tournament. He and Larry Nelson were a stroke behind D.A. Weibring at the conclusion of 54 holes of play. For the first time, however, the Western Open ended after 54 holes. Heavy rains had ravaged Butler National in the week leading up to the championship, causing flood delays that forced officials to shorten the event to three rounds.

Norman was tied for the lead after the first and second rounds, but came up with a final-round 69 to Weibring's 68 on a course made up of nine holes from Butler National and nine from the adjacent Oak Brook Golf Club, the village-owned course.

Before the 1987 tournament ever started, officials had considered moving it from flood-damaged Butler National to Olympia Fields. But Oscar Miles, Butler's course superintendent, assured officials that, barring more rain, the four rounds could be played. Backed by an army of course workers, helicopters, "Water Hog" cleaners, and unperturbed by such annoyances as collapsed tents and concession stands in Salt Creek, Miles would have pulled it off. More rain fell on Friday, however, forcing a flood delay and the ultimate decision to shorten the tournament and to use part of the Oak Brook layout.

By then, the unusual at Butler National had become expected. Three years earlier, a plane crash on Sunday morning nearly overshadowed the drama of the

Watson-Norman playoff that afternoon. A single-engine Cessna with three aboard had been circling over Butler National for an aerial photography shoot. The plane lost power, and the pilot brought it down as gently as he could on the Oak Brook municipal course. All three aboard were injured, with one suffering a broken neck. Fortunately, no spectators—who watched in disbelief as the plane glided silently over the Butler clubhouse—were injured.

Playoffs, with up to a quartet of players, were relatively regular occurrences in the 1980s. A four-man logjam, the first in the Western Open since the 1950s, occurred in 1986, when Tom Kite, finishing nearly two hours ahead of the final group, set what turned out to be a target score of 2-under 286. Seven different players would hold the lead during the day. Eventually, the rest of the field came back to Kite, with Fred Couples, Nick Price, and David Frost matching his score.

That elite group took on the par-4 16th hole to start

sudden-death, and Kite came up the instant winner via a 7-foot birdie putt set up by a 112-yard downhill, downwind sand wedge. The kicker? Five more players, including who else but Norman, were another stroke back.

"This game, I don't understand it," Kite said later. "I'll die and not understand it. There are days you shoot a really good score, and somebody beats you. Then this happens. I've got no clue."

Norman could say the same thing.

For that matter, so could Peter Jacobsen, who was in position to win back-to-back Western Opens, only to squander the lead twice down the stretch. In 1988, Jacobsen became the target of a death threat during Sunday's round: "A man with a black eye patch will kill Peter Jacobsen," a mysterious voice said in a call to Butler National. Tournament officials increased security but did not interrupt Jacobsen to tell him of the threat. Unaware of the commotion, Jacobsen was the

Greg Norman and Tom Watson are pensive during their 1984 sudden-death playoff.

The 1987 Western Open was shortened following flooding at Butler National.

Jim Benepe has just seen Peter Jacobsen's approach bounce into Salt Creek, giving him the 1988 Western Open title.

co-leader in the closing holes with Jim Benepe, who had earned All-America honors on Northwestern's golf team and was bankrolled by a group from Skokie Country Club.

In the championship via a sponsor exemption, Benepe was playing in his first PGA Tour event. He played with the confidence of a veteran for 71 holes. Then, a 45-foot, three-putt bogey on the final hole dropped him a stroke behind Jacobsen and had the twenty-four-year-old cursing himself as he checked his scorecard. In the fairway, Jacobsen was 165 yards from the pin. He thought a hint of a breeze was in his face. There was no breeze.

He pulled out a 6-iron. That was too much club by almost two clubs. Jacobsen almost hit Salt Creek, behind the green, on the fly. His ball flew the green and bounced into the drink. He was on his way to a double-bogey, and a stunned Benepe went from loser to winner in a flash.

"I played myself out of it," Jacobsen said.

"I'm numb," said Benepe, who had won the Western Junior in 1982 and was the medalist in the 1986 Western Amateur.

Jacobsen had a two-stroke lead with four holes to play the following year, only to see McCumber come back and force a playoff. Jacobsen's par putt on the first playoff hole spun out, a second disappointment in as many years.

For all the excitement in the 1980s, by far the most dramatic championship came in 1985. It had been 75 years since the amateur Chick Evans beat the pros and captured the match-play Western Open of 1910. It had been some 30 years since amateur Doug Sanders had won the Canadian Open. Since then, a few amateurs had led early in tournaments, and Jim Simons had led going into the final round of the 1971 U.S. Open. Sanders had been the last to win.

Then came Scott Verplank, the best amateur of the day. He had won the U.S. Amateur at Oak Tree in 1984 and the Western Amateur at Point O'Woods in 1985.

Amateur sensation Scott Verplank always got out of trouble with panache during the 1985 Western Open.

He was confident, could putt, and would prove unflappable.

He won the 82nd Western Open. He virtually dominated it, leading the first three rounds outright with rounds of 68-68-69. Then, veteran Jim Thorpe—whose back-to-back 66s in the middle rounds brought him into contention—scored a final-round of par 72 in a drizzle while Verplank stumbled to a 2-over 74. There would be a sudden-death playoff.

Verplank had played sensationally in fashioning his lead. In his opening round, he was 3-under after 15 holes. He was on fire, and he would get hotter. On the par-4 16th, Verplank faced a 12-foot sidehill putt that, if missed, could roll well past the hole. It was exactly 6 p.m.

Verplank drew back his putter, and . . .

SCREEEEE! On the other side of the hedges and fence, out on Jorie Boulevard, a siren went off, produced by a passing police car.

Not that Verplank knew it. He drained the right-to-left putt for a birdie 3 and finished with a 4-under 68, the leader. The look in his eyes was that of someone who would drop a birdie putt in an earthquake. He wasn't just playing to play. He was playing to win.

"I'm surprised," Verplank told disbelieving reporters after signing his scorecard. "I'm not saying I've got any

Jim Thorpe placed second behind Verplank at the 1985 Western Open, but still earned first money...

kind of chance. I wasn't even looking at the scoreboard. When did I think I could lead? When I birdied No. 16."

Verplank's second round 68 featured six birdies in the final eight holes, a dazzling performance. There were 33,900 golf fans at Butler National. Many of them had come to see Nicklaus, making his first appearance since 1981. As the day progressed, the crowd turned its attention to Verplank, the amateur sensation.

"I just tried to get ahold on what's going on," Verplank said. "Today, I got ahold of it and it came out pretty good. And I won't try to think about winning until the opportunity presents itself."

When asked if he could imagine winning the Western Open in his wildest dreams, he said, "I don't have wild dreams."

There was no need to, so wild was the reality. Almost every big name around, up to and including Nicklaus and Seve Ballesteros, was in the field, and here, after a third straight round in the 60s, was the kid leading the field. Thorpe trailed Verplank by two and was three in front of a fivesome tied for third.

"It'll be pretty much like match play," figured Thorpe.

"It may get that way in the final few holes, but I'm just going to try and play my game," Verplank plotted. "I've looked at PGA Tour scores for the last five years,

and you never know when somebody's going to go bananas on Sunday."

Nobody did, and it came down to Verplank and Thorpe. They were in the last pairing. Thorpe tied Verplank with a 10-foot birdie on the 8th hole. It was now a 10-hole tournament. It was match play.

When Thorpe dropped a 6-iron a foot from the pin on the par-3 11th, he figured to move in front. Instead, Verplank ran in a 50-footer for a deuce to stay tied. Thorpe finally took the lead when Verplank three-putted for the first and last time all week on the next hole, but Thorpe gave the lead back, and then some, on the treacherous 14th. Thorpe's tee ball splashed into Teal Lake, and Verplank again led by a stroke.

Thorpe answered with a tying 25-foot birdie at the par-5 15th, and made an All-American scrambling par on the 18th after snap-hooking his tee shot against the fence. He saved par with a 15-foot putt, and the twosome prepared for sudden death.

Thorpe and Verplank were in the same situation. Each could focus on getting his name on the J.K. Wadley Trophy. Thorpe, as the low professional, had annexed the $90,000 first prize, and like Verplank, didn't have to concern himself with money. Now they were playing for glory.

They halved the 16th hole with par 4s. On the 459-yard par-4 17th, it became a chipping contest when Verplank and Thorpe each missed the green with their approaches. Verplank chipped to five feet, but Thorpe's chip left him twice as far away. Thorpe missed his putt, Verplank made his, and history was made.

"I was never really nervous today except on the 17th (in the playoff)," Verplank explained. Even then, he wasn't in a completely unfamiliar situation. "I asked myself, 'How many five-footers straight uphill have you had in your life?' That's the putt I practice every day."

Thus concluded another unpredictable Western Open, one fully in keeping with the 1980s, the decade when anything could happen and everything did.

...while Verplank became the first amateur in 75 years to capture the venerable title.

FIND THAT TROPHY!

The George S. May Memorial Trophy, last seen almost 20 years ago.

Somewhere, perhaps at the bottom of the Little Calumet River in northeastern Illinois, buried under silt and sludge, down in the muck with car bumpers and the other effluvia of modern civilization, is the George S. May Memorial Trophy. Or maybe the silver behemoth was melted down and sold at the height of the precious metals boom of the late 1970s and early 1980s. It may now exist in the form of several thousand charm bracelets.

Nobody knows for sure, just as nobody knows who, how, or even when the May Trophy was spirited out of the Western Golf Association's headquarters sometime between November 1979 and the following spring. Nobody knows who called with a ransom demand after the theft became public months later.

Nobody knows much of anything, except that the May Trophy was valuable, both in cash and sentimental value. Donated to the WGA by Alice May, the widow of George S. May, and their daughter Dorothy, late in 1962, the trophy was originally the symbol of May's World Championship of Golf, played annually at his Tam O'Shanter Country Club in Niles, Illinois, from 1943 through 1957.

George S. May never did anything small, whether it was awarding a purse or ordering a trophy. Excluding the base, his idea of a proper trophy for a World Championship was 31 inches in circumference and weighed 28 pounds. Few trophies in the world of sports, a world of big trophies, outdid this prize in the audacity department.

The WGA renamed it the George S. May Memorial Trophy and added a massive four-sided wooden base, with silver plaques listing the winners of the Western Open, Western Amateur, Western Junior, and May's original World Championship. Beginning in 1963, it was displayed at every WGA championship and various other functions in the course of the year.

The rest of the time, it was not in the trophy cases in the entrance hall to WGA headquarters. Too big to display, it was crated up and housed in a room in a corner of the building's basement.

"It was a paralyzing thing," recalled Marshall Dann, the WGA's executive director at the time. "You couldn't give it to somebody. Too big."

Instead, players posed hugging it after winning a WGA title, as at the 1979 Western Amateur, its last public appearance.

When the WGA's maintenance man opened the crate in advance of the WGA's annual meeting in May of 1980, the big silver cup was missing. The crate was still occupied by the wooden base. Nothing else had been touched, upstairs or downstairs, including other crated trophies.

A preliminary investigation by the Golf police and the insurance company liable for the tab turned up no clues. Only after the news of the theft and the posting of a $1,000 reward was reported did the trail begin to heat up.

Three days later, the phone rang in WGA public relations director Brian Fitzgerald's office. "I've got your trophy," said a streetwise voice. "I've got your trophy and I'm willing to deal."

Fitzgerald didn't recognize the voice as one of his many friends who had been calling. He asked the voice how he could be sure the May was on the other end of the line.

"It's sittin' right here in front of me. Go ahead, ask me anything about it."

Fitzgerald began to quiz the mystery man, and began to believe that he had the trophy. Then the caller got down to business. He wanted more than $1,000. He knew the market.

"Hell, I put $210 out of my own pocket to buy the thing from a pawn shop," said the voice. Fitzgerald nearly dropped the phone.

"I saw the TV and they showed it on there, and I thought that thing looked familiar. I'd seen it a couple days earlier in this shop. Course, you gotta understand, this wasn't exactly a regular pawn shop, you know what I mean."

Fitzgerald called in Dann for further negotiations and verification that the May was indeed still in two pieces (its lid was removable, which the WGA and the caller, but few others, knew). The caller decided he wanted $4,500 for his $210 "investment."

"It will take a little time and a few phone calls to get approval on $4,500," Dann told the voice, "but let me work on it over the weekend. Can you call us back on Monday?"

The voice agreed. Dann notified the Golf police, which called in the FBI and Illinois State Police. The trail was hot. Any call on Monday would be traced.

There was no call. Not Monday, not Tuesday, not ever. The voice had gotten cold feet.

The reward was raised to $4,500, not the usual figure for a reward for anything, in an effort to flush the caller out.

That didn't work. The trail was cold again.

Fast-forward from springtime to summer, just prior to the 1980 Western Open, a time when a million details must be addressed. The phone rang again. It was a young gymnastics instructor with a story to tell.

He owned a speedboat, and on a lovely June night, he and his girlfriend motored up the Little Calumet River, stopping under the Interstate 57 bridge for a quiet moment alone.

It was near midnight. A car stopped abruptly on the highway above. Then, in a flash, there was what he called a "silvery object that looked like a small garbage can" flying through the air, splashing into the water half a football field away. Simultaneously, another glint in the moonlight came from a smaller object, hitting the surface farther away.

The car sped off. With the report from the gym instructor, the trail was, well, wet.

It was also considered warm enough to undertake a search. The insurance company arranged for a Chicago Fire Department search-and-rescue team, accompanied by Dann, Fitzgerald, and the gym instructor, to go on a hunt for the May Trophy on Monday, June 30, 1980. That happened to be the first day of Western Open week at Butler.

Wherever a diver would go, black silt would cloud the water. It was a search by feel that yielded spare tires, a baby carriage—thankfully empty—and sundry other items, but not the prize of prizes.

"Those guys were terrific," Fitzgerald recalled. "But they said at the start that it was very unlikely we would find it."

The divers searched for nine hours, knowing that between the sighting and the search, countless barges had come through the river, moving the mucky bottom generally toward Lake Michigan. For all they knew, the trophy, cup and lid, was a half-mile downstream, or already in the lake, or buried completely.

One day was enough. The effort had been made. The George S. May was declared officially, unalterably, completely lost. The insurance company paid the claim. The trail is still cold. ◻

Tom Watson has to lean around the May Trophy to be seen after winning the 1977 Western Open.

McCUMBER MONDAYS

Mark McCumber didn't mind playing on Monday if it was the Western Open.

For Mark McCumber, the best day of a tournament—payday—doesn't always come on Sunday.

At the Western Open, it twice came on Monday. McCumber, unique among the Western Open's multiple champions, won both of his titles on a Monday, once by playing 36 holes, once by playing just one.

He came from behind in one championship and survived in a playoff in the other. He was healthy the first time, ailing the second time.

The common denominator was that McCumber, the only player to win multiple Western Opens in the 1980s, stood tall down the stretch.

His first title came in the 1983 championship, which concluded with 36 holes on Monday because of a severe rainstorm that began at mid-morning Friday. The rainfall flooded over a third of the course and did not abate until Saturday night. That forced the second round to Sunday and made a double round on Monday the only way to squeeze in the full four laps of Butler National.

McCumber, who made the cut by only four strokes, opened the day seven in arrears of leader Tom Watson and caught up in the morning,

scoring a 4-under-par 68. Meanwhile, Watson shot an uncharacteristic 3-over 75.

Watson was the crowd favorite among the gallery of 18,700, but he struggled all day. McCumber, playing in a group three holes ahead of Watson, had a brief lead early in the final round. Watson rallied to tie and eventually took a lead he held until late in the round.

A birdie on the 15th drew McCumber within a stroke, and an 18-foot birdie on the last hole tied Watson, who by then was playing the 15th. McCumber was in the house at 4-under 284.

It would prove to be enough. Watson bogeyed the 15th to drop a stroke behind, then missed three straight birdie putts, settling for pars. He had a 25-footer on the home hole, and just missed on the low side.

For McCumber, then thirty-one, it was a big win, only the second of his career and measurably more important than his 1979 triumph in the Doral-Eastern Open.

"With the heritage it has, that it was once considered one of the majors, to have my name on the trophy next to Watson and Casper and

With runner-up Peter Jacobsen in the background, Mark McCumber expresses his appreciation to the 750 fans who turned out on a Monday morning for one hole of a sudden-death playoff.

a birdie on the par-3 13th. He was 14 under par, a new low for any stage of the Western Open at Butler National.

McCumber halved the lead with his own birdie on the 13th, and moved into a tie when Jacobsen botched his way to a bogey 6 on the par-5 15th. And while McCumber would manage a series of routine pars from that point, Jacobsen was hanging on, especially on the par-4 17th, where a blast out of wet sand in a greenside bunker forced a 15-foot par-saving putt. He made it, parred 18, and then watched McCumber do the same thing with the sun sliding below the northwest horizon, just before a rare summer fog, caused by the unseasonable cool, began to form.

Even before McCumber finished, it had been decided a sudden-death playoff, if necessary, would start at 9 a.m. Monday morning on the first tee.

The playoff would not go past the first green. Jacobsen hit his too-short wedge on the front edge of the green, some 40 feet from the pin. McCumber noted a wind shift and ripped a sand wedge 10 feet from the cup. Jacobsen lagged to three feet. Now McCumber had a shot at a birdie and a win.

"I knew the putt broke four or five inches, and I thought I made it," said McCumber. "I thought I made it the entire time, until it burned the right (high) side of the hole."

He finished up, tapping in for par, and for a reason.

"It swings the momentum, makes his putt just a little longer."

Now Jacobsen had to make his three-footer to advance to the second tee. He made a good stroke, but the ball caught the bottom edge of the hole and did a classic 360, staying aboveground.

"I have mixed emotions the way it ended," said McCumber, a good friend of Jacobsen. "I'm sorry to see it for his sake. I didn't mind it for mine."

McCumber's second Western Open championship was worth more than twice as much as his first ($180,000 versus $72,000), and put him in a class with a list of multiple winners that goes back to the start of the century and Willie Anderson. ◻

Nicklaus—I'm very gratified," he said.

McCumber made 140 strokes on that Monday in 1983 to win. Six years later, he took four strokes on Monday and won.

Another rainstorm, this one a Sunday cloudburst, delayed final round play for 3 1/2 hours. After 54 holes, McCumber and Larry Mize, at 10-under 206, had led Peter Jacobsen and Paul Azinger by a stroke.

At the beginning of the week, Jacobsen was still trying to come to grips with his overcooked 6-iron into Salt Creek that handed the Western title to Jim Benepe the year before.

McCumber, meanwhile, was patrolling Butler National with an aching back, one which had flared up 11 weeks earlier, during the Players Championship, and was troubling him again. By Saturday, he was limping to tees and had a case of the lefts, all caused by the back.

"It's an adventure," McCumber said. "It's enough to stand on the 14th tee with the tournament on the line, but when you don't know if you're going to be able to swing or not, it's really tough."

Sunday, his back would face its greatest test. McCumber was warmed up and had played six holes when the sirens sounded and play was suspended for the looming storm, which not only rinsed Butler National, but cooled the air. When action resumed, McCumber was tied with Jacobsen at 12-under.

Jacobsen, playing ahead, took a two-stroke lead on McCumber with

17

POINTING OUT
PRO PROSPECTS

*R*obert Trent Jones once said, "The vitality of golf is that it offers man his own personal challenge for combat. He attacks the course and par. It's my job to create the pitfalls that defend the course against easy conquest, because the shattering of par without this challenge is a fraud. The punishment should fit the crime."

At the Point O'Woods Golf & Country Club, nestled in a forest adjacent to Interstate 94 just outside of Benton Harbor, Michigan, Jones created one of his masterpieces.

Known worldwide for designs that favor length and

Point O'Woods Golf & Country Club offers beauty and a brawny course simultaneously.

huge greens, he came up with a different scheme for the Point, a course that can play several ways, with the potential for crime and resultant punishment evident no matter what the configuration. Listed at about 6,900 yards, par can range from 70 to 72, and the yardage can vary by some 200 yards, as the situation warrants.

Because of that, it quickly became evident that the Point's sublime layout was not just a fine country club course but one uniquely suited to the special challenge of match play. "The Peerless Point," Chick Evans called it.

Unlike medal—or stroke—play, where many, if not most, players are content to settle for par and don't get too aggressive in their search of birdies, man-to-man matches tempt the aggressive player to take chances in

The name of every Western Amateur champion is on the George R. Thorne Trophy.

order to win holes. In match play, the boldest players gamble as if they're in Las Vegas and the next roll of the dice decides if they're taking the bus or the plane home.

Jones built flexibility into the course, and the implementation of his concept by Point O'Woods members and Western Golf Association officials makes the course the perfect setting for the Western Amateur.

The second hole, for instance, is a par 5 with a second shot that demands a carry over a ravine, one complete with pond, for those going for the green. Layup means a possible birdie. Going for it means anything from eagle to a high number. Likewise, the dogleg third hole can play as a par 5, at a shortish 461 yards, or as a 436-yard par 4.

It's the eighth hole, a par 4, that is the most intriguing on the course. A short par 4, there's a cliff to the left and behind the green, and a pond behind trees to the right. At 321 yards, the standard for stroke-play qualifying, it's a 3-wood or 2-iron and wedge for most players.

Then comes match play, when the tee is moved up to the front of the tee box. From there, it's 277 yards to the center of the green, and tempting. Very tempting. Drive the green and putt for an eagle. Miss it, and lose the hole.

"The shot better not be over one-tenth of 1 percent in error," said Jones.

Ben Crenshaw is typical of those who have won the Western Amateur at the Point, doing so in 1973...

...then going to professional success, including a win in the 1992 Western Open.

The back side also offers thrills. The 12th can play as a par 4 or par 5, depending on the tee placements, while the par-5 15th is more like a par 4, gently falling down a grade to a reachable plateau green.

"I developed a system to change the tee blocks," longtime WGA Director Chuck Eckstein, the lead rules official for the Western Amateur for decades, remembered. "One day I forgot to change them on the 12th from practice rounds to the tournament and they played from the back. The players yelled like hell that they couldn't reach the green in two."

Even reaching the 12th in two offers no guarantees, for the green is a 12,000-square foot affair with more rolls than a breakfast buffet. And the par-3 17th, where countless matches have been decided, offers an all-water carry over its 207 yards of Michigan real estate.

First held at the Point O'Woods in 1963—when Tom Weiskopf emerged on the national scene—and brought back for an encore in 1965, the Western Amateur has been held at the Point continuously since 1971. In that time, virtually every major American professional golf star has had his moment in the amateur sun at Point O'Woods.

"It's a great golf course," said Eckstein. "I've also worked with the USGA, and they've never drawn the crowds for the U.S. Amateur that the Point O'Woods got."

WGA Executive Director Don Johnson also noted the support the Western Amateur receives. "Point O'Woods provides a quality, championship venue for our Western Amateur," he said. "More importantly, the members at Point O'Woods have enthusiastically supported this championship for many years. We're look-

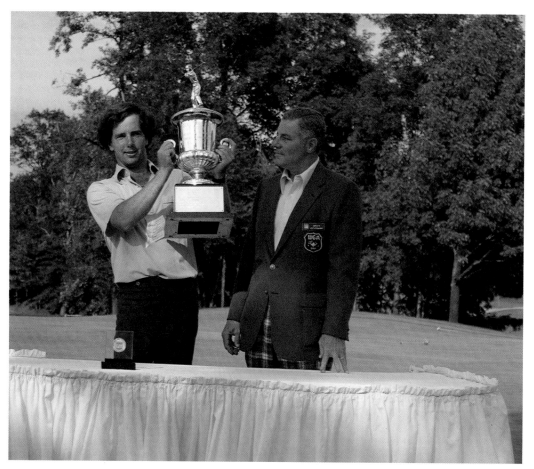

Mark O'Meara won the qualifying medal in the 1980 Western Amateur, but was swept aside once match play began. With O'Meara at the medalist trophy presentation is 1980-81 WGA President Bruce K. Goodman.

ing forward to working together with the members in the coming years to further build on the Western Amateur's rich tradition."

For many amateur golfers, Point O'Woods has provided a barometer for future success in professional golf. Through 1998, six Western Amateur winners at the Point had won professional majors and five had won the Western Open. Tiger Woods, 1994 Western Amateur champion, made both lists in 1997 with his wins in the Masters and the Motorola Western Open. Weiskopf, who won the 1963 Western Amateur, and Ben Crenshaw, the 1973 Western Amateur champion, also hold wins in majors and the Western Open.

When Sweet Sixteen match play qualifiers are taken into account, the number of major winners having passed through the Point reached 20 in 1997 with

Woods' Masters victory and Justin Leonard's British Open title. Leonard won the Western Amateur in 1992 and 1993.

Those of a certain age can remember like yesterday when Ben Crenshaw was the medalist in qualifying two years running, capturing the championship in the second year.

"To this day, Ben Crenshaw still calls me Mister," Eckstein marveled.

Then they will tell you that the year after, 1974, saw one of the great matches in Western Amateur history, with Curtis Strange and Jay Haas dueling in an 18-hole final that went to the second extra hole before Strange triumphed.

The nineteen-year-old beat his Wake Forest teammate after going 4-down through six holes, leading after 15, and hanging on to go past the 18th green. Strange, foreshadowing the grit he would show in winning back-to-back U.S. Opens, won with a two-putt birdie on the par-5 second. The victory capped a week of survival against a field that included Jerry Pate, Craig Stadler, Gary Hallberg, Gary Koch, and Mike Donald.

"The one big thing about a tournament like this is you just hate to go this far and lose in the semis or finals," Strange said at the time. "So you just dig back a little further."

There was the magical year of 1980, when Mark O'Meara was the medalist but didn't get to a final match that saw Hal Sutton win his second straight

Lanny Wadkins survived a 20-hole match with Tom Kite to advance to the 1970 Western Amateur final at Wichita Country Club.

crown by defeating David Ogrin 4 and 3. Some call 1980 magical because the Western Amateur was played at all, scarcely a week after winds of tornadic force tore through the picturesque grounds and wreaked havoc.

It is hindsight based on the knowledge of what players have done as professionals, for the most part, that makes most of those Western Amateurs stand out today, though all of the above players had impressive resumes in college and other amateur events.

Similarly, nobody knew just how good Scott Verplank was playing when he won the 1985 Western Amateur. The U.S. Amateur champ the year before, Verplank won everything in sight on the 1985 amateur circuit, but the quality of his dominance was certified when, less than a month after winning at the Point, he defeated a stellar field of professionals to win the Western Open.

By 1963, when Weiskopf scored a 5 and 4 victory over Labron Harris, Jr., the Western Amateur had assumed its present configuration. A dramatic change in the championship in the mid-1950s eventually shortened the playing from seven days to five, but made the golf more intense.

Previously, 36 holes of qualifying set the stage for match play beginning with a round of 64 players. Win six matches, with the semis and finals at 36 holes, and you were the champ.

In 1955, at the suggestion of longtime WGA Director Cameron Eddy, the stroke-play portion of the proceedings was doubled to 72 holes, with a cut after 36. Only eight qualified for match play. That weeding was considered too severe, and beginning in 1956, the top 16 qualifiers made match play.

Immediately, using a phrase perhaps taken from high school basketball tournament lore, the qualifiers became known as the Sweet Sixteen. Beginning in 1961, when Jack Nicklaus won at the New Orleans Country Club, all four matches were 18-hole affairs, compacting the match-play portion into two frantic days.

The championship, which prior to 1955 had the potential to play 144 holes or more

Michael Jordan, player No. 23 on the pairing sheet, played in the 1991 Western Amateur at the invitation of WGA officials. He scored 85-81 and missed the 36-hole cut by 15 strokes.

comfortable shoes to last the week.

So testing is the current Western Amateur format that it has been suggested several times as the model for a PGA Tour match-play tournament. The Tour's administrators haven't acted on that notion yet, but all one needs to do is look through the Western Amateur records to see what drama they're missing.

In 1970, the last Western Amateur not played at Point O'Woods, the gallery at Wichita Country Club was treated to one of the great showdowns between professional stars-to-be when Lanny Wadkins needed to go to the 20th hole to knock off Tom Kite in the semifinals.

"Tom had played great all week," Wadkins recalled a few years later. "After beating him, the finals [a 4 and 2 win over Charlie Borner] seemed easier."

The Western Amateur has from its inception in 1899 been regarded as one of the major amateur events, ranked by players with the U.S. Amateur and British Amateur. Because the Western Amateur awards exemptions to a wide range of players with proven credentials, it often has a stronger field than either the USGA or R&A. There are usually 60-odd places available for the hundreds who attempt to qualify for the Western Amateur in what is known as prequalifying.

An exemption, of course, is no guarantee of success. The match-play format brings with it the possibility for upsets. Witness 1976, when John Stark, a member of the Houston golf team, made it into the field through prequalifying, fought his way into the Sweet Sixteen, then stunned everyone to win the championship. Stark's title, capped by a 3 and 1 win over Mick Soli in the final, ranks as the biggest pure shocker in Western Amateur history.

More recently, favorites have triumphed. In 1991, when Michael Jordan's first appearance in a non-celebrity event drew the biggest first-round crowd ever, Phil Mickelson defeated Justin Leonard 2 and 1 in the championship match. Mickelson, who played with Jordan and Ohio State's Chris Smith the first two days,

in seven days, now offered 144 holes in five days.

The Western Amateur champion of today still must survive 72 holes of qualifying, with a cut to the low 50 after 36 holes and to the low 16 after 72 holes. Then as a Sweet Sixteen qualifier, he must win four, 18-hole matches in two days. He not only has to be a fine player, he must be physically fit, mentally tough, and wear

Phil Mickelson's silky putting stroke helped defeat plucky Justin Leonard 2 and 1 in the 1991 Western Amateur championship match. Leonard won the crown the following two years.

had already won Tucson's Northern Telecom Open earlier in the year and entered the Western Amateur as a heavy favorite.

The next two years, Leonard assumed the favorite's role. He won in 1992, surviving a semifinal assault from Chris Riley that included a 2-2-2 outburst on the ninth through 11th holes. In 1993, he successfully defended his title with a 6 and 4 win over Danny Green, who would win the 1997 Western Amateur. In 1994, Eldrick "Tiger" Woods made up for missing the Sweet Sixteen the year before by beating fellow Californian Riley 2 and 1 in the finals.

All of this excitement has taken place on a course that not only ranks as difficult and intriguing, but as one of the more beautiful layouts anywhere. On rolling land, and with the lowest-hanging branches removed from towering oaks and maples, one can see flags fluttering on greens hundreds of yards away in many areas. The course's combination of challenge and condition-ing—combined with the hospitality extended by the galleries and the Point members—has earned the Western Amateur the title of "the Masters of amateur golf."

That is not hyperbole. Some years ago, the WGA surveyed players past and present, and received rave reviews.

"During my two years at the Western, I was very impressed with the galleries and their conduct," Peter Jacobsen recalled. " No matter where the pins are cut, the course plays tough and is a true championship test. I will always believe the Western Amateur is the toughest amateur event to win!"

Jerry Pate recalled another unique element of the Western Amateur. The match-play action is broadcast on two radio stations in the Benton Harbor-St. Joseph area. WHFB and WSJM both provide live play-by-play commentary from the course. In 1974, decades before drawing a check for commentary on TV, Pate was drafted as an unpaid analyst for the Strange-Haas final.

Andy North had to go to the last hole to beat Barney Thompson in the 1971 Western Amateur final.

3-iron dead right, also into the woods. Andy ran it up 30 feet away on the green, and Curtis boldly ran it over the green into the trap.

"Curtis got set, the gallery quieted, then everybody erupted when he chipped it in from the trap. The crowd had barely settled down when Andy rolled home his own birdie putt and everyone cheered. Nobody believed they could both make such fantastic pressure birdies. Andy won the match 1 up, and then the championship."

Bean's winning par putt on the home hole was set up by an astonishing shot, a desperation slash at his ball in a water hazard to the front left of the green. It stopped three feet from the cup.

Of all the dramatic holes at the Point, the one best remembered is the par-3 ninth, a 192-yard carry over water to a narrow green perched on the edge of a cliff with a bunker in the prime bailout position.

Or, as Tom Watson put it, "Don't be short...or right...or left...or over!"

"It is designed for both difficulty and beauty," said Dr. Gil Morgan. "But after you have your par, you are glad to have it behind you."

And, figured Andy North, the 1971 winner, "Sweet memories are made when (it's) birdied."

Always a favorite gallery hole—it's beautiful, and besides, there's a must-visit Wilbur's homemade ice cream stand nearby—the ninth is the place to see and be seen. In 1992, everybody watching in the third round of qualifying saw Todd Demsey smack a soaring 4-iron that one-hopped into the cup for an ace and a $10,000 donation to the Evans Scholars Foundation in his name from M&W Tire in Benton Harbor.

That's the Western Amateur at Point O'Woods, where the big names of the future hone their skills in one of the grandest tournaments in amateur golf.

Twenty-three years later, Johnny Miller added his cogent commentary on WHFB as his son Andy Miller fought his way to the 1997 final, and a loss to Danny Green on the first extra hole of the championship match.

Scott Simpson should have been on the radio in 1975. Here's how he remembered the critical 15th hole in the semifinal match between Strange and Andy Bean, which he called "the most exciting I've ever seen."

"Andy hit his second way right in the woods," Simpson recalled. "Curtis had driven perfect but hit a

WEISKOPF REMEMBERS

The squawk over the walkie-talkie was short and direct.

"Tom Weiskopf wants to see you right now," went the message. "He's teed off. He's in the middle of the first fairway."

The message was for Marshall Dann, the WGA's executive director at the time. It came from the first tee in the 1969 Western Open at Midlothian Country Club in Midlothian, Illinois.

"Oh-oh," said Dann.

Weiskopf teeing off was one thing and being teed off was another, and the radio message sent mixed signals to Dann. He left the WGA's headquarters trailer and took off in a cart toward the first fairway.

"I caught him before his third shot, and said, 'Tom, is there anything I can do for you?' Dann recalled. "He said, 'Stand there while I play this shot.' He played it, went up and putted out, and said, 'C'mon over to the second tee.'

"'When did I first play with you?' he asked me, knowing it was 1964, when he got into the Western Open, his first tour event, for winning the Western Amateur the year before. 'I won $487.50, and here's a check for that amount for the Evans Scholars Foundation.'"

Over the years, Weiskopf continued to donate an amount equal to that check he earned with a tie for 30th place in 1964. In 1982 he upped the ante when, after five top-six finishes in the championship, he finally broke through and added the Western Open crown to his Western Amateur title. Then, he announced he would donate $4,875 from the winning check.

"Maybe there's a little bit of destiny in this game," Weiskopf said.

Tom Weiskopf's win in the 1963 Western Amateur earned him an invitation to the 1964 Western Open. Western Amateur Tournament Chairman George Webb presents the trophy.

There is some charity as well. Weiskopf is one of many touring professionals who have donated to the Evans Scholars Program over the years. Among the members of the Par Club are former Western Open winners Arnold Palmer, Jack Nicklaus, Hale Irwin, Tom Watson, Ben Crenshaw, Nick Price, and Tiger Woods.

TIGER MASTERS
THE WESTERN AMATEUR

James F. Ashenden, Jr. vividly remembers Saturday, August 6, 1994, the day he witnessed the coming of Tiger Woods.

Playing in a quarterfinal match in the Western Amateur, Woods sank a 40-foot par-saving putt to halve the first hole of sudden death, then drained a 20-foot, downhill eagle putt on the next hole to defeat a charging Chris Tidland.

"When Tiger Woods made those two putts to win that match, we had a foretaste of what was going to happen with that man's career," said Ashenden, a Western Golf Association director and past president.

Woods, soon to enter his freshmen year at Stanford, won his next two matches to claim the 1994 Western Amateur title—his first victory in a major amateur championship. Later that same month, Woods won the first of three straight U.S. Amateur titles.

Most remarkable about Woods' win at the Western Amateur, Ashenden noted, was that Woods' final two putts came after Tidland, an Oklahoma State standout, had turned in six straight birdies—including a 60-foot chip-in on the 18th—to send the match into sudden death.

"With six holes to play, Tiger was 4 up, and he played the last six holes in two-under-par," Ashenden said. "How could he possibly not win?" But Tidland's sextuplet birdie string pulled the match all square after 18.

"It looked like it was Chris Tidland's day to shine," said Ashenden, who followed the action in sudden death after joining the match on the 15th hole of the championship's annual venue, Point O'Woods Golf & Country Club in Benton Harbor, Michigan.

The playoff started on the par-4 first hole at the Point. Tidland dropped his approach shot onto the center of the green, about 20 feet from the cup. Woods, after pulling his drive, had a good lie from the left rough. Then disaster nearly struck.

"Tiger airmailed his approach out of the rough and hit a lady standing on the back of the green. The ball dropped about four or five feet behind the green," Ashenden said. "If he hadn't hit that lady, he would have been another 30 feet past the green."

Still, Woods faced a nearly impossible shot, with the pin tucked near the back edge of the green, which sloped severely away from him. His

Tiger Woods wowed the crowds at the Point in 1994 the way he wows them now on the pro circuit.

pitch rolled 40 feet past the cup.

"So now, Chris appeared to have the match won. He had an easy two-putt up the hill for par."

Woods remained undaunted. He stepped up to his ball and drained the 40-foot putt to save par and send the match to a second playoff

hole. "I had this funny feeling ... I saw the line of my putt," he told reporters after the match. "I stood over it and said, 'Just hit it, and it will go in.' Just a fluke thing that happened at the right time."

Tidland birdied the short, par-5 second, but Woods calmly knocked in a 20-foot, downhill, breaking eagle putt to win the match and advance to the semifinals.

"How could anyone play the last eight holes in a match in seven under par as Tidland did ... and lose?" Ashenden quizzed. "But he did, because here was Tiger making a 40-foot putt and then a 20-foot eagle putt. You could almost see the future for Tiger Woods, when he overcame that kind of a comeback by his opponent to win. I've never seen anything like it. It is now a fond memory of a spectacular competitor at the beginning of his outstanding career."

Woods followed his quarterfinal win with more routine victories in the semifinals and finals to claim his first and only Western Amateur title. "This win means a lot to me," said Woods. "All the big tournaments I've won until now have been junior tournaments. This is a great tournament on a great golf course. It really is the Masters of amateur golf."

Less than three years later, Woods stunned the golf world with his record-breaking victory in professional golf's Masters at Augusta National.

Jim Ashenden and others who witnessed Woods' match against Tidland at Point O'Woods weren't surprised.

In fact, WGA officials had been watching Tiger Woods mature as a golfer since 1992, when Woods competed in his first WGA tournament, the 75th Western Junior.

The match-play portion of the championship was held at the prestigious Chicago Golf Club, that Wheaton enclave which dates back to the end of the last century and the beginnings of golf in the Chicago area. WGA officials made sure everybody who was anybody in the ever-changing junior game was invited to play.

As a result, the Western Junior had one of its finest fields and some famous names.

Nicklaus, for one—Michael Nicklaus, Jack and Barbara's youngest, with a swing and gait that looked just like his father's.

And Woods—Eldrick Woods, already known by the nickname of "Tiger," and already displaying, while rough-edged, the game that would make him famous later in the decade.

By the time of the 1992 Western Junior, sixteen-year-old Woods had played in the Los Angeles Open (thanks to the invitation of future WGA Tournament Director Greg McLaughlin), and had won a U.S. Junior and a pair of American Junior Golf Association events. Even then, the lanky kid with the easy smile and the plus 3.2 handicap index attracted

reporters simply by arriving on the scene. He gave them plenty to write about.

"My goals have always been kind of high," he said. "My dad tries to tone that down sometimes, because I get so goal-conscious that sometimes I lose my focus."

Young Woods would qualify for the 32-player match-play portion of the championship, winning his first-round match against eighteen-year-old Jason Enloe of Decatur, Illinois, on the 20th hole. Woods was 1 down with four holes left, but came back by making three straight birdies. He then watched Enloe sink an impossible putt on the home hole to force extra holes. Woods finally won the match on Chicago Golf's stout second hole, a 440-yard par-4 with a routine two-putt.

"It was like two fighters out there," Woods said. "Who was going to crack? We both did, and then saved it."

Woods would be knocked out in the quarterfinals the following afternoon, falling 3 and 1 to Ted Purdy of Scottsdale, Arizona, after beating medalist Kevin Mihailoff of Naples, Florida, 3 and 2. "I didn't have it," Woods said after his six-bogey quarterfinal performance.

John Curley of Osterville, Massachusetts, won the title, beating John Bernatovitz of Akron, Ohio, 4 and 2. But Woods, foreshadowing his future, made the headlines. ◘

Tiger Woods accepts a WGA medal from WGA Director and Western Junior Chairman John Kretzschmar for making the quarterfinals of the 1992 Western Junior at Chicago Golf Club, his first WGA appearance.

THE STORM

The tremendous storm that ravaged Point O'Woods just before the 1980 Western Amateur caused rules changes that benefit golfers today.

All things considered, 1980 was not a great year for course conditions in Western Golf Association championships. The greens at Butler National Golf Club died shortly before the club hosted the Western Open in early July. Later that month, 100-mile-per-hour winds tore through the Point O'Woods Golf & Country Club just 10 days before the start of the Western Amateur.

The dying greens at Butler National may have been an embarrassment, but golfers can putt on dead grass. Dead trees littering the entire Point O'Woods course in Benton Harbor, Michigan, posed a greater challenge.

If it wasn't a tornado that hit the Point O'Woods that year, it might as well have been. The heavily wooded Point lost 200 trees. Rather, they weren't lost. They were everywhere: uprooted, cracked in half, torn apart and deposited randomly. Trees fell in fairways, onto greens and into ponds. The Point was a mess. The course was closed with the Western Amateur looming.

Point O'Woods members—led by Bob Gerbel, who also was a WGA director—worked alongside staff and cleanup crews to bring the course to playability. For days, the sound of chain saws and heavy logging apparatus filled the air. The Point looked and sounded more like a lumber mill than a golf course.

The dawn-to-dusk efforts paid off. By Wednesday, July 30, when the championship opened, the Point was playable, albeit with special local rules established for the occasion.

"There was one concession that got the most attention," recalled Marshall Dann, then the WGA's executive director. "Because of the trees on the golf course, we ruled that a tree that was attached to its roots was still a tree. A tree that was not attached was ruled to be ground under repair.

"I called P.J. Boatwright of the USGA to tell him, and he

These rules allowed the Amateur to proceed despite stumps and debris strewn across the course.

said, 'You can't do it that way, because that's not the rule, but you've got to do it that way, or you don't have a tournament.'"

Today, check the USGA/R&A Decisions on the Rules of Golf, and you will eventually come to Decisions 25/7, 25/8, and 25/9, all of which have to do with trees in various states of distress. Having considered the situation at the 1980 Western Amateur, the rules makers decided that not only do unattached trees now qualify as ground under repair because they are "material piled for removal," but fallen trees still attached can be ruled as ground under repair at the discretion of the committee.

The Western Amateur, operating in 1980 with its own makeshift "storm" rules, turned into a dandy. U.S. Amateur champion Mark O'Meara was the medalist in qualifying but fell to Fred Couples on the 19th hole in the quarterfinals. Couples was knocked out in the semifinals by David Ogrin, the pride of Waukegan, Illinois, on the third hole of sudden death, and Ogrin, in turn, fell to defending champion Hal Sutton 4 and 3 in the title match. ◻

David Ogrin and Fred Couples before their 1980 Western Amateur semifinal match. Ogrin won on the third hole of sudden death.

Hal Sutton, seen here with the George S. May Trophy in 1979, beat David Ogrin 4 and 3 in the 1980 championship match.

CHAPTER

18

"WELCOME TO COG HILL"

*I*t is midday in the second round of the 1997 Motorola Western Open at Cog Hill Golf & Country Club in Lemont, Illinois.

On the golf course, affectionately and accurately named Dubsdread, Justin Leonard is fashioning a cozy 8-under-par 64, good enough to make him the leader after 36 holes. Eldrick " Tiger" Woods, who would end up winning this 94th edition of the Western Open, has yet to assert himself, but thousands are in his gallery.

Off the course, in the air-conditioned comfort of the media tent, Cog Hill Chairman Joe Jemsek is having lunch. Jemsek, the old pro who made public-course

Cog Hill Golf & Country Club has been a mecca for Chicago-area golfers since it opened during the Roaring '20s.

golfers feel more like kings than commoners, usually holds court at lunchtime, telling old stories and picking up gossip from the morning rounds. On this particular Friday, Jemsek is alone and spies a reporter looking for a free lunch. He motions the scribe over.

"You know what?" Jemsek says without prompting. "I wouldn't have this here if it wasn't for the caddies."

In two sentences, Joe Jemsek, a caddie early in the century, had summed up why he volunteered to turn over his golf course to the Western Golf Association in the fall of 1990, when the fallout from the Shoal Creek controversy meant the Western Open could no longer be played at Butler National Golf Club in Oak Brook. Faced with moving its venerable championship to a new site, the WGA had started an immediate search for a Chicago-area club willing to serve as host.

"We were concerned," said WGA Executive Director Donald D. Johnson. "Unlike other tournaments, where the money goes to the Jaycees or the United Way, our money goes to one charity—the Evans Scholarships for caddies." Without a mutually beneficial agreement with a new host club, the tournament's profitability could be threatened, resulting in less money for caddie scholarships.

The Western Open needed help. Caddies, those put through college by the Evans Scholars Foundation, needed help. An old caddie, one who made himself a success without the benefit of college, wasn't going to stand by and see scholarships disappear. Certainly, Cog Hill had built a fine reputation without the Western Open. But there was something else at stake here. Doing what is right.

Joe Jemsek would do what was right. The publicity, and there would be plenty for Jemsek and his Cog Hill domain, would be a bonus.

This was the Shoal Creek controversy in simple terms. Several weeks before the 1990 PGA Championship, the second to be held at the Birmingham, Alabama, country club, Shoal Creek founder Hall Thompson said he saw no way blacks would become members of the private club.

"The country club is our home and we pick and choose who we want," Thompson told the *Birmingham Post-Herald*. "I think we've said we don't discriminate in every other area except the blacks."

Thompson promptly said that he was misquoted, then apologized. It didn't matter. From the story's publication on June 21, 1990, criticism grew. The PGA of America, followed by the PGA Tour and USGA, quickly formulated criteria for hosting tournaments that forbade discrimination in memberships. Shoal Creek hosted the PGA only after a black was admitted as an honorary member.

The PGA Tour's new rule stated that clubs discriminating "on the basis of race, religion, sex, or national origin" would not be allowed to host events.

The Western Open, a co-sponsored PGA Tour event, and subject to the Tour's rules, would be affected immediately. Butler National's bylaws said nothing about race, religion, or national origin, and its membership reflected that. Sex, though, was another matter. Butler National was a men-only club, was chartered as such, and was going to remain as such.

So the Western Open, a championship for which Butler National's course was designed, would abruptly be leaving the club it had called home since 1974.

Jemsek quickly offered Cog Hill's facilities to the WGA. It was an offer the WGA could not refuse. Jemsek gave the course to the WGA rent-free, while the WGA paid for upgrades to course infrastructure to accommodate television, scoreboards, and all the other trappings of modern tournament life.

"This is a nationally ranked facility owned and operated by the Jemsek family, which has had a lifelong commitment to golf," Johnson said in announcing the agreement. "We look forward to our partnership."

The new agreement meant the WGA would add a great course to its roster, one with perhaps fewer chances for unmitigated disaster than Butler National proffered in a round, but one with great shot values, greens that invited the holding of one's breath, and the length necessary for the modern-day game. And unlike Butler, which was built on a flood plain, Dubsdread is situated on a fast-draining bluff. The Western Open's

Joe Jemsek ordered Cog Hill's Dubsdread course built in 1964, then offered it to the WGA for the Western Open in the late fall of 1990.

problems with massive floods would be no more.

Cog Hill also had 250 acres of parking and, in Dubsdread's routing, a layout which had plenty of room for spectators.

In moving from Butler National to Dubsdread, the Western Open went from strength to strength. Dubsdread had been designed by Dick Wilson and Joe Lee as a quality, championship layout. Since its opening in 1964, the course already had hosted three U.S. Public Links championships—two for men and one for women—the 1988 Western Junior, and a never-ending series of qualifying events for USGA championships. Everyone knew the course would be ready for the professionals. The only question was whether the professionals would like it.

They did. The 1991 Western Open saw Dubsdread open to rave reviews.

"I think you gained something moving from Butler," said Bob Gilder, who owned (and still owns) the Butler National course record of 8-under-par 64. "This is the best public golf course I've ever played. I don't think the TPC courses stand up to all this."

Virtually everyone liked Dubsdread. Several professionals voiced the opinion that a U.S. Open could be played on Dubsdread. (In 1997, the USGA brought the U.S. Amateur to Cog Hill but has so far not awarded its Open to the Lemont layout.)

Dubsdread's first Western Open lived up to the championship's expect-the-unexpected standard, delivering a shocking finish on a level with the first Western Open played at Butler National.

At Butler in 1974, Tom Weiskopf surrendered the lead to Tom Watson on the final holes. At Cog Hill in 1991, Greg Norman surrendered the lead to Russ Cochran on the final holes.

The Great White Shark led by five strokes standing on the 11th tee and lost. Cochran birdied the 15th and 16th, the latter on a 35-foot putt, to get into position. Norman waved him by with bogeys on the 13th (via an unplayable lie in a jungle to the front left of the green), the 14th (three putts from 16 feet), the 15th (a mammoth tee shot hooked into the woods to the left), and the 16th (an approach landing in a lady's purse). Needing a birdie on the 18th to tie Cochran, Norman took a bogey and lost by two strokes. He had turned a potential 66 into a 71 and a second place finish, just one stroke in front of Fred Couples in third.

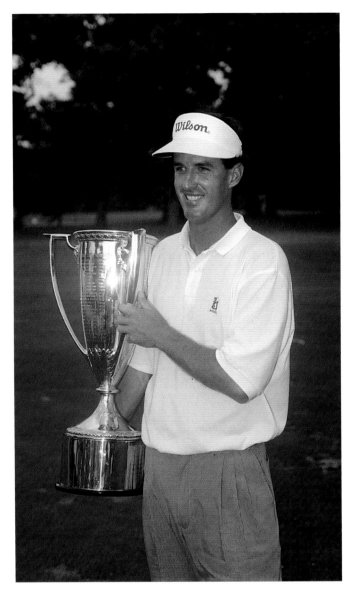

Timely birdies by Russ Cochran, combined with Greg Norman's collapse, brought Cochran the first Western Open title determined at Cog Hill.

"I stubbed my toe," said Norman more than once. "I had a chance to win fairly easily. I have to take it philosophically."

He had opened the round with three birdies and a hole-out eagle (a 5-iron on the par-4 fourth) in the first five holes, then faded.

Cochran, the only left-handed player in the field, captured his first victory on the PGA Tour.

The real winner, though, was Dubsdread. The fans turned out as expected, the players loved it almost uniformly, and the feel during the week was that of a major.

"We had a very successful week," Johnson declared when the tournament concluded. "We had a great field, the players loved the course and we had large crowds every day. It's almost too good to be true."

At the same time, there was a genuine feeling of good fellowship throughout the grounds. Whether it was an Evans Scholar directing traffic in the parking lots, Joe Jemsek or his son, Frank, greeting fans at the course's front gate, or friends gathering at the great amphitheater by the par-3 14th (nicknamed "Pork Chop Hill" after the tasty sandwiches sold there), the Western Open at Cog Hill had developed the atmosphere of a county fair.

There was a moment during the third round in 1991 that captured the essence. In just 30 seconds, if one was leaning against the right tree, one could hear a roar from the sixth green (Couples making a birdie to take the lead), a roar from the seventh green (Illinois' own Gary Hallberg sinking a critical par putt), and a roar from the fifth green (Norman making a birdie to match Couples at 11-under). It was terrific entertainment.

There was more the following year, when Norman was second again, this time to Ben Crenshaw, who triumphed after a final round that saw four players hold the lead at various junctures and 11 players still within four strokes late in the afternoon.

"Golf is strange," said Crenshaw after winning for the first time in more than two years. He won by a stroke, making a birdie on the par-4 17th, then watching as Norman's bid for a birdie on the last hole, a curling uphill 15-footer, stopped six inches short of dead center.

The drama, which included Couples making a bid and Chip Beck making a double-bogey on the penultimate hole to drop from contention, attracted 38,000 to Dubsdread. The crowd, the largest in Western Open history to that point, removed any doubts that the championship might not draw in Lemont. By the win-

Greg Norman was the runner-up the first three years the Western Open was played on Dubsdread.

ter of 1992-93, the Jemseks and the WGA had agreed on a new 10-year deal that would make the Western Open a fixture at Cog Hill through 2002.

Nick Price soon became a fixture in the winner's circle. One of the three players vanquished by Tom Kite in the 1986 playoff, Price ran away with the 1993 Western Open. He opened with an 8-under 64 and finished with a total of 19-under 269, one off the tourna-

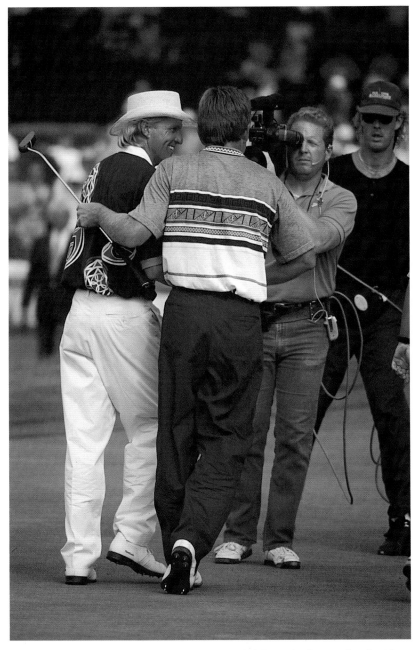

In 1993, Norman could do nothing but congratulate Nick Price after he romped to the title.

the adjacent Mount Assisi Academy, Price quipped: "That'll help." Things began to happen. Kraft made a birdie from a bunker on the par-3 12th, but played the last six holes 3-over, including a 5-5 finish on the closing par 4s. His bogey on the home hole, which Price had also bogeyed in the group ahead, was set up by an approach that slid into a bunker to the right of the green. He needed to get close to a pin on the edge of a slope—a shot with no margin for error—and ended up 25 feet below the hole. Facing that putt to tie Price, he missed.

"It was my tournament to win or lose," Kraft said.

His to lose, finally. And Price's to win for the second year running. The win also marked the first successful Western Open title defense since Jack Nicklaus in 1967-68. Price, buoyed by the victory, went on to win the British Open and PGA Championship in the following few weeks, becoming the first player to annex a Western-British-PGA triple in a calendar year.

In 1995, Price's opening round 3-over 75 was his first over-par round in the Western Open since it moved to Dubsdread. He had been a cumulative 44-under-par the previous four years. He wouldn't win three Westerns in a row, as Ralph Guldahl had in 1936-37-38, finishing tied for 13th. But he was only four strokes off the pace, as the 92nd Western Open, the first played for a $2 million total purse, saw a battle for the lead that seemed to involve half the field.

Sunday's final round didn't separate the field, but congested it. Near the end of the round, an astonishing 19 players were within four shots of the lead, which was held by Billy Mayfair.

Mayfair walked to the 18th green unaware that he still was in a tie for the lead. Caddie Dan Heber knew the score, however, and told Mayfair that the right-to-left 5-footer for birdie he was looking at on the final hole was worth making. So he made it, took sole possession of the lead at 9-under, and ended up the winner.

Before making the winning putt "I bent over and I thought I broke a rib because I couldn't get any air into

ment record. His wire-to-wire triumph was the first in the Western Open in 60 years. Norman, five strokes behind, was runner-up for the third straight year and for a record fifth time overall.

In 1994, Price had a tougher time. The long birdie putts didn't fall as frequently. With five holes to play, he trailed Greg Kraft by three strokes. However, on the 14th tee, after posing for a picture taken by a nun from

Annually, the crowds climb the hill behind the 14th green at Cog Hill to watch the action and soak up the sun.

Nick Price rarely strayed from the fairways during his 1993 championship march.

me," said Mayfair after regaining his color. "So if you think there isn't pressure out here, there is."

Mayfair, in typical Western fashion, saw others fold under that pressure. Brett Ogle took the scenic route to oblivion. John Huston caught a case of four-putts. Steve Lowery and Jay Haas crashed.

Bob Estes, the leader with three holes to play, claimed malfunctioning scoreboards had led him to believe he was tied for the lead, not in the lead. Thinking he needed a birdie to win, he made a bad swing on the 16th fairway, one that sent his ball to the left and double-bogey land. The scoreboards? Nobody had used that one before. "I definitely would have been leaning on that shot just a little bit to keep it to the right if I'd known I had a one-shot lead," he said.

None of the runners-up needed an excuse in the 1996 Motorola Western Open. None of them were close enough to Steve Stricker to need one. Stricker won by eight strokes, the largest margin in a Western Open in 44 years.

His last 41 holes, he was 14-under-par. In one 18-hole stretch, from the 14th in the second round through the 13th in the third, he needed but 61 strokes, 11 under regulation. Had that been on a No. 1 through No. 18 journey, it would have been a course record by two strokes, supplanting the efforts of Jeff Sluman in 1992 and John Adams in 1993. Or take Stricker's inward nine on Friday and his outward nine on Saturday—a pair of 31s, good for a 62 in more standard circumstances.

And all because his wife and caddie Nicki put the spurs to him while they waited on the 14th tee on Friday.

"I was down on myself," Stricker recalled. "Then she got on me. I snapped back at her. When I get going this way, my fuse is pretty short. I didn't yell at her, but I got pretty testy.

"I went by the ropes by myself and thought. I got

Price's wire-to-wire 1993 win was the first in the Western Open since Macdonald Smith's at Olympia Fields in 1933.

Billy Mayfair accepts the mammoth winner's check from Motorola officials Bob Weisshappel and Christopher Galvin after his surprise 1995 win.

frustrated in a good way. I freewheeled it from then on."

Stricker, who had opened with a 7-under 65, finished at 18-under 270, eight strokes ahead of Billy Andrade and Jay Don Blake, who were rumored to be playing the same golf course.

The same feeling came over players at times in 1997, when Tiger Woods visited the Motorola Western Open for the first time as a professional. When his intention to play was revealed on January 9, the WGA phones overloaded. One new phone system later, ticket orders cascaded in, and when the gates opened, the largest crowds in the history of the championship poured onto the Cog Hill grounds.

Woods was not the first of black or Asian heritage to play in the Western Open. In 1930, Atlanta-born Robert Ball, by then living in Chicago and running a miniature golf operation on Wabash Avenue, made the

first of two appearances. He missed the cut at Indianwood near Detroit, and again failed to make the final 36 holes in 1931 at Miami Valley Golf Club in Dayton, Ohio.

In both cases Ball broke an informal color barrier that became formal by the WGA's adoption of a "Caucasians only, except by invitation" rule, prominently placed on the entry blank, from1932, eleven years before the PGA of America adopted a similar restriction, to 1948. Whether the rule was directed at Ball personally, or he happened to be caught up in it, has not been determined.

Not until 1956 did the barrier fall, when Ted Rhodes and Charlie Sifford played in the Western Open. It took that long because starting in 1950, the WGA used the PGA's membership regulations to determine eligibility of professionals in the Western Open.

Undoubtedly, the 1956 Western Open's setting, the racially-advanced city of San Francisco, and the use of the U.S. Army-owned Presidio course, helped the barrier come down. Rhodes finished tied for 35th, earning $110, while Sifford missed the cut.

In 1935, a barnstorming group of six Japanese golfers was invited to tee it up in the Western Open at South Bend Country Club, the first from the Orient to play. Five of the six made the cut, with Kanekichi Nakamura finishing 15th and winning $50.

What the galleries of 1997 saw was a splendid exhibition.

Woods, like Jack Nicklaus 35 years earlier, could do things to and with a golf ball that others could not. Take his second shot on the 568-yard par-5 ninth hole in the second round. Mere mortals would have laid up after driving into the right rough, with a stand of trees in the way. Not Woods, who gambled from 236 yards out and hit a slicing 2-iron to within yards of the green.

The throngs prompted WGA officials to implement a helicopter shuttle service to transport some of the Tour professionals from their hotels to the course. A different air force would have been needed to stop Woods. He scored a three-stroke victory, one made more memorable by the Sunday gallery of 49,462 and their enthusiastic support of Tiger's quest for yet another win.

Woods had come into the tournament as the favorite. He already had won the 1997 Masters and four other events since joining the PGA Tour in the fall of 1996. Woods' ultimate victory was lent a mystical aura by the crowd, as thousands of fans spilled onto the fairway to follow him on his victorious walk down Dubsdread's famed 18th fairway. There had never been a scene like it in the near-century-long history of the Western Open, or in the history of golf in the United States, for that matter.

"I didn't really see them," said Woods later, when Cog Hill was beginning to return to normal. "I was facing forward. I didn't want to look back. I had to finish out the hole, and the hole's not behind me."

A few words from Nicki Stricker, Steve Stricker's wife and caddie, was what it took to send Steve off on a birdie binge that brought him the 1996 Western Open crown.

Presently, it was, and Woods became the seventh player to win both the Western Open and Western Amateur, joining Scott Verplank, Andy Bean, Ben Crenshaw, Tom Weiskopf, Jack Nicklaus and, of course, Chick Evans as double winners.

In one short week in July, Tiger Woods had enhanced his young legend, and the WGA saw its Open championship enhanced in kind.

Tiger Woods and a few thousand of his closest friends on the final fairway in 1997.

Mike Tirico (left), ABC-TV golf host, presents WGA Executive Director Don Johnson and WGA President H. Grant Clark, Jr. with the 1998 Metropolitan Golf Writers Association's Bing Crosby Tournament Sponsor Award. The award recognizes the WGA's dual sponsorship of the Western Open and the Evans Scholars Foundation, the tournament's sole charitable beneficiary.

The magical finish of the 1997 Western was the highlight of Tiger Woods' summer.

THE WESTERN'S EVANS SCHOLARS

They're everywhere at Cog Hill Golf & Country Club during Motorola Western Open week.

They're working behind the scenes, working at jobs that are thankless, and working at jobs that often don't afford them much time to watch golf.

They are Scholars and Alumni of the Evans Scholars Program.

Continuing a tradition that dates from 1962, when the Western Open was anchored in the Chicago area, the Scholars and Alumni help in many aspects of the massive operation, from parking cars to working in gallery control.

When pro-am guests drive up to the Cog Hill clubhouse, an Evans Scholar greets them, takes their clubs, makes sure they know who they'll be playing with, and wishes them a great day.

When thousands of cars descend on the Lemont area, every one of them driven by a golf fan intent on getting into the parking lots in the shortest available time, the Scholars and Alumni point them in the right direction.

When bad weather threatens and the players have to be evacuated, Scholars and Alumni assist in driving the player shuttles.

Thanks to these Scholars and Alumni, much of the load is lifted from Tournament Director Greg McLaughlin's back.

"In 1997, we had a problem with our will-call (ticket pickup) site," McLaughlin recalled. "Boom! Five alumni took it over. Problem solved. And in the parking lots, we have over 250 Scholars and Alumni working every day."

That year, Scholars even made it onto Dubsdread doing what comes naturally: caddying. At the behest of 1987 Western Open champion D.A. Weibring, current Evans Scholars were invited to caddie for PGA Tour players during the Chick Evans Memorial Pro-Am. The PGA Tour players donated the pro-am purse to the Evans Scholars

Evans Scholar Brian Shell, president of the Indiana University chapter, caddied for Tiger Woods in the 1997 Chick Evans Memorial Pro-Am.

Foundation. It was a reminder of the days from 1962 through 1986, when local caddies carried players' bags during the Western Open itself. It also was one more way to help preserve Chick Evans' dream of sending caddies to college. ◻

Prospective Evans Scholars of long ago bone up on caddie technique by reading the WGA's "Pin Pointers" brochure.

When WGA people need things done at the Western Open, it's the Evans Scholars who carry the load, including Dick Daniels (above), an Evans Scholars alumnus and WGA director.

Traffic jams are minimized at Cog Hill thanks to the hard-working Evans Scholars and Alumni in the parking lots.

Evans Scholars are on hand during the Western Open to tell their story.

This Evans Scholars promotional campaign commissioned in 1990 by Centel, then the sponsor of the Western Open, featured not models, but authentic Scholars Robert Dugdale (Northwestern '90) and Stacie Young (Northwestern '91).

THE FUTURE

Today, the Western Golf Association and the Evans Scholars Foundation are strong, both financially and in leadership. But what of the future? What of the caddie population? Will country clubs have caddies 20, 40, 100 years from now? Will the cost of college tuition, the biggest single bill the Evans program has to pay, spiral out of control?

What of the Western Open, which has grown into a major source of funding for the Evans Scholarships? Could its days be threatened by the trend toward mammoth PGA Tour purses?

These are some of the questions the WGA faces as the millennium turns. WGA officials are confident the organization is strong enough to meet the challenges ahead.

"I see us as very strong," says H. Grant Clark, Jr., the WGA's president in 1998 and 1999. "We can look back at our first 100 years with pride and, since 1930, with great satisfaction in the success of the Evans Scholarships.

"Our tournaments continue to rank among the most prestigious in the nation, golf is growing in popularity, and the development of the Evans Scholars Program speaks for itself," Clark said. "We can see the evidence in the Evans Scholars, in their career accomplishments and in what they've given back to the program in terms of donations."

The WGA's achievements are clear. So, too, are the challenges.

"First, we must maintain strong caddie programs. Our success depends on the game of golf itself, on the support we receive from our member clubs," Clark said. "That support comes not only in the form of dollars but through the maintenance of strong caddie programs.

"At many of our member clubs, caddie programs continue to thrive," he added. "However, at some of the new clubs, particularly those built as real-estate developments, caddies are very tough to find. At new clubs, it's a tough sell, no question about it."

Sometimes a special effort is required to maintain caddie programs at traditional clubs as well, even those historically affiliated with the WGA.

"The Country Club of Florida—founded by one of the Western Golf Association's most prominent leaders, Carleton Blunt—used to have caddies and dropped them a few years ago," Clark recalled. "Now, they're trying to establish a caddie program again, but the older members are all used to riding. And the area is less populated

WGA President H. Grant Clark, Jr., before the painting of Chick Evans in the WGA's Directors Room.

with youth. I've talked to the professional there about using forecaddies. That's a good compromise. We've had cases where forecaddies have qualified for the Evans scholarship."

The WGA has developed a broad-based caddie information program to assist clubs and public courses in promoting walking and the use of caddies.

For club officials, the WGA offers a comprehensive Caddie Operations Manual that outlines the hows and whys of starting and maintaining a caddie program.

For caddies, the WGA offers a videotape, "Caddie Your Way to College," which provides a review of the basics of both caddying and the Evans Scholars Foundation. Accompanying the video is a caddie instruction manual that lists the duties and responsibilities of a caddie. Additionally, since the late 1940s, the WGA has provided "Honor Caddie" badges to clubs to award to their best caddies each year.

A caddie services director, employed seasonally, works with individual clubs in developing and maintaining caddie programs and conducts informational seminars on such topics as the recruitment and training of caddies.

All of the above has helped buttress caddie programs across the country. In Chicago, for example, the WGA assisted in the development of a caddie program at Jackson Park Golf Course, a municipally-owned course on the city's south side. Jackson Park, which celebrates its 100th anniversary in 1999, had not had caddies walk its grounds for decades when WGA and Jackson Park officials began building the foundation for today's caddie program. Now, Jackson Park not only actively promotes the use of caddies, several of the course's caddies have earned Evans Scholarships.

"Jackson Park definitely is one of our success stories, and there are many more," said WGA Executive Director Donald D. Johnson. "We have actively sought to assist in the development of caddie programs in areas where the use of caddies has declined, yet where there are many young men and women who would benefit from both the experience of caddying and the unique opportunity provided by an Evans Scholarship."

So far, the WGA's supportive stance has kept caddies in the forefront at many of its member clubs and has provided the Evans Scholars Foundation with an ample number of worthy scholarship candidates.

"Our base for caddie scholarships has held firm," Johnson said. "There's no question that there's a correlation between the health of caddie programs and the number of applications we receive for Evans Scholarships, and in the past several years we've had more candidates than ever. Certainly we're concerned about the potential for a decline in caddie programs, but we believe we're taking the necessary steps to ensure caddies will be a part of golf for a long, long time."

One of those steps was the WGA's strong support of the National Club Association's 1997 dispute with the Internal Revenue Service regarding caddies. The IRS sought to have caddies, long considered as independent contractors, reclassified as club employees. That change threatened the future of the caddie industry in the United States. The IRS has since backed down from its stance, and presently there is legislation in Congress to exempt caddies from full-time employee status.

Robert L. McMasters, an Evans Scholar Alumnus and the WGA's president in 1996 and 1997, helped lead the campaign for new legislation. "We were pro-active and wrote letters, but it would have fallen on deaf ears without Congress taking the IRS to the woodshed," said McMasters, who believes the ultimate threat to caddies might come not from

An early Honor Caddie badge.

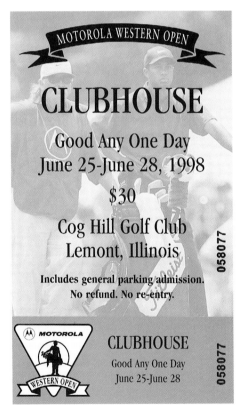

Individual Western Open ticket buyers are a big part of the Evans Scholars Foundation's continuing success.

233

A quintet of WGA Presidents, Carleton Blunt (1957), William F. Souder, Jr. (1962-63), Tom King (1964-65), Harold Moore (1958-59), and James Royer (1960-61) gather in the mid-1960s.

the cart, but from society's changing values.

"Short-term, caddie programs are still going to be strong," he says. "Long-term, the question is this: Are families into teaching their kids the work ethic? In Space Age America, kids are in poverty because of a lack of love. A lot of kids today don't have direction. To sign up to caddie at 6 a.m., to work all day, to hang around the caddie yard, it's a great opportunity. That's where we have to educate families."

Clark, McMasters, and Johnson all believe the caddie tradition must, and will, be preserved.

Johnson, himself a caddie in his high school days, can't conceive of the concept of a caddieless golf society.

"I don't see it happening," he says, noting the strong Midwestern tradition of golfing with a caddie. "Our directors and other club leaders have worked hard in recent years to promote the merits of walking and taking a caddie. It's the traditional way to play the game, it's the best way to play, and many golfers today, young and old, agree.

"We will continue to work hard to reach into areas where young people need and want to improve themselves through education and, as evidenced by the Jackson Park program and others, our efforts are paying dividends," Johnson said. "Many families today still do believe in and practice the work ethic, and they definitely believe in the value of a college education. Our job is to find those families in need and to educate them on the merits of caddying and of applying for an Evans Scholarship.

"The quality of the parents and of the young people we meet with and talk to at our selection meetings reinforces my faith not only in the future of caddie programs, but in the future of our society," added Johnson.

When future caddies do apply for the Evans Scholarships, the WGA will need the funds necessary to keep pace with the increasing costs of college. That is the second challenge the WGA faces as it enters its second century. Fortunately, the financial picture is much brighter today than it was a decade ago.

"We were a hand-to-mouth organization from 1930 to 1988," says Johnson. "We were borrowing money to pay our bills. Our goal every year was to raise enough money from the Par Club and Bag Tag programs to pay the tuition."

The WGA directorate in 1976 (left to right) Front row: Rex Bruno, George Garvey; Middle row: Nels Ulseth, Mike McDermott, Elon Ellis, Carleton Blunt, Leo Lederer, Chick Evans, Chuck Simmons; Back row: Bruce Goodman, Ells Widermann, Tom Reynolds, Bob Bohnen, Joe Ewen, Dick Campbell, Gene Firmine.

The WGA, adversely affected by the high interest rates of the 1970s, no longer is forced to take out loans and repay them from fund-raising proceeds. Now, the money is in the bank, earning interest before the checks to colleges are written. Plus, the McGuigan Endowment Fund, established in the 1980s, has provided a rainy-day cushion.

The program's growth over seven decades has dictated a corresponding need for greater fiscal responsibility. When the WGA began sponsorship of the Evans Scholars Program in 1930, tuition at Northwestern University was $300 a year. Two caddies received scholarships.

"In 1997, our tuition bill was over $4 million for the first time; that with 810 kids in college. In 1999, the tuition bill is expected to exceed $5 million," Johnson notes. "You can see the need for fund-raising if we want to keep this program at the current level. We want to keep up with the rising cost of tuition and somewhat expand the program.

"The ultimate goal is to have 1,000 Evans Scholars in college," he said. "That goal gets harder and harder to reach, because we have no control over tuition."

On the tournament side, the WGA also has little control over the size of the Western Open's purse. The PGA Tour encourages organizers of each event to increase their prize money as much as possible.

The Western Golf Association is governed by volunteer officers and directors, while a full-time staff conducts day-to-day operations. Among the WGA leaders are, in front (from left): Michael L. McDermott, Gregory T. McLaughlin, Bruce K. Goodman, James F. Ashenden, Jr., H. Grant Clark, Jr., Donald D. Johnson, Robert M. Alsteen, Rexford E. Bruno, and Bruce Korn. In back (from left) are: Raymond L. Fahrmeier, Lloyd F. McGlincy III, Robert L. McMasters, Roger J. Mohr, Gordon H. Ewen, John P. Hanna, Sam J. DiGiovanni, David U. Cookson, Raymond B. Anderson, David J. Shaw and James E. Moore.

In 1995, with the support of corporate title sponsor Motorola, the purse for the Motorola Western Open jumped from $1.2 million to $2 million just two months before the championship. PGA Tour officials and professionals applauded the move. The increase in PGA Tour purses has continued, however, and by 2003, the Tour hopes that virtually all tournaments will be awarding $3.5 million for four days of playing golf.

Johnson, who led the successful search for Motorola's backing in the early 1990s, when Sprint decided not to renew a deal previously negotiated by Centel, believes the Western Open's future is secure despite the growing costs.

"It would have to be something drastic that would cause us to consider abandoning the Western Open," said Johnson.

That possibility was last considered in the late 1950s and early 1960s, when purses increased dramatically and television became a major force in professional golf.

As long as corporate America and, more to the point, corporate Chicago, is willing to step forward, however, the Western Open will continue to hold its position as one of the world's oldest golf championships and one that, through pro-ams and ticket sales, provides a healthy slice of the Evans program's operating budget.

Also, golf fans in the Chicago area have supported the Western Open in increasing numbers. The tournament has enjoyed record crowds throughout the 1990s. The game of golf is growing in popularity, and golf fans are flocking to professional tournaments to see the world's best players perform. Increased television exposure and ancillary revenues have helped professional golf's position as one of the nation's healthiest spectator sports.

"The 1990s have been good years for professional golf, and we've enjoyed many of the related benefits as the sponsoring organization of Chicago's only PGA Tour event," Johnson said. "With the presence of Tiger Woods and many other young stars on the professional circuit, we see our sport continuing to grow in popularity."

Another reason for optimism is the WGA's penchant for attracting and then following capable leaders. Through the past century, the WGA has been guided by a series of visionary men, leaders such as Arthur Bowen, who pushed for the formation of the Associated Golf Clubs of Chicago in 1899, and David Forgan, who suggested naming the new group the Western Golf Association.

They were followed by leaders such as Chick Evans, who by convincing WGA leaders Charles Pfeil and Joe Busch to back his scholarship plan, set the WGA on a new course. Since 1930, the WGA's focus has moved away from conflict with the USGA over who controlled golf in the United States and toward the greater goal of benefiting society through the education of deserving caddies.

Then came leaders such as Carleton Blunt, who helped propel the Evans Scholars Program to new heights in the 1940s and 1950s. His work has been enhanced and perpetuated by the many past presidents of the WGA, the trustees of the Evans Scholars Foundation and, in recent years, countless Evans Scholars Alumni.

Indeed, one of the WGA's strongest assets is the Alumni base of Evans Scholars, who

Time seems to stand still at WGA headquarters in Golf, even as the progress of the Evans Scholars goes forward.

since 1992 have donated over $1 million a year to the program.

"That's the biggest single change," says Educational Director James E. Moore. "Their numbers, and their participation at all levels. We like to say that you become an Evans Scholar for four years but remain for a lifetime as an Alumnus."

The philosophy of working together fostered by longtime Educational Director Roland F. "Mac" McGuigan, who died in 1991, remains a legacy that builds in most Scholars the understanding that they are not only graduates of their particular university but of the Evans program as well.

"When freshmen move to campus, they find they've become part of a group that cares about them," Moore says. "You feel part of a group as a freshman because of the New Scholars Program. That safety net catches a big percentage of them. It's kind of a Big Brother and Big Sister program. The upperclassmen mentor the underclassmen. And the Alumni mentor the upperclassmen."

Chick Evans and his dedication to the education of caddies remains the focus of the Evans Scholars "family."

For some years, the WGA's informal slogan has been "Keep Chick's Dream Alive." Now, two decades after Chick Evans' death, with the Scholars who knew him approaching and going beyond middle age, with his victories in championship competition 75 years and more distant, there is another objective: Keep Chick's Memory Alive.

"I think our organization has done an excellent job of maintaining his profile, especially among the Evans Scholars," said WGA President Grant Clark.

Given that Evans' name is the foundation's name, that the phrase Evans Scholars is carved into the headquarters building's facade, that his picture and story still are given a prominent place in the Western Open's annual program, and that people still tell Chick Evans stories, there is really no need to worry.

Chick's memory is every bit as alive as the dream.

So, too, are the golf championships that Chick and his contemporaries at the WGA loved so much. Today, the Western Open, the Western Amateur, and the Western Junior remain among the nation's premier golf championships.

"We are fortunate and proud to be one of the nation's two oldest national golf organizations and to still be sponsoring annual championships for professional, amateur and junior golfers," said Clark. "Golf is our middle name, and it is a love of golf that has proved to be the common bond throughout our history. Our founders created the Western Golf Association to further the interests of golf and golfers in what then was considered the western United States."

Now, 100 years later, the WGA—with more than 500 member clubs—is one of the leading golf associations worldwide.

"If you look at where we are today, having sponsored more than 270 golf championships during the past century while also nurturing the nation's largest individually funded scholarship program, I think our founders would be proud of the work they started and which we are continuing," Clark said.

The true force behind the Western Golf Association's success has not been the strength or contributions of one individual or even a handful of leaders, explained Clark, the WGA's 57th president.

"All of our progress has been accomplished through the spirit, generosity, and hard work of thousands of volunteers, hundreds of thousands of donors, and the many friends of golf we have made in the past century," he noted. "We are an organization that has prospered for one reason: our mission of educating caddies and conducting national championships is centered around the greatest game ever played, a game that ultimately develops a passion and pride in those who play it, a game that inspires in all of us a sense that our goal truly is not whether we win or lose but how we play the game.

"I think the Western Golf Association and those who have supported it the past 100 years have played the game very well," Clark added. "They have left a legacy of scholarships and championships that will serve as an inspiration to all of us as we successfully carry on this worthwhile work well into the twenty-first century."

WGA PRESIDENTS

YEARS	PRESIDENT	CLUB
1899	**Hobart C. Chatfield-Taylor**	Onwentsia Club
1900-1901	**George R. Thorne**	Midlothian CC
1902	**William Holabird**	Glen View Club
1903	**Edward P. Martin**	Belmont CC
1904	**B.F. Cummins**	Belmont CC
1905	**Alan L. Reid**	Chicago Golf Club
1906	**Phelps B. Hoyt**	Glen View Club
1907-1908	**Albert R. Gates**	Calumet CC
1909	**Charles F. Thompson**	Homewood CC
1910	**Horace F. Smith**	Nashville G&CC
1911	**William Heyburn**	Louisville CC
1912-1913	**John D. Cady**	Rock Island Arsenal GC
1914	**Franklin L. Woodward**	Denver CC
1915-1916	**George R. Balch**	Cincinnati GC
1917-1919	**Charles F. Thompson**	Homewood CC
1920	**Wilbur H. Brooks**	Mayfield CC
1921-22	**Albert R. Gates**	Skokie CC
1923-1925	**Charles O. Pfeil**	Memphis CC
1926-1927	**Hobart P. Young**	Exmoor CC
1928-1929	**Robert M. Cutting**	Hinsdale GC
1930-1931	**Leslie S. Gordon**	Indian Hill Club
1932-1933	**R. Arthur Wood**	Exmoor CC
1934-1935	**Norman B. Freer**	Hinsdale GC
1936	**Henry C. Bartholomay**	Lake Geneva CC
1937-1938	**Gorton Fauntleroy**	Chicago Golf Club
1939-1940	**Leslie L. Cooke**	Bob O'Link GC
1941-1942	**Theodore C. Butz**	Exmoor CC

YEARS	PRESIDENT	CLUB
1943-1944	**William T. Woodson**	Flossmoor CC
1945	**Theodore C. Butz**	Exmoor CC
1946-1947	**James L. Garard**	Glen View Club
1948-1949	**Maynard G. Fessenden**	Bob O'Link GC
1950-1951	**Jerome P. Bowes, Jr.**	Exmoor CC
1952	**Gordon E. Kummer**	Milwaukee CC
1953-1954	**Stanley J. McGiveran**	Inverness Club
1955-1956	**James L. O'Keefe**	Evanston GC
1957	**Carleton Blunt**	Glen View Club
1958-1959	**Harold A. Moore**	Indian Hill Club
1960-1961	**James M. Royer**	Knollwood Club
1962-1963	**William F. Souder, Jr.**	Glen View Club
1964-1965	**Thomas V. King**	Evanston GC
1966-1967	**Adelor J. Petit, Jr.**	Knollwood Club
1968-1969	**Boyd J. Simmons**	Indian Hill Club
1970-1971	**Mark H. Cox**	Park Ridge CC
1972-1973	**George M. Bard**	Barrington Hills CC
1974-1975	**Thomas A. Reynolds, Jr.**	Shoreacres
1976-1977	**Robert G. Bohnen**	Hinsdale GC
1978-1979	**Gordon H. Ewen**	Indian Hill Club
1980-1981	**Bruce K. Goodman**	Lake Shore CC
1982-1983	**Michael L. McDermott**	Evanston GC
1984-1985	**Rexford E. Bruno**	La Grange CC
1986-1987	**Henry Bartholomay III**	Glen View Club
1988-1989	**Sam J. DiGiovanni**	Olympia Fields CC
1990-1991	**James F. Ashenden, Jr.**	Skokie CC
1992-1993	**Robert M. Alsteen**	Exmoor CC
1994-1995	**Raymond B. Anderson**	Oak Park CC
1996-1997	**Robert L. McMasters**	Red Run GC
1998-1999	**H. Grant Clark, Jr.**	Glen View Club

THE WGA CHAMPIONSHIPS

THE WESTERN OPEN

Played for the J.K. Wadley Trophy and a money prize. Conducted at match play, 1910-1911.

Year	Champion	Score	Runner-Up	Score	Course
1899	Willie Smith	156	Laurie Auchterlonie	156	Glen View G&PC
	Playoff: Smith 74, Auchterlonie 84				
1901	Laurie Auchterlonie	160	David Bell	162	Midlothian CC
1902	Willie Anderson	299	Willie Smith	304	Euclid C
			W.H. Way	304	
1903	Alex Smith	318	Laurie Auchterlonie	320	Milwaukee CC
			David Brown	320	
1904	Willie Anderson	304	Alex Smith	308	Kent CC
1905	Arthur Smith	278	James Maiden	280	Cincinnati GC
1906	Alex Smith	306	John Hobens	309	Homewood CC
1907	Robert Simpson	307	Willie Anderson	309	Hinsdale GC
			Fred McLeod	309	
1908	Willie Anderson	299	Fred McLeod	300	Normandie GC
1909	Willie Anderson	288	Stewart Gardner	297	Skokie CC
1910	a-Chick Evans	6 & 5	George A. Simpson		Beverly CC
	Medalist: Chick Evans, 71				
1911	Robert Simpson	2 & 1	Tom McNamara		Kent CC
	Medalist: James Simpson, 152				
1912	Macdonald Smith	299	Alex Robertson	302	Idlewild CC
1913	John J. McDermott	295	Mike Brady	302	Memphis CC
1914	Jim Barnes	293	Willie Kidd	294	Interlachen CC
1915	Tom McNamara	304	Alex Cunningham	306	Glen Oak CC
1916	Walter Hagen	286	Jock Hutchison	287	Blue Mound CC
			George Sargent	287	
1917	Jim Barnes	283	Walter Hagen	285	Westmoreland CC

Year	Champion	Score	Runner-Up	Score	Course
1919	Jim Barnes	283	Leo Diegel	286	Mayfield CC
1920	Jock Hutchison	296	Jim Barnes	297	Olympia Fields CC
			C.W. Hackney	297	
			Harry Hampton	297	
1921	Walter Hagen	287	Jock Hutchison	292	Oakwood C
1922	Mike Brady	291	Laurie Ayton	301	Oakland Hills CC
			Jock Hutchison	301	
1923	Jock Hutchison	281	Bobby Cruickshank	287	Colonial CC, Memphis
			Leo Diegel	287	
			Walter Hagen	287	
			Joe Kirkwood	287	
1924	Bill Mehlhorn	293	Al Watrous	301	Calumet CC
1925	Macdonald Smith	281	Leo Diegel	287	Youngstown CC
			Johnny Farrell	287	
			Emmett French	287	
			Walter Hagen	287	
			Bill Mehlhorn	287	
1926	Walter Hagen	279	Harry Cooper	288	Highland G&CC
			Gene Sarazen	288	
1927	Walter Hagen	281	Al Espinosa	285	Olympia Fields CC
			Bill Mehlhorn	285	
1928	Abe Espinosa	291	Johnny Farrell	294	North Shore CC
1929	Tommy Armour	273	Horton Smith	281	Ozaukee CC
1930	Gene Sarazen	278	Al Espinosa	285	Indianwood G&CC
1931	Ed Dudley	280	Walter Hagen	284	Miami Valley GC
1932	Walter Hagen	287	Olin Dutra	288	Canterbury GC
1933	Macdonald Smith	282	Tommy Armour	288	Olympia Fields CC
1934	Harry Cooper	274	Ky Laffoon	274	CC of Peoria

Playoff: Cooper 67, Laffoon 67. Second playoff: Cooper 66, Laffoon 69.

Year	Champion	Score	Runner-Up	Score	Course
1935	Johnny Revolta	290	Willie Goggin	294	South Bend CC
1936	Ralph Guldahl	274	Ray Mangrum	277	Davenport CC
1937	Ralph Guldahl	288	Horton Smith	288	Canterbury GC

Playoff: Guldahl 72, Smith 76

Year	Champion	Score	Runner-Up	Score	Course
1938	Ralph Guldahl	279	Sam Snead	286	Westwood CC
1939	Byron Nelson	281	Lloyd Mangrum	282	Medinah CC

Year	Champion	Score	Runner-Up	Score	Course
1940	Jimmy Demaret	293	Toney Penna	293	River Oaks CC
	Playoff: Demaret 70, Penna 74				
1941	Ed "Porky" Oliver	275	Ben Hogan	278	Phoenix CC
			Byron Nelson	278	
1942	Herman Barron	276	Henry Picard	278	Phoenix CC
1946	Ben Hogan	271	Lloyd Mangrum	275	Sunset CC
1947	Johnny Palmer	270	Bobby Locke	271	Salt Lake CC
			Ed "Porky" Oliver	271	
1948	Ben Hogan	281	Ed "Porky" Oliver	281	Brookfield CC
	Playoff: Hogan 64, Oliver 73				
1949	Sam Snead	268	Cary Middlecoff	272	Keller GC
1950	Sam Snead	282	Jim Ferrier	283	Brentwood CC
			E.J. "Dutch" Harrison	283	
1951	Marty Furgol	270	Cary Middlecoff	271	Davenport CC
1952	Lloyd Mangrum	274	Bobby Locke	282	Westwood CC
1953	E.J. "Dutch" Harrison	278	Ed Furgol	282	Bellerive CC
			Fred Haas	282	
			Lloyd Mangrum	282	
1954	Lloyd Mangrum	277	Ted Kroll	277	Kenwood CC
	Playoff: Mangrum 3, Kroll 4				
1955	Cary Middlecoff	272	Mike Souchak	274	Portland GC
1956	Mike Fetchick	284	Jay Hebert	284	Presidio GC
			Doug Ford	284	
			Don January	284	
	Playoff: Fetchick 66, Hebert 71, Ford 72, January 75				
1957	Doug Ford	279	George Bayer	279	Plum Hollow GC
			Gene Littler	279	
			Billy Maxwell	279	
	Playoff: Ford 4-3-4, Bayer 4-3-5, Littler 5, Maxwell 5				
1958	Doug Sanders	275	Dow Finsterwald	276	Red Run GC
1959	Mike Souchak	272	Arnold Palmer	273	Pittsburgh FC
1960	Stan Leonard	278	Art Wall	278	Western G&CC
	Playoff: Leonard 3, Wall 4				
1961	Arnold Palmer	271	Sam Snead	273	Blythefield CC
1962	Jacky Cupit	281	Billy Casper	283	Medinah CC

Year	Champion	Score	Runner-Up	Score	Course
1963	Arnold Palmer	280	Julius Boros	280	Beverly CC
			Jack Nicklaus	280	
	Playoff: Palmer 70, Boros 71, Nicklaus 73				
1964	Juan "Chi Chi" Rodriguez	268	Arnold Palmer	269	Tam O'Shanter CC
1965	Billy Casper	270	Juan "Chi Chi" Rodriguez	272	Tam O'Shanter CC
			Jack McGowan	272	
1966	Billy Casper	283	Gay Brewer	286	Medinah CC
1967	Jack Nicklaus	274	Doug Sanders	276	Beverly CC
1968	Jack Nicklaus	273	Miller Barber	276	Olympia Fields CC
1969	Billy Casper	276	Rocky Thompson	280	Midlothian CC
1970	Hugh Royer	273	Dale Douglass	274	Beverly CC
1971	Bruce Crampton	279	Bobby Nichols	281	Olympia Fields CC
1972	Jim Jamieson	271	Labron Harris, Jr.	277	Sunset Ridge CC
1973	Billy Casper	272	Larry Hinson	273	Midlothian CC
			Hale Irwin	273	
1974	Tom Watson	287	J.C. Snead	289	Butler National GC
			Tom Weiskopf	289	
1975	Hale Irwin	283	Bobby Cole	284	Butler National GC
1976	Al Geiberger	288	Joe Porter	289	Butler National GC
1977	Tom Watson	283	Johnny Miller	284	Butler National GC
			Wally Armstrong	284	
1978	Andy Bean	282	Bill Rogers	282	Butler National GC
	Playoff: Bean 4, Rogers 5				
1979	Larry Nelson	286	Ben Crenshaw	286	Butler National GC
	Playoff: Nelson 3, Crenshaw 4				
1980	Scott Simpson	281	Andy Bean	286	Butler National GC
1981	Ed Fiori	277	Greg Powers	281	Butler National GC
			Jim Simons	281	
			Jim Colbert	281	
1982	Tom Weiskopf	276	Larry Nelson	277	Butler National GC
1983	Mark McCumber	284	Tom Watson	285	Butler National GC
1984	Tom Watson	280	Greg Norman	280	Butler National GC
	Playoff: Watson 4-4-3, Norman 4-4-4				
1985	a-Scott Verplank	279	Jim Thorpe	279	Butler National GC
	Playoff: Verplank 4-4, Thorpe 4-5				

Year	Champion	Score	Runner-Up	Score	Course
1986	Tom Kite	286	Fred Couples	286	Butler National GC
			Nick Price	286	
			David Frost	286	

Playoff: Kite 3, Couples 4, Price 5, Frost 5

Year	Champion	Score	Runner-Up	Score	Course
1987	D.A. Weibring	207	Greg Norman	208	Butler National GC
			Larry Nelson	208	and Oak Brook GC

Shortened to 54 holes by flood.

Year	Champion	Score	Runner-Up	Score	Course
1988	Jim Benepe	278	Peter Jacobsen	279	Butler National GC
1989	Mark McCumber	275	Peter Jacobsen	275	Butler National GC

Playoff: McCumber 4, Jacobsen 5

Year	Champion	Score	Runner-Up	Score	Course
1990	Wayne Levi	275	Payne Stewart	279	Butler National GC
1991	Russ Cochran	275	Greg Norman	277	Cog Hill G&CC
1992	Ben Crenshaw	276	Greg Norman	277	Cog Hill G&CC
1993	Nick Price	269	Greg Norman	274	Cog Hill G&CC
1994	Nick Price	277	Greg Kraft	278	Cog Hill G&CC
1995	Billy Mayfair	279	Jay Haas	280	Cog Hill G&CC
			Justin Leonard	280	
			Jeff Maggert	280	
			Scott Simpson	280	
1996	Steve Stricker	270	Billy Andrade	278	Cog Hill G&CC
			Jay Don Blake	278	
1997	Eldrick "Tiger" Woods	275	Frank Noblio	278	Cog Hill G&CC
1998	Joe Durant	271	Vijay Singh	273	Cog Hill G&CC

a-Amateur

THE WESTERN AMATEUR

Played for the George R. Thorne Trophy (championship), and the Cameron Eddy Trophy (medalist).

Year	Champion	Margin	Runner-Up	Medalist	Course
1899	David Forgan	6 & 5	Walter Egan	David Forgan (84)	Glen View
1900	William Waller	1 up	William Holabird, Jr.	Walter Smith (161)	Onwentsia
1901	Phelps B. Hoyt	6 & 5	Bruce Smith	Fred Hamlin (176)	Midlothian
				Walter Egan (176)	
1902	H. Chandler Egan	1 up, 37 holes	Walter Egan	H.C. Egan (163)	Chicago Golf
1903	Walter Egan	1 up	H. Chandler Egan	all match-play	Euclid
1904	H. Chandler Egan	6 & 5	D.E. Sawyer	H.C. Egan (144)	Exmoor

Year	Champion	Margin	Runner-Up	Medalist	Course
1905	H. Chandler Egan	3 & 2	Walter Egan	Guy Miller (157)	Glen View
1906	D.E. Sawyer	1 up, 37 holes	Warren Wood	W.C. Fownes, Jr. (153)	Glen Echo
1907	H. Chandler Egan	5 & 4	Herbert Jones	D.E. Sawyer (160)	Chicago Golf
				K.P. Edwards (160)	
				W.I. Howland, Jr. (160)	
1908	Mason Phelps	6 & 5	H.W. Allen	K.P. Edwards (152)	R. Arsenal
1909	Chick Evans	1 up	Albert Seckel	Warren Wood (146)	Homewood
1910	Mason Phelps	2 & 1	Chick Evans	Harry Legg (140)	Minikahda
1911	Albert Seckel	8 & 7	Robert Gardner	Paul Hunter (154)	Detroit
1912	Chick Evans	1 up	Warren Wood	Warren Wood (69)	Denver
1913	Warren Wood	4 & 3	E.P. Allis	Chick Evans (151)	Homewood
1914	Chick Evans	11 & 9	James Standish, Jr.	Chick Evans (147)	Kent
1915	Chick Evans	7 & 6	James Standish, Jr.	Paul Hunter (150)	Mayfield
1916	Heinrich Schmidt	7 & 6	Douglas Grant	H. Schmidt (145)	Del Monte
1917	Francis Ouimet	1 up	Ken Edwards	Donald Edwards (150)	Midlothian
1919	Harry Legg	2 & 1	R. Bockenkamp	Clarence Wolff (146)	Sunset Hill
1920	Chick Evans	5 & 4	Clarence Wolff	Bobby Jones (139)	Memphis
1921	Chick Evans	3 & 2	Rudy Knepper	Rudy Knepper (144)	Westmoreland
				H.R. Johnston (144)	
1922	Chick Evans	5 & 4	George Von Elm	Chick Evans (143)	Hillcrest
1923	Chick Evans	6 & 4	W.H. Gardner	Jess Sweetser (143)	Mayfield
1924	H.R. Johnston	1 up	Albert Seckel	Arthur Sweet (141)	Hinsdale
1925	Keefe Carter	3 & 2	Russell Martin	Dexter Cummings (138)	Lochmoor
1926	Frank Dolp	6 & 5	Bon Stein	H.R. Johnston (141)	White Bear YC
1927	Bon Stein	2 & 1	Eddie Held	Charles Hunter (147)	Seattle
1928	Frank Dolp	4 & 3	Gus Novotny	Johnny Dawson (141)	Bob O'Link
1929	Don Moe	1 up, 37 holes	Gilbert Carter	Don Moe (144)	Mission Hills
1930	John Lehman	4 & 2	Ira Couch	John Lehman (147)	Beverly
				Chick Evans (147)	
1931	Don Moe	9 & 7	M. McNaughton	Eddie Hogan (140)	Portland
1932	Gus Moreland	5 & 4	Ira Couch	John Lehman (137)	Rockford
1933	Jack Westland	3 & 2	Rodney Bliss	Zell Eaton (141)	Memphis
1934	Zell Eaton	4 & 3	Spec Goldman	Zell Eaton (144)	Twin Hills
1935	Charles Yates	5 & 3	Rodney Bliss	Rodney Bliss (142)	Broadmoor
1936	Paul Leslie	2 & 1	Bob Frazer	Matt Zadalis (138)	Happy Hollow
1937	Wilford Wehrle	1 up	Chuck Kocsis	Charles Yates (137)	Los Angeles
1938	Bob Babbish	1 up	M. McCarthy	Burleigh Jacobs, Jr. (139)	South Bend

Year	Champion	Margin	Runner-Up	Medalist	Course
1939	Harry Todd	2 & 1	Larry Moller	Spec Stewart (137)	Oklahoma City
1940	Marvin Ward	3 & 1	George Victor	Art Doering (142)	Minneapolis
				Jim Ferrier (142)	
1941	Marvin Ward	3 & 2	Harry Todd	Harry Todd (141)	Broadmoor
1942	Pvt. Pat Abbott	7 & 6	B. McCormick	Marvin Ward (141)	Manito
1946	Frank Stranahan	1 up	Marvin Ward	Frank Stranahan (141)	Northland
				Marvin Ward (141)	
				Smiley Quick (141)	
1947	Marvin Ward	1 up	Frank Stranahan	Marvin Ward (141)	Wakonda
1948	Skee Reigel	3 & 1	James T. McHale	Laurence Glosser (139)	Wichita
1949	Frank Stranahan	5 & 4	Walter Cisco	John Wagner (145)	Bellerive
1950	Charlie Coe	7 & 6	Robert Goldwater	James T. McHale (143)	Dallas
				Dale Morey (143)	
				Leonard White (143)	
				Morris Williams (143)	
1951	Frank Stranahan	7 & 6	James Blair III	Frank Stranahan (139)	South Bend
1952	Frank Stranahan	3 & 2	Harvey Ward, Jr.	John Coyle (141)	Exmoor
				Don Cherry (141)	
1953	Dale Morey	8 & 6	Richard Norton	Frank Strafaci (140)	Blythefield
1954	Bruce Cudd	1 up, 37 holes	Philip Getchell	Maj. H. Williams (142)	Broadmoor
1955	Eddie Merrins	1 up, 37 holes	Hillman Robbins, Jr.	Don Bisplinghoff (276)	Rockford
1956	Mason Rudolph	6 & 4	Jack Parnell	Don Bisplinghoff (2 73)	Belle Meade
1957	Dr. Edgar Updegraff	9 & 8	Joe Campbell	Bob Pratt (289)	Old Warson
				Phil Rodgers (289)	
1958	James "Billy" Key	3 & 2	Mason Rudolph	James "Billy" Key (286)	CC of Florida
				Mason Rudolph (286)	
				Edwin Hopkins, Jr. (286)	
1959	Dr. Edgar Updegraff	7 & 5	Charles Hunter, Jr.	Dr. Arthur Butler (278)	Waverley
1960	Tommy Aaron	default	Bob Cochran	Pfc. Phil Rodgers (281)	Northland
1961	Jack Nicklaus	4 & 3	James "Billy" Key	Ron Weber (278)	New Orleans
1962	Art Hudnutt	1 up	Melvin Stevens	Labron Harris, Jr. (281)	Orchard Lake
1963	Tom Weiskopf	5 & 4	Labron Harris, Jr.	Don Voth (294)	Point O'Woods
1964	Steve Oppermann	3 & 2	Dr. Edgar Updegraff	Dr. Edgar Updegraff (277)	Tucson
1965	Bob Smith	1 up, 19 holes	George Boutell	Marty Fleckman (290)	Point O'Woods
1966	Jim Wiechers	1 up	Ron Cerrudo	Marty Fleckman (282)	Pinehurst
1967	Bob Smith	3 & 1	Marty Fleckman	Bob Smith (280)	Milburn
1968	Rik Massengale	3 & 1	Kemp Richardson	Bob Barbarossa (280)	Grosse Ile

Year	Champion	Margin	Runner-Up	Medalist	Course
1969	Steve Melnyk	3 & 1	Howard Twitty	Pat Fitzsimons (283)	Rockford
1970	Lanny Wadkins	4 & 2	Charlie Borner	Tom Kite (273)	Wichita
1971	Andy North	1 up	Barney Thompson	Allen Miller (284)	Point O'Woods
				Tom Watson (284)	
1972	Gary Sanders	1 up	Dr. Gil Morgan	Ben Crenshaw (282)	Point O'Woods
1973	Ben Crenshaw	4 & 3	Jimmy Ellis	Ben Crenshaw (286)	Point O'Woods
1974	Curtis Strange	1 up, 20 holes	Jay Haas	Curtis Strange (278)	Point O'Woods
1975	Andy Bean	1 up	Randy Simmons	Bob Byman (289)	Point O'Woods
				Keith Fergus (289)	
				Bill Mallon (289)	
				Randy Simmons (289)	
1976	John Stark	3 & 1	Mick Soli	Bob Byman (289)	Point O'Woods
1977	Jim Nelford	2 & 1	Rafael Alarcon	Lee Mikles (284)	Point O'Woods
1978	Bob Clampett	2 up	Mark Wiebe	Vance Heafner (283)	Point O'Woods
1979	Hal Sutton	1 up	Mike Gove	Joe Rassett (275)	Point O'Woods
1980	Hal Sutton	4 & 3	David Ogrin	Mark O'Meara (280)	Point O'Woods
1981	Frank Fuhrer	2 & 1	Curt Byrum	Willie Wood (283)	Point O'Woods
				Ed Luethke (283)	
1982	Rick Fehr	5 & 3	Tommy Moore	Rick Fehr (272)	Point O'Woods
1983	Billy Tuten	2 up	Kent Kluba	Roy Biancalana (282)	Point O'Woods
1984	John Inman	3 & 2	Rocco Mediate	Scott Verplank (270)	Point O'Woods
1985	Scott Verplank	1 up	Dave Peege	Scott Verplank (278)	Point O'Woods
1986	Greg Parker	3 & 1	Robert Huxtable	Jim Benepe (279)	Point O'Woods
1987	Hugh Royer III	3 & 2	Craig Perks	Len Mattiace (276)	Point O'Woods
1988	Chris DiMarco	1 up	Bill Lundeen	Tom Carr (276)	Point O'Woods
1989	David Sutherland	2 & 1	Tony Mollica	Doug Martin (271)	Point O'Woods
1990	Craig Kanada	4 & 2	Greg Griffin	Scott Frisch (281)	Point O'Woods
1991	Phil Mickelson	2 & 1	Justin Leonard	Phil Mickelson (279)	Point O'Woods
1992	Justin Leonard	2 up	David Howser	John Harris (280)	Point O'Woods
1993	Justin Leonard	6 & 4	Danny Green	Jason Gore (277)	Point O'Woods
1994	Eldrick "Tiger" Woods	2 & 1	Chris Riley	Bud Still (279)	Point O'Woods
1995	Patrick Lee	2 & 1	Robert Floyd	Mathew Goggin (274)	Point O'Woods
				Justin Roof (274)	
1996	Joel Kribel	2 & 1	Brett Partridge	Joel Kribel (274)	Point O'Woods
1997	Danny Green	1 up, 19 holes	Andy Miller	Arron Oberholser (271)	Point O'Woods
1998	Michael Henderson	1 up	Shawn Koch	Alberto Ochoa (277)	Point O'Woods

THE WESTERN JUNIOR

Played for the W.A. Alexander Cup (champion, 1914-1992), the Milt Woodard Trophy (champion, 1993-present), and the Adelor J. Petit, Jr. Trophy (medalist).

Year	Champion	Margin	Runner-Up	Medalist	Course
1914	Charles Grimes	6 & 5	Lawson Watts	John Simpson (76)	Chicago Golf
1915	DeWitt Balch	2 & 1	Moritz Loeb	John Simpson (83)	Midlothian CC
1916	John Simpson	4 & 3	Ben Buffum	Ben Buffum (76)	Hinsdale CC
1917	Frederick Wright	5 & 4	Richard Haight	Dewey Weber (72)	Exmoor CC
1919	Howard Sassman	4 & 3	Clyde Kennedy	R.E. Rolf (76)	Flossmoor CC
1920	Harold Martin	1 up, 19 holes	Walter Crowe	Dexter Cummings (77)	Bob O'Link C
1921	Burton Mudge, Jr.	5 & 3	Jack Wenzler	Alex Bush (77)	Belle Meade CC
1922	Kenneth Hisert	4 & 2	Burton Mudge, Jr.	Stanley Arndt (76)	Olympia Fields
1923	Ira Couch	2 & 1	Emerson Carey, Jr.	Ira Couch (76) Emerson Carey, Jr. (76)	Westmoreland
1924	Eldridge Robinson	3 & 2	Donald Carrick	H.J. Foley (78)	Briargate CC
1925	Emerson Carey, Jr.	6 & 5	Fred S. Lyon	Joe Palettie (72) Donald Carrick (72) Merritt Joslyn (72)	Big Oaks CC
1926	Sam Alpert	2 & 1	Francis Clary	Art Tveraa (73)	Edgewater CC
1927	Albert Hakes	1 up, 37 holes	Pat Ennis	Robert Stewart (75) David Gernon (75)	Indian Hill C
1928	Dick Mullin	5 & 4	Tom Cooley	Dick Mullin (73)	Glen View C
1929	Fred Lyon	5 & 4	William Redmond	Fred Lyon (72)	LaGrange CC
1930	C.K. Collins	5 & 4	William Chambers	C.K. Collins (75)	Flossmoor CC
1931	Robert Cochran	7 & 6	Charles Becka	John H. Root (73)	Midlothian CC
1932	John Banks	7 & 5	Willie Meike	John Banks (75) Willie Meike (75)	Medinah CC
1933	Frank Bredall	2 up	James Black	Ross Manarchy (71)	Normandie CC
1934	Fred Haas, Jr.	3 & 2	Bob Jones	Fred Haas, Jr. (71) Ralph Ackerman (71) Elton Hill (71) Keith Johnson (71)	Hinsdale CC
1935	Fred Haas, Jr.	7 & 6	Walter Burkemo	Fred Schwarze (71)	Oakland Hills
1936	Sid Richardson	4 & 3	Joe Franco	Joe Fall, Jr. (72)	Sunset Ridge
1937	John Holmstrom	1 up, 38 holes	Bert McDowell	Earle Wilde (68)	Cherry Hills

Year	Champion	Margin	Runner-Up	Medalist	Course
1938	Charles Betcher	3 & 2	Bert McDowell	Bert McDowell (73)	U. of Minnesota
1939	Sam Kocsis	1 up	William Courtright	David Osler (74)	U. of Michigan
				Chase Fannon (74)	
1940	Ben Downing	5 & 4	Harry Deas	James McCarthy (74)	Mill Road Farm
1941	Ben Downing	7 & 6	Mark Weidman	John Stolz, Jr. (76)	Iowa State
1942	William Witzleb	2 & 1	John Krejci	William Norwell (75)	Elmhurst CC,
					Ridgemoor CC
1946	Mac Hunter	1 up, 38 holes	Bob Abrahams	Bob Olsen (76)	Iowa State
1947	Tom Veech	1 up	Art Wyatt	George Dayiantis (74)	Northwestern
				Gene Coulter (74)	
1948	Gene Coulter	4 & 2	Bob Olsen	John Hare (71)	Purdue
1949	Dean Lind	2 & 1	Norm Dunlap	Reggie Myles (73)	U. of Michigan
1950	Dean Lind	7 & 6	Warren Dailey	Billy Casper (71)	Burke Memorial GC
				Tom Crabbe (71)	
1951	Hillman Robbins, Jr.	3 & 2	Tom Brennan	Eddie Merrins (68)	Finkbine GC
1952	Don Nichols	4 & 3	Sam Sadler	Tom Washburn (70)	U. of Minnesota
1953	Henry Loeb	5 & 3	John Fry	Phil Rodgers (69)	Stanford
1954	Herbert Klontz	1 up	Robert MacMichael	Ronald Schwarzel (70)	U. of Illinois
1955	Gerald McFerren	1 up	Bob Magnussen	Don Essig III (73)	Manor CC
				Larry Reich (73)	
1956	Dick Foote	3 & 1	Deane Beman	Deane Beman (147)	U. of Michigan
				Cyrus Northrop (147)	
1957	Don Essig III	5 & 3	Jack Moore	Don Essig III (146)	Purdue
1958	Jack Rule	5 & 4	C.A. Smith III	Gary Liotta (142)	Finkbine GC
1959	Steve Spray	9 & 7	Dave Leon	Richard Youngberg (144)	U. of Illinois
1960	Labron Harris, Jr.	9 & 8	Jim Mooney	Labron Harris, Jr. (147)	U. of New Mexico
1961	Phil Marston	2 & 1	Dick Killian	Jim Jamieson (141)	Michigan State
1962	George Shortridge	1 up, 23 holes	Dave Gumlia	Jim Jamieson (143)	U. of Minnesota
1963	George Boutell	4 & 3	Fred Ewald	Jim Wiechers (136)	Ohio State
1964	Jim Wiechers	3 & 1	Greg Pitzer	Chris Scena (148)	Air Force Acad.
1965	John Richart	3 & 2	Jim Herring	Dave Hanten (137)	Finkbine GC
1966	Ross Elder	3 & 2	Steve Cisco	Danny May (140)	Indiana
				Drue Johnson (140)	
1967	Mike Goodart	4 & 3	Andy North	Paul Purtzer (140)	Purdue GC
1968	Don Hawken	4 & 2	Andy North	Bruce Ashworth (140)	Stanford GC
1969	Jim Simons	6 & 5	Bruce Ashworth	Dennis Walters (140)	U. of Illinois

Year	Champion	Margin	Runner-Up	Medalist	Course
1970	Jeff Reaume	4 & 3	David Newquist	Niles Bakke (146)	U. of Michigan
1971	Richard Brooke	3 & 2	Gary Gant	Jay Haas (141)	U. of Iowa
1972	Dennis Sullivan	5 & 4	Todd Crandall	Fred Ridley (138)	Ohio State GC
1973	Tommy Jones	4 & 3	Rich Ritter	Tommy Jones (143)	Duke U. GC
1974	Edwin Fisher Jr.	1 up	Brad Bettin	Jon Chafee (141)	U. of Minnesota
1975	Britt Harrison	2 & 1	John Jones	Larry Rinker (137)	Stillwater CC
1976	Gary Hallberg	1 up	Tom Hershner	Doug Thomas (139)	Eugene CC
1977	Gary Wilks	5 & 3	David Abell	Fred Couples (138)	Purdue GC
1978	Bob Clampett	2 & 1	Eric Evans	Bob Clampett (136)	U. of New Mexico
1979	Willie Wood	6 & 4	Jay Kent	Mark Brooks (142)	U. of Alabama
				Brad Jones (142)	
1980	Eugene Elliott	3 & 2	Mark Thaxton	Kelly Clair (140)	Purdue GC
1981	Gregg VanThaden	2 up	Brian Tennyson	Greg Tebbutt (141)	Ohio State GC
1982	Jim Benepe	4 & 3	Todd Anderson	Jim Benepe (143)	Travis Pointe CC
1983	Brad Meek	1 up	Mike Swartz	Todd Hamilton (137)	Lincolnshire Fields CC, U. of Illinois
1984	Steve LaMontagne	5 & 4	Jim Sowerwine	Sean Pappas (139)	Lone Palm GC
1985	Don Edwards	3 & 2	Chuck O'Brien, Jr.	Michael Bradley (140)	Ohio State GC
1986	Jon Worrell	2 & 1	Brad McMakin	Steve Stricker (138)	Duke U. GC
1987	Jim Furyk	7 & 5	Pat Carter	David Morland (140)	Michigan State
1988	Chris Smith	5 & 4	Craig Kanada	Keith Sbarbaro (145)	Cog Hill G&CC
				Phil Mickelson (145)	
1989	Craig Darling	3 & 2	David Barsantee	Russell Simenson (136)	U. of Illinois
1990	Kelly Mitchum	2 & 1	Bobby Cochran	Robert Dean (141)	Pinehurst #4, Pinewild CC
1991	Trip Kuehne	1 up	Donnie Darr	Brian Bartolec (136)	Michigan State
				Grant Masson (136)	
				Hank Schlissberg (136)	
1992	John Curley	4 & 2	John Bernatovicz	Kevin Mihailoff (139)	Chicago Golf
1993	Michael Jones	1 up	Brian Payne	Brian Payne (143)	Univ. Ridge GC
1994	Brad Elder	2 & 1	Ben Curtis	Brad Elder (66)	U. of Michigan
1995	James Driscoll	4 & 3	Thomas Parker	Mark Catalano (139)	The Homestead
1996	Andy Rapp	3 & 2	Carl Pettersson	Jeremy Wilkinson (141)	Edina CC
1997	Nick Cassini	4 & 3	Jonathan Rusk	Nick Cassini (137)	East Lake GC
1998	David Wagenseller	3 & 2	Brady Stockton	Hunter Mahan (141)	Exmoor CC
				Nick Manthey (141)	
				Jon Turcott (141)	

AUTHOR'S NOTE

T here is no better field to cover in sports than golf, not only because it doesn't have night games, with the imminent deadlines that plague newspaper reporters, but because of the people in it.

Many are associated with the Western Golf Association. Over the years, I had pestered WGA communications maven Gary Holaway about a centennial book, so when he called to ask if I was interested in working on one, the only possible answer was in the affirmative. Having already nominated myself, I had to accept.

By then, I'd been covering the Western Open since 1979, the Western Amateur since 1990, and I'd also covered the Western Junior and Evans Scholars selection meetings. I thought I knew plenty. Instead, I discovered how much nobody knew.

The WGA, for all of its good work on courses and in the classrooms, had been ignored. Other histories of American golf, worthy in all other respects, had mentioned it and the Evans Scholars only in passing.

Fine. Reporters like to snoop for a scoop. This was historical snooping. Much was discovered, but, alas, the George S. May Memorial Trophy is still at large.

This is more than a fresh history of the WGA's role in the game and in society over the last century. We have tried to focus on the big picture, but we took side trips as space allowed. Chick and the Haig and Arnie and Jack and Tiger are all here, plus less familiar names such as Carleton Blunt, the driving force in the growth of the Evans program for a half-century.

There are many to thank, starting inside the WGA with Executive Director Don Johnson, Educational Director Jim Moore, Centennial Committee Chairman Rich Peterson, and Gary Holaway, an early backer. They were enthusiastic in their support and helpful in their criticism.

They've also been generous with their time, a trait common among all who wear the WGA's Green Coat, whether staffers or volunteer directors. Thanks also go to all at WGA headquarters who helped me find things, including controller Wayne Janik, who found the date a trophy was acquired, Ann Gerdom, who assisted with editing, and Barry Deach, who, before he left the WGA, took on the insane task of organizing a massive archive of photos that had gone untouched for years. Many are in this book.

At Sleeping Bear Press, the kudos go to Brian Lewis for agreeing to take on the project, and to Lynne Johnson and Adam Rifenberick for fine-tuning it.

Bob Verdi, a good friend and competitor whose well-chosen words and phrases are now found in not only the *Chicago Tribune* but also *Golf World* and *Golf Digest* as well, was extremely supportive from the start.

At the *Daily Southtown,* Mike Waters, the sports editor at the time this baby was conceived, was gracious enough to let me play hooky even more than usual, and Mike Deacon, in charge of the department more recently, has been similarly generous.

Author Cal Brown kept me aimed in the right direction. Francis Trimble of the Texas State Golf Hall of Fame called one day with a question, and ended up far more helpful to me than I was to her. A tip of the cap to them, and to Northwestern University archivist Patrick Quinn.

Others who went above and beyond in giving advice were Reid Hanley, Chris Krug, Rory Spears, Lindsey Willhite, and Len Ziehm.

Interviews, prowling the WGA's own archives, and independent research were the main sources of the information. Scanning thousands of newspaper microfilm reels in libraries as near as the Harold Washington Library in downtown Chicago and as distant as Buffalo, New York, fleshed out the bare details. The kind folks at the Arlington Heights (Illinois) Memorial Library, which features late hours, got to know me well as I chuckled over the wit of the *Chicago Tribune's* Charlie Bartlett.

Also crucial was the coverage provided by *Golf World.* In the first few decades after its 1947 inception it covered the game intimately. I poured over hundreds of issues dating to the magazine's start.

Like golf, writing is a game in which perfection is unattainable. Any error that has snuck in is mine. I'm reminded of a day in the late-1980s, when a PGA Tour representative told Charlie Kimmel, who invented the modern art of scoreboard calligraphy at the 1932 Western Open, that he'd gotten the cut wrong on his mammoth board.

Charlie disagreed.

"The computer says so," said the Tour guy.

Charlie looked at his painstaking work and began counting again. As he did, those of us who came to depend on him for statistics as well as banter, sided with our sage and suggested that the Tour check its computer. Soon the word came from the back of the room that all of us expected.

"Charlie, you're right. The computer missed someone."

Whoever fed the stats in, messed up. It was a case of garbage in, garbage out. The aim from the start has been to make this work live up to Charlie Kimmel's no-garbage standard.

- Tim Cronin

P H O T O   C R E D I T S

The photographs that have been included in this book have been provided by the Western Golf Association with the following exceptions:

Acme Newspictures, Inc., 65 (right)
Associated Press, 66 (top), 135
Alex Bremmer, 109 (top)
Fran Byrne, vi (top)
Central News Photo Service, 67 (right)
Chicago Historical Society, xiv, 4, 79
Chicago Photographers, 158
Chicago Tribune, 185 (left), 194 (top)
The Curtis Studios, 68
The Daily Southtown, back flap
The Daily Times, 144
The Glen View Club, cover painting
J.P. Graham, 43
International News Photos, Inc., 25, 29 (left), 49, 56, 134, 140 (right)
Kenebry Photography, 179
Keystone View Company, 40, 171 (left)
Mike Klemme/Golfoto, 216
Koehne Photography, 103 (right)
F.A. Kuehn & Co., 97 (bottom)
R.B. Leffingwell/Chicago Sun-Times, 187 (top)
MacGregor and Company, 57
Sidney L. Matthew, 37
Milwaukee Journal Photo, 127 (left)
Alex J. Morrison, 151

Moulin Studios, 137
Bruce Newnum, 208
Pacific & Atlantic Photos, 31, 33, 48 (left), 65 (left)
PGA Tour, 225
George S. Pietzcker, 44
Reames Studio, 97 (top), 98, 155, 160
Bob Ringham, 192
Rotofotos, 60
Rick Sharp, 146, 147, 220
Steffens-Chicago, 51
Terry's Photography, 164, 165 (bottom), 180
Paul Thompson, 17
Town & Country Photographers, 90 (bottom), 101 (left), 107 (left)
Underwood & Underwood, 58, 69
Underwood & Underwood/Corbis Bettmann, 54
United States Golf Association, i, 22, 29 (right), 32, 148
UPI/Corbis-Bettmann, 53, 132, 152, 184
Wide World Photos, Inc., 12, 59 (bottom), 63, 67 (left), 70, 73 (top), 74, 75, 76, 142
William R. Witteker Photography, 124